EXPLORATION

of the

VALLEY

of the

AMAZON,

1851–1852

William Lewis Herndon (Courtesy of the United States
Naval Academy Museum, Annapolis, Maryland)

EXPLORATION
of the
VALLEY
of the
AMAZON,
1851–1852

William Lewis Herndon

Edited and with a Foreword by

Gary Kinder

Grove Press
New York

Published simultaneously in Canada
Printed in the United States of America

Library of Congress Cataloging-in-Publication Data
Herndon, William Lewis, 1813–1857.
 Exploration of the valley of the Amazon / made under the direction of the Navy
Department, by Wm. Lewis Herndon and Lardner Gibbon.
  p. cm.
  ISBN 0-8021-3704-0
  1. Amazon River Valley—Description and travel. 2. Amazon River Valley—Discovery
and exploration—American. 3. Brazil—Description and travel. 4. Peru—Description and
travel. 5. Bolivia—Description and travel. I. Gibbon, Lardner. II. United States. Navy
Dept. III. Title.
F2546 .H56 2000
981'.104—dc21   00-024491

Design by Laura Hammond Hough

Grove Press
841 Broadway
New York, NY 10003

00 01 02 03   10 9 8 7 6 5 4 3 2 1

Contents

❦

LIST OF PLATES   ix

MAP   x

FOREWORD   xiii

Chapter I

INTRODUCTORY

United States ship Vandalia—*Valparaiso—Santiago—*
Preparatory orders—Lima—Means of information—Conquests
of the Incas in the Montaña—First explorations
of the Spaniards—Madame Godin

4

Chapter II

INTRODUCTORY

Orders—Investigation of routes—River Beni—Cuzco route—
Preparations for the journey—The start

19

Chapter III

*Passports—Means of defence—The road—Narrow pass—
Bridge—Tribute money—Dividing line between the Coast and
the Sierra—Varieties of the potato—Mines of Párac—Narrow
valley—Summit of the Cordillera—Reflections*

32

Chapter IV

*Mines of Morococha—A Yankee's house—Mountain of
Puy-puy—Splendid view—Lava stream—Chain bridge at
Oroya—Descent into the valley of Tarma—American
physician—Customs—Dress—Religious observances—Muleteers
and mules—General Otero—Farming in the Sierra—Road to
Chanchamayo—Perils of travel—Gold mines of Matichacra—
View of the Montaña—Fort San Ramon—Indians of
Chanchamayo—Cultivation*

59

Chapter V

*Division of the party—Acobamba—Plain of Junin—
Preservation of potatoes—Cerro Pasco—Drainage of the mines*

94

Chapter VI

*Departure from Cerro Pasco—Mint at Quinua—Chinchao
Valley—Huallaga River*

115

Chapter VII

*Itinerary—Tingo Maria—Vampires—Blow-guns—Canoe
navigation—Shooting monkeys—Salt hills of Pilluana*

139

Chapter VIII

*Pongo of Chasuta—Chasuta—Sta. Cruz—Antonio, the
Paraguá—Laguna—Mouth of the Huallaga*

169

Chapter IX

*Entrance into the Amazon—Upper and lower missions of
Mainas—Conversions of the Ucayali—Trade in Sarsaparilla—
Advantages of trade with this country*

189

Chapter X

*River Ucayali—Sarayacu—The missionaries—The Indians of
the Ucayali*

199

Chapter XI

*Upper Ucayali—M. Castelnau—Length of navigation—Loss of
the priest—Departure from Sarayacu—Iquitos—Mouth of the
Napo—San José de los Yaguas—State of Indians of Peru*

220

Chapter XII

*Caballococha—Alligators—Indian incantations—Tabatinga—
River Yavari—San Paulo—Making* manteiga—*River Juruá—
River Japurá*

240

Chapter XIII

*Egas—Trade—Lake Coari—Mouth of the Rio Negro—
Barra—Trade—Productions*

261

Chapter XIV

*Town of Barra—Foreign residents—Population—Rio Negro—
Connexion with the Oronoco—River Purus—Rio Branco—
Vegetable productions of the Amazon country*
276

Chapter XV

*Departure from Barra—River Madeira—Villa Nova—Cocoa
plantations—Obidos*
289

Chapter XVI

*Santarem—Population—Trade—River Tapajos—
Diamond region*
302

Chapter XVII

*Departure from Santarem—Monte Alegre—Prainha—
River Xingu—Great estuary of the Amazon—India-rubber
country—Method of collecting and preparing the India-rubber—
Bay of Limoeiro—Arrival at Pará*
304

Chapter XVIII
Pará
320

Chapter XIX
Resumé
334

List of Plates

PLATE 1—*Cathedral of Lima*   9

PLATE 2—*Yanacoto*   37

PLATE 3—*Hacienda de Mayoc*   42

PLATE 4—*San Mateo*   45

PLATE 5—*Summit of the Cordillera*   55

PLATE 6—*Mountain of Puy-puy*   62

PLATE 7—*Oroya*   66

PLATE 8—*Tarma*   72

PLATE 9—*Fort San Ramon*   85

PLATE 10—*Cerro Pasco*   106

PLATE 11—*Miner*   110

PLATE 12—*Ore carrier*   111

PLATE 13—*Givaro*   156

PLATE 14—*Givara*   210

PLATE 15—*Zaparo* (Hunter)   265

PLATE 16—*Zaparo* (Fisher)   317

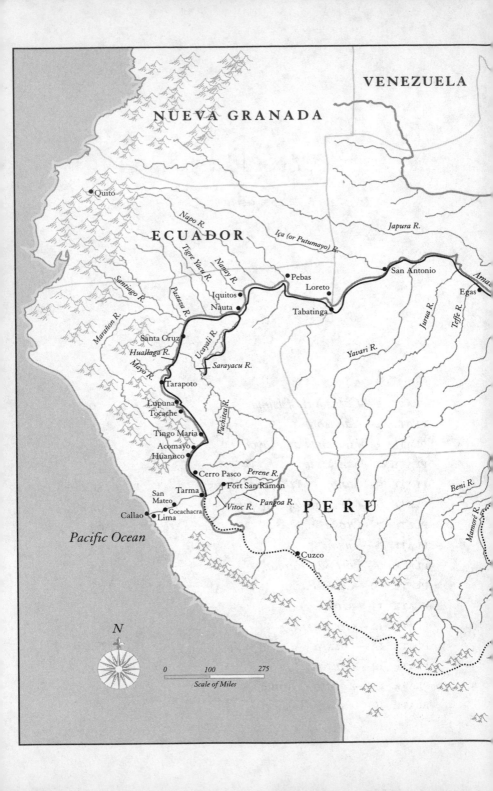

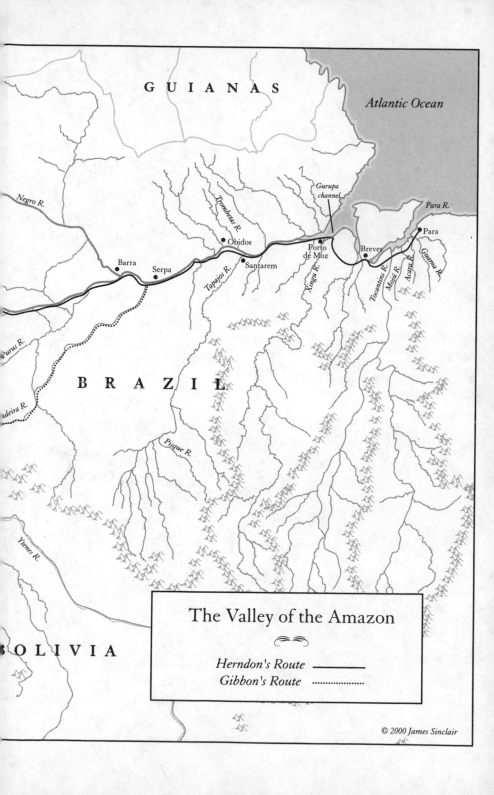

GUIANAS

Atlantic Ocean

Negro R.

Trombetas R.

Obidos

Gurupa channel

Para R.

Porto de Moz

Para

Barra

Serpa

Santarem

Breves

Tapajos R.

Xingu R.

Tocantins R.

Moju R.

Acara R.

Guama R.

urus R.

B R A Z I L

adeira R.

Pisque R.

Yenes R.

BOLIVIA

The Valley of the Amazon

Herndon's Route ——————
Gibbon's Route ·················

© 2000 James Sinclair

Foreword

EXPLORATION OF THE VALLEY OF THE AMAZON, by William Lewis Herndon, is an adventure through the most exotic land on earth and a journey into the soul of a singular man. I first became acquainted with his work as I was researching a book about another event that occurred later in his life.

In 1857, five years after he had returned from the Amazon, Herndon commanded a 280-foot side-wheel steamer, the S.S. *Central America*, delivering passengers to and from the California gold rush. In September of that year, Herndon steamed into a hurricane two hundred miles off the Carolina coast. Storm winds rose to over a hundred knots, the hull sprung a leak, and sea water rushed into the hold, dousing the boiler fires. Without steam to drive his engines, Herndon could not bring his bow into the weather, and the ship fell off into the trough of the sea.

In his hands, Herndon held the lives of sixty women and children and over five hundred men. He ordered the men to form bailing lines with pitchers, bowls, and basins, anything that would hold water. They were seasick and had had little food or sleep for two days, yet they bailed without stopping for thirty hours, some of them passing out from exhaustion. But their efforts kept the ship afloat a little longer, and in that tiny window of time took place one of the most dramatic rescues in the annals of the sea: Captain Herndon safely transferred every woman and child and fifty of the men from the crippled steamer to a two-masted brig tossing in the storm nearly five miles to the lee.

As I was writing *Ship of Gold in the Deep Blue Sea,* the story of the sinking of the *Central America* and the recovery of her gold cargo in the 1980s, I kept asking myself, What man could inspire so many others to work so hard under conditions so overwhelming? What man could take an oath never to abandon his ship, then live that oath as he stood on the weather deck on a dark night engulfed by a raging sea, facing his own imminent death?

To understand more about what motivated him, I read his account of the Amazon exploration, and I was stunned by his scholarship and insight. He was unusually diverse in his knowledge of academics and human nature. He was religious but neither zealous nor judgmental; humble but not incapable of issuing orders; sensitive but not incapable of being stern; unafraid of physical danger, yet forgiving of those who were.

Herndon was a slight man who wore thin gold spectacles. When he commanded the *Central America* on her last voyage, he was forty-three and balding, with a red beard running the edge of his jaw from temple to temple. Though he looked more like a professor or a banker than a sea captain, he had been at sea since he was fifteen, in the Mexican War and the Second Seminole War, in the Atlantic and the Pacific, the Mediterranean and the Caribbean.

In 1850 the Secretary of the Navy had appointed Herndon to lead the first American expedition into the mysterious and foreboding territory known as the Valley of the Amazon, from the trickling headwaters of the Amazon's tributaries sixteen thousand feet high in the Peruvian Andes, to Pará, Brazil, where the river emptied into the Atlantic four thousand miles away.

"The route by which you may reach the Amazon River is left to your discretion," read Herndon's orders. "It is not desired that you should select any route by which you and your party would be exposed to savage hostility, beyond your means of defence and protection. . . . Arriving at Pará, you will embark by the first opportunity for the United States, and report in person to this department."

Herndon departed Lima, Peru, on May 20, 1851, and arrived at Pará nearly a year later, traveling the distance by foot, mule, canoe, and small boat. He compiled lists, kept timetables, took boiling points, recorded the weather, studied the flora, and measured and skinned small animals and birds. But he filed his report to the Navy as a narrative, not only cataloging his scientific and commercial observations, not only presenting his studies of the meteorology, anthropology, geology, and natural history of the Amazon, but also rendering his experiences with natives and nature as colorful scenes that exposed the legends and the beauty and the curious customs of the region, creating one of the finest accounts of travel and discovery ever written. It was an explorer's intimate portrait of an exotic land before the outside world rushed in.

Herndon described vampire bats, poisonous blowdarts, and serpents eighteen feet long. He encountered painted blue men with earlobes drooping to their shoulders, and trees so large that the shot from his fowling piece could not reach the lowest branch. His report so far surpassed his superiors' expectations that instead of the obligatory print run of a few hundred copies for Congress, the Secretary of the Navy ordered ten thousand copies in the first run; three months later, he ordered another twenty thousand, and the book became an international best-seller. Herndon recounted his adventures with such insight, such compassion and wit, and such literary grace that he came to symbolize the new spirit of exploration and discovery sweeping mid-nineteenth-century America.

Herndon rendered the exotic Amazon so vivid in the imagination of one young man in Keokuk, Iowa, that the young man quit his job in a print shop and headed for Brazil. He wrote to his brother, "I shall take care that Ma and Orion are plentifully supplied with South American books. They have Herndon's report now." He went by way of Cincinnati, down the Ohio and the Mississippi, figuring that when he got to the end, he would book passage on the next ship out of New Orleans bound for Pará, Brazil. Once there, he would work his way up the Amazon into its tributaries to experience the region Herndon had brought to life in his report. But in New Orleans, he discovered that there was not then, nor had there ever been, a ship leaving for Pará. He was stuck at the dock in New Orleans with little more than the experience of having traveled down the Mississippi and a recollection of boatmen sounding "mark twain." Had Herndon's book not inflamed the imagination of the young Samuel Clemens, Clemens might never have traveled the backwater where he later set so many of his stories, or changed his name, or gone on to write of Tom Sawyer and Huckleberry Finn.

For the next century, Herndon's report was out of print, until a heavily edited version was briefly revived in 1952. For years I have thought that his account had to be one of the greatest chronicles of travel and exploration ever written; parts of it are some of the finest writing of any kind I have ever read.

Reading the journal, four things come clear: One, Herndon

was physically tough, the only officer who could walk over the Andes at sixteen thousand feet and not take sick from the altitude.

Two, he placed great value on friendship and the companionship of other men: At one juncture he decided to split his party and send half of his men along a different route under the command of a junior officer. "I had deliberated long and painfully on the propriety of this separation," wrote Herndon. "I knew that I was depriving myself of a pleasant companion and a most efficient auxiliary.... I felt again that ... swelling of the heart and filling of the eyes that I have so often been called upon to endure in parting from my friends and comrades...."

Three, he possessed the fearless, insatiable curiosity of an explorer, determined to experience one region of the Amazon populated by descendants of the Inca, who a hundred years earlier had destroyed every Catholic mission in the territory and forbade whites to enter. Two years earlier they had routed a Catholic priest who led an armed complement of 150 men.

Four, he delighted in beauty, of sound, color, texture, and form; he possessed an aesthete's eye for the exquisite. He could command a warship, and he could stand in awe of a spider's web. On August 16, 1851, he wrote,

> Lovely morning. On stepping out of the house my attention was attracted by a spider's web covering the whole of a large lemon-tree nearby. The tree was oval and well shaped, and the web was thrown over it in the most artistic manner, and with the finest effect. Broad, flat cords were stretched out, like the cords of a tent, from its circumference to the neighboring bushes; and it looked as if some genie of the lamp, at the command of its master, had exhausted taste and skill to cover with this delicate drapery the rich-looking fruit beneath.

Herndon could translate Latin, Spanish, Portuguese, occasionally quotes from all three, and from poetry. I cannot imagine a more
cultured, sensitive, or capable man, one more at home in society,
with natives, books, and science, as well as at the helm. It was as
though one chamber of his heart beat to the call of the wild, and
another hummed the tune of an artist's muse.

Beyond the heroics and the aesthetics, what made Herndon's
account so charming was his refusal to take himself too seriously.
One afternoon he accompanied a native into the woods to watch him
bring down a large bird with a blowgun. "I admired the stealthy and
noiseless manner with which he moved through the woods, occasionally casting a wondering and reproachful glance at me as I would
catch my foot in a creeper and pitch into the bushes with sufficient
noise to alarm all the game within a mile round."

Some of Herndon's observations seem a century ahead of their
time. He frequently lamented the native women's lot: to do all the
work only to be mistreated, often beaten, by the men; he also observed that, in their strict roles, even women in Peruvian and Brazilian society felt stifled.

But two of his sentiments I find curious, one disturbing: First,
Herndon's obvious reverence for the territory and his unabashed,
contradictory recommendation that it be developed quickly and
fully. Second, that the development, if necessary, come at the
expense of the native tribes. Reflecting his own industry and the energetic, "Manifest Destiny" mood of America in the mid-nineteenth
century, Herndon saw the Amazon territory as bursting with possibility and seemed perplexed by the natives' inability to appreci-
ate the potential. In his eyes, one of the main impediments to the
growth of the region was the natives' complacency, and here we
see the only other inconsistency I can discern in his writings: He
seems at once disdainful of and amused by the laziness. He com-

pares the mind of the Indian to that of an infant, and he adds that
there are intelligent men "who scruple not to say that the best use
to which an Indian can be put is to hang him, that he makes a bad
citizen and a worse slave." Yet he seems enamored of, almost wist-
ful for, the *"dolce far niente"* of the tropical climes, which he calls
the "principal charm" of Pará.

"Men in these countries are not ambitious," he wote.

> They are not annoyed, as the more masculine people of colder
> climates are, to see their neighbors going ahead of them. They
> are contented to live, and to enjoy, without labor, the fruits
> which the earth spontaneously offers. . . . I have very little
> doubt but that the bold and ambitious Englishman, the spir-
> ited and cosmopolitan Frenchman, and the hardy, persever-
> ing, scheming American, who likes little that anyone should
> go ahead of him, would alike, in the course of time, yield to
> the relaxing influence of a climate that forbids him to labor.

Perhaps he distinguished between the native of the field and
forest and the citizen of the city. Nevertheless, the next step in his
vision seems shocking in today's political climate. In 1852 he mused,
"Civilization must advance, though it tread on the neck of the savage, or even trample him out of existence. . . . [T]hrow open the
country to colonization, inducing people to come by privileges and
grants of land. I am satisfied that in this way, if the Indian be not
improved, he will at least be cast out, and that this glorious country
may be made to do what it is not now doing—that is, contribute its
fair proportion to the maintenance of the human race."

Respecting his integrity and his judgment as I do, I find this
fascinating commentary. Were he to take the same journey today,
I believe that the same sensitive and cultured man would find little

reason to recommend the steps he outlined near the end of his journal in 1852:

> Let us now suppose the banks of these streams settled by
> an active and industrious population, desirous to exchange the
> rich products of their lands for the commodities and luxuries
> of foreign countries; let us suppose introduced into such a coun-
> try the railroad and the steamboat, the plough, the axe, and the
> hoe; let us suppose the land divided into large estates, and cul-
> tivated by slave labor, so as to produce all that they are capable
> of producing: And with these considerations, we shall have no
> difficulty in coming to the conclusion that no territory on the
> face of the globe is so favorably situated, and that, if trade there
> is once awakened, the power, the wealth, and grandeur of an-
> cient Babylon and modern London must yield to that of the
> depots of this trade that shall be established at the mouths of
> the Oronoco, the Amazon, and the La Plata.

I find it eerie to read the journal now and realize that though
I know what will happen to him a few years later, he has no idea
what lies ahead; that while trying to save the lives of the women
and children and the five hundred heroic men on the *Central
America,* he will sacrifice his own in the worst disaster at sea in
American history. I consider it a privilege to introduce you to the
remarkable man who lived that oath, and who led the first American expedition into the Valley of the Amazon, William Lewis
Herndon.

—Gary Kinder

Editor's Note

HERNDON FILLED his original account with the names of scores of minor political characters, geographical references, and tribes in the region. He quoted liberally from local sources and references, including exports and costs that today are of little interest. At each hamlet he reported the crops grown and the minerals extracted, and he sounded for depth at every bend of the river, all information required by his superiors. But the majority of these observations only slow his otherwise rich and sympathetic portrait of this exotic land, so I have deleted whole paragraphs, and occasionally a sentence or clause, whose inclusion seemed too detailed, caused confusion, or required too much explanation.

33D CONGRESS, }   HO. OF REPS.   { EXECUTIVE,
1st Session. }   { No. 53.

EXPLORATION

OF THE

VALLEY OF THE AMAZON,

MADE UNDER DIRECTION OF

THE NAVY DEPARTMENT,

BY

WM. LEWIS HERNDON AND LARDNER GIBBON,
LIEUTENANTS UNITED STATES NAVY.

PART I.
BY LIEUT. HERNDON.

WASHINGTON:
ROBERT ARMSTRONG, PUBLIC PRINTER
1854.

LETTER OF THE SECRETARY OF THE NAVY,

COMMUNICATING

A REPORT OF AN EXPLORATION OF THE VALLEY OF THE AMAZON AND

ITS TRIBUTARIES, MADE BY LIEUT. HERNDON, IN CONNECTION WITH

LIEUT. GIBBON.

JANUARY 6, 1854—*Resolved,* That there be printed, for the use of the members of the House, ten thousand extra copies of the report of the Secretary of the Navy communicating the reports of the exploration of the river Amazon and its tributaries, made by Lieutenants Herndon and Gibbon, with the accompanying maps and plates.

APRIL 13, 1854—*Resolved,* That there be printed twenty thousand additional copies of the reports of the surveys and explorations of the river Amazon, with the plates and maps accompanying, by Lieutenants Herndon and Gibbon—two hundred and fifty copies for distribution by Lieutenant Herndon, and two hundred and fifty copies by Lieutenant Gibbon, and the remainder for the use of the members of the House.

To the Senate and House of Representatives:

I herewith transmit a communication from the Secretary of the Navy, accompanied by the first part of Lieut. Herndon's Report of the Exploration of the Valley of the Amazon and its tributaries, made by him, in connexion with Lieut. Lardner Gibbon, under instructions from the Navy Department.

MILLARD FILLMORE.

WASHINGTON, *February* 9, 1853.

I

NAVY DEPARTMENT, *February* 7, 1853.

To the PRESENT.

SIR: In compliance with the notice given in the annual
report of this department to the President, and communi-
cated to Congress at the opening of its present session, I have
the honor herewith to submit the first part of the Report of
Lieut. Herndon, of the Exploration of the Valley of the
Amazon and its tributaries, made by him, in connection
with Lieut. Lardner Gibbon, under instructions from this
department, dated the 15th of February, 1851.

I am happy to be able to inform you that Lieut. Gibbon
reached Pará on his homeward journey some weeks ago,
and may very soon be expected to arrive in the United
States. When he returns, Lieut. Herndon will have all the
materials necessary to complete his report, and will devote
himself to that labor with the same assiduity which has
characterized his present work.

I would respectfully beg leave to suggest that, in
submitting this report to the House of Representatives, it be
accompanied with a request to that body, if it should think
proper to direct the printing of this valuable document, that
the order for that purpose may include all the remaining
portions of the report which may hereafter be furnished; and
that the order for printing shall include a suitable direction
for the engraving and publication of the maps, charts, and
sketches, which will be furnished as necessary illustrations of
the subjects treated of in the report.

I have the honor to be, with the highest consideration,
your obedient servant,

JOHN P. KENNEDY.

WASHINGTON CITY, *January 26, 1853.*

To the Hon. JOHN P. KENNEDY,

Secretary of the Navy.

SIR: I have the honor to submit part first of the Report of an Exploration of the Valley of the Amazon, made by me, with the assistance of Lieut. Lardner Gibbon, under instructions of the Navy Department, bearing date February 15, 1851.

The desire expressed by the department for an early report of my exploration of the Amazon, and the general interest manifested in the public mind with regard to the same, have induced me to lay before you at once as full an account of our proceedings as can be made before the return of my companion.

The general map which accompanies the report is based upon maps published by the Society for the diffusion of Useful Knowledge, but corrected and improved according to my own personal observations, and on information obtained by me whilst in that country.

The final report of the expedition will be submitted as soon after Lieut. Gibbon's return as practicable. I am in daily expectation of intelligence about him. At the latest accounts (26th of July, 1852) he was at Trinidad de Moxos, on the Mamoré, in the republic of Bolivia, making his preparations for the descent of the Madeira.

I have the honor to be, very respectfully, your obedient servant,

WM. LEWIS HERNDON,
Lieut. U.S. Navy.

Chapter I

INTRODUCTORY

United States ship Vandalia—*Valparaiso—Santiago—*
Preparatory orders—Lima—Means of information—Conquests
of the Incas in the Montaña—First explorations of the
Spaniards—Madame Godin

ATTACHED TO THE U.S. SHIP VANDALIA, of the Pacific squadron,
lying at anchor in the harbor of Valparaiso, in the month of August, 1850, I received a communication from the Superintendent
of the National Observatory, informing me that orders to explore
the Valley of the Amazon would be sent by the next mail steamer.

The ship was then bound for the Sandwich Islands, but Captain Gardner, with that kindness which ever characterized his
intercourse with his officers, did not hesitate to detach me from
the ship, and to give me permission to await, at Valparaiso, the
arrival of my instructions.

The officers expressed much flattering regret at my leaving the
ship, and loaded me with little personal mementos—things that
might be of use to me on my proposed journey.

On the sixth of August I unexpectedly saw, from the windows
of the club-house at Valparaiso, the topsails of the ship mounting
to the mastheads; I saw that she must needs make a stretch in-shore

to clear the rocks that lie off the western point of the bay, and desirous to say farewell to my friends, I leaped into a shore-boat and shoved off, with the hope of reaching her before she went about. The oarsmen, influenced by the promise of a pair of dollars if they put me on board, bent to their oars with a will, and the light whaleboat seemed to fly; but just as I was clearing the outer line of merchantmen, the ship came sweeping up to the wind, and as she gracefully fell off on the other tack, her royals and courses were set; and bending to the steady northeast breeze, she darted out of the harbor at a rate that set pursuit at defiance. God's blessing go with the beautiful ship, and the gallant gentlemen, her officers, who had been to me as brothers.

Owing to the death of President Taylor, and the consequent change in the Cabinet, my orders were delayed, and I spent several weeks in Valparaiso, and Santiago, the capital of Chili. This time, however, was not thrown away: My residence in these cities improved my knowledge of the Spanish language, and gave me information regarding the Bolivian tributaries of the Amazon which I probably could have got nowhere else.

The city of Santiago is situated in a lovely plain at the very foot of the cordillera. The snowy summits of this chain, painted in bold relief against the hard, gray sky of the morning, have a very singular and beautiful appearance; they seem cut from white marble, and within reach of the hand. It is almost impossible to give an idea of the transparency of the atmosphere at this place. I was never tired of watching, from a little observatory, the stars rising over these mountains. There was nothing of the faint and indistinct glimmer which stars generally present when rising from the ocean; but they burst forth in an instant of time, in the full blaze of their beauty, and seemed as if just created.

Chili, in arts and civilization, is far ahead of any other South American republic. There are many young men of native families, educated in the best manner in Europe, who would be ornaments to any society; and the manners of the ladies are marked by a simple, open, engaging cordiality that seems peculiar to Creoles. I do not know a more pleasant place of residence than Santiago, except for two causes: one, earthquakes, to the terrors of which no familiarity breeds indifference; the other, the readiness of the people to appeal to the bayonet for the settlement of political differences, or in the struggle for political power. These two causes shook the city and society to their foundations a few months after I left it.

On the twentieth of January, 1851, I received the following instructions from the Hon. William A. Graham, Secretary of the Navy:

NAVY DEPARTMENT, *October 30, 1850.*

SIR: Proceed to Lima, for the purpose of collecting from the monasteries, and other authentic sources that may be accessible to you, information concerning the headwaters of the Amazon and the regions of country drained by its Peruvian tributaries. You will then visit the monasteries of Bolivia for a like purpose, touching the Bolivian tributaries of that river, should it in your judgment be desirable.

The object of the department in assigning you to this service is with the view of directing you to explore the Valley of the Amazon, should the consent of Brazil therefore be obtained; and the information you are directed to obtain is such as would tend to assist and guide you in such exploration, should you be directed to make it.

As this service to which you are now assigned may probably involve the necessity of the occasional expenditure of a small amount on government account, you are furnished with a bill of credit for one thousand dollars, for which you will account to the proper office.

Also, enclosed you will find a letter of introduction to Messrs. Clay and McClung, chargés d'affaires near the governments of Peru and Bolivia.

Respectfully, &c.,
WILLIAM A. GRAHAM.

As I had obtained from my Santiago and Valparaiso friends all the information that I would be likely to get in the cities of Bolivia, I determined to proceed to Lima, and accordingly embarked on board the mail boat of the twenty-sixth.

My residence in Valparaiso had made new friends and established new ties, that I found painful to break; but this is the lot of the navy officer: Separated from his family for years, he is brought into the closest and most intimate association with his messmates, and forms ties which are made but to be broken, generally by many years of separation. Taken from these, he is thrown among strangers, and becomes dependent upon their kindness and hospitality for the only enjoyments that make his life endurable. Receiving these, his heart yearns towards the donors; and my Valparaiso friends will readily believe that I was sad enough when compelled to leave them.

I arrived in Lima on the sixth of February. This city has changed greatly since I was here twenty years ago. Though we had bullfights on the accession of the new president, yet the noble amphitheatre was not crowded as in old times with the *élite* and fashion of Lima, but seemed abandoned to the vulgar. The ladies have given up their peculiar and most graceful national costume, the *Saya y Manto,* and it is now the mark of a ragged reputation. They dress in the French style, frequent the opera, and, instead of the *Yerba de Paraguay,* called *matté,* of which they used a great quantity formerly, they now take tea. These are causes for regret, for one likes to see nationality preserved; but there is one cause for congratulation (especially on the part of sea-going men, who have sometimes suffered), the railroad between Lima and Callao has broken up the robbers.

But with these matters I have nothing to do. My first business at Lima was to establish relations with the accomplished and learned superintendent of the public library. This gentleman, who is an ecclesiastic and a member of the Senate, has so high a character for learning and honesty that, though a partisan politician and a member of the opposition to the new government, he preserves (a rare thing in Peru) the respect and confidence of all. He placed the books of the library at my disposal, and kindly selected for me those that would be of service.

The sources of information, however, were small and unsatisfactory. The military expeditions into the country to the eastward of the Andes left little or no reliable traces of their labors. The records of the exploration of the Jesuits were out of my reach, in the archives of Quito—at that time the head of the diocese, and the starting point of the missions into the interior—and nearly all that I could get at were some meagre accounts of the operations of the Franciscans.

Though the information obtained in Lima was not great, I still think that a slight historical sketch of the attempts to explore the Montaña* of Peru, made since the conquest of that country by Pizarro, will not be uninteresting.

---

*Montaña (pronounced Montanya) is the name given by the Peruvians to any wooded country, *monte* being the Spanish term for a thick and tangled forest. As there is no other wooded country in Peru except to the eastward of the Andes, the term applies only to the eastern slope, and the level country at the base of the mountains, stretching as far as the confines of Brazil.

Modern books upon the subject—such as Prescott's *Peru;* Humboldt's *Narrative;* Von Tschude's *Travels;* Smith's *Peru As It Is;* Condamine's *Voyage on the Amazon*—were all consulted, and, together with oral communications from persons who had visited various parts of the Valley of the Amazon, gave me all the information within my reach, and prepared me to start upon my journey at least with open eyes.

The attention of the Peruvian government was directed to the country east of the Andes even before the time of the Spanish conquest. The sixth Inca, Rocca, sent his son, at the head of fifteen thousand men, with three generals as companions and advisers, to the conquest of the country to the northward and eastward of Cuzco, inhabited by Indians called Antis. The young prince added a space of thirty leagues in that direction to the dominions of his father, but could reach no further on account of the roughness of the country and the difficulties of the march. The tenth and great Inca, Yupanqui, sent an expedition of ten thousand men to pursue the conquests. These reached the Montaña, and, embarking on rafts upon the great river Amarumayo, fought their way through tribes called Chunchos, till they arrived, with only a thousand men, into the territory of tribes called Musus. Finding their numbers now too small for conquest, they persuaded these Indians that they were friends, and, by their superior civilization, obtained such an ascendency among them that the Musus agreed to send ambassadors to render homage and worship to the "Child of the Sun," and gave these men of the Inca race their daughters in marriage, and a place in their tribe.

Years afterwards, the Incas and their descendants desired to return to Cuzco; but in the midst of their preparations they received intelligence of the downfall of their nation, and settled finally among the Musus, who adopted many of the laws, customs, usages, and worship of the Incas.

I have little doubt of the truth of this account, for even at the present day may be found amongst the savages who dwell about the headwaters of the Ucayali, the Purus, and in the country between the Purus and Beni, traces of the warlike character of the mountain race, and that invincible hatred of the white man which the descendants of the Incas may well be supposed to feel. This determined hostility and warlike character prevented me from embarking upon the Chanchamayo to descend the Ucayali and was the cause why I could not get men to ascend the Ucayali from Sarayacu.

This character is entirely distinct from that of the Indians of the plains everywhere in South America, who are, in general, gentle, docile, and obedient, and who fear the white man with an abject and craven fear.

Love of dominion and power had induced the Indian princes of Peru to waste their treasures and the lives of their subjects in the subjugation of the Montaña. A stronger passion was now to urge a stronger people in the same direction. Stories of great empires, which had obtained the names of Gran Pará and El Dorado, filled with large and populous cities, whose streets were paved with gold; of a lake of golden sand, called Parima; of a gilded king, who, when he rose in the morning, was smeared with oil, and covered with gold dust blown upon him by his courtiers through long reeds, and of immense mineral and vegetable treasures, had for some time filled the ears and occupied the minds of the avaricious conquerors.

Hernando Pizarro fitted out two expeditions. These men, led on by the report of the Indians, who constantly asserted that the rich countries they sought lay yet farther to the eastward, penetrated, it is supposed, as far as the Beni; but, overcome by danger, privation, and suffering, they returned with no results, save marvellous stories of what they had seen and learned, which inflamed the curiosity and cupidity of others. These parties were generally accompanied by an ecclesiastic, who was the historian of the expedition. Some idea may be formed of the worthlessness of their records by examining a few of the stories related by them. Here is one:

> Juan Alvarez Maldonado made an expedition from Cuzco in the year 1561. He descended the eastern range of the Andes, and had scarcely cleared the rough and rocky ground of the slope when his party encountered two pigmies. They shot the female, and the male died of grief six days afterwards.
>
> Following the course of the great river Mano downwards, at the distance of two hundred leagues they landed upon a beach, and a piquet of soldiers penetrated into the woods. They found the trees so tall as to exceed an arrow-shot in height, and so large that six men, with joined hands, could scarcely circle them. Here they found lying upon the ground a man, five yards in height, members in proportion, long snout, projecting teeth, vesture of beautiful leopard skin, short and shrivelled, and, for a walking-stick, a tree, which he played with as with a cane. On his attempting to rise, they shot him dead, and returned to the boat to give notice to their companions. These went to the spot, and found traces of his having been carried off. Following the track towards a neighboring hill, they heard such shouts and vociferations that they were astounded, and, horror-stricken, fled.

These are of the number of stories which, inflaming the cupidity of the Spaniards, led them to brave the perils of the wilderness in search of El Dorado. They serve to show at this day the little confidence which is to be placed in the relations of the friars concerning this country; I do not imagine, however, that they are broad lies. The soldiers of Maldonado evidently mistook monkeys for pigmies, and some beast of the forest, probably the tapir, for a giant.

But the defeated followers of one faction, flying from before the face of the still victorious Pizarros, did find to the eastward of Cuzco a country answering, in some degree, to the description of the fabulous El Dorado. They penetrated into the valleys of Carabaya, and found there washings of gold of great value. They subjugated the Indians, built the towns of San Juan del Oro and others, and sent large quantities of gold to Spain. On one occasion they sent a mass of gold in the shape of an ox's head, and of the weight of two hundred pounds, as a present to Charles V. The Emperor, in acknowledgment, gave the title of "Royal City" to the town of San Juan del Oro, and ennobled its inhabitants. The Indians, however, in the course of time, revolted, murdered their oppressors, and destroyed their towns. Up to the last three years this has been a sealed country to the white man. I shall have occasion to refer to it again.

It is not to be expected that information of an exact and scientific character could be had from the voyages of adventurers like these. They were mere soldiers, and too much occupied in difficulties of travel, conflicts with Indians, ambitious designs, and internal dissentions, to make any notes of the topography or productions of the countries they passed through.

But a task that had baffled the ambition and power of the Incas and love of gold, backed by the indomitable spirit and courage of the hardy Spanish soldier, was now to be undertaken by men who were urged on by a yet more absorbing passion than either of these. I mean missionary zeal—the love of propagating the faith.

The first missionary stations established in the Montaña were founded by two Fathers of the holy company of the Jesuits in 1737. They commenced operations at the village of St. Francis de Borja, founded in 1634 and situated on the left bank of the Marañón, not far below where it breaks its way through the last chain of hills that obstructs its course.

In the same year (1637), according to a source (whose statements, I think, are always to be received *cum grano salis*), a Portuguese captain ascended the Amazon with a fleet mounting forty-seven large guns. After an eight months' voyage from Pará, he arrived at the port of Payamino, on the river Napo. I am unable to find out how far up the Napo this is; but leaving his fleet there, the captain went with some of his officers by land to Quito. The Royal Audience of that city determined to send explorers with him on his return, and two Jesuit Fathers were selected for that purpose, and directed to report to the King of Spain.

The Spanish government, then occupied with the rebellion of Portugal, could lend no aid to the missionaries, and one of the Jesuit Fathers returned to Quito in 1643. He appealed to the Royal Audience, and to the college of the Jesuits at that city, for help to the missions, and the latter institution furnished him with five or six missionaries. These were well received by the Indians, and prosecuted their labors with such success that in the year 1666 they had formed thirteen large and populous settlements in the country, bordering on the upper Marañón, and near the mouths of the Pastaza, Ucayali, and Huallaga.

About this time the Franciscans commenced pushing their explorations and missionary operations from Lima, by the way of Tarma and Jauxa, into the Montaña, drained by the headwaters of the Ucayali; and here we begin to get a little topographical information, and the map may now be consulted in elucidation of the text.

About this time the Franciscans, also penetrating from Tarma by the valleys of Chanchamayo and Vitoc, established the missions of the Cerro de la Sal and the Pajonal. The Cerro de la Sal is described as a mountain of rock and red earth, with veins of salt of thirty yards in breadth, to which the Indians, for many miles around, were in the habit of repairing for their supply. The Pajonal is a great grassy plain, enclosed between the river Pachitea and a great bend of the Ucayali. It is about 120 miles in length from north to south, and ninety from east to west; and I judge from its name, and some imperfect descriptions of it, that it is a very fine grazing country.

In the year 1712 Padre Francisco de San José established a college at the village of Ocopa, in the Andes, a few leagues from Jauxa. By his zeal and abilities he induced many European monks, of the order of St. Francis, to come over and join him in his missionary labors. These men labored so successfully that up to 1742 they had established ten towns in the Pajonal and Cerro de la Sal, and had under their spiritual direction ten thousand converts. But in this year an Indian of Cuzco, who had been converted and baptized as Juan Santos, apostatized from the faith; and, taking upon himself the style and title of Inca, and the name of Atahuallpa, excited to rebellion all the Indians of the plain, and swept away every trace of the missionary rule, some seventy or eighty of the priests perishing in the wreck.

It is quite evident that no distaste for the Catholic religion induced this rebellion; for in the year 1750, eight years afterward, the Marquis marching into this country for the punishment of the rebels, found the church at Quimiri, on the river Perené, in perfect order, with candles burning before the images. He burned the town and church. And six years after this, when another entrance into this country was made by a general, he found the town rebuilt, and a large cross erected in the middle of the plaza, or public square. I have had occasion myself to notice the respect and reverence of these Indians for their pastors, and their delight in participating in the ceremonial and sense-striking worship of the Roman Church.

It remains but to speak of the conversions of the Ucayali, which are the only trophies that now remain of the zeal, patience, and suffering of these devoted men. The missions established on the Ucayali were lost by insurrections of the Indians in 1704. In 1726 the converted Indians, about the head of canoe navigation on the Huallaga, discovered a wooded plain, which was named Pampa del Sacramento, from the day of its discovery being the festival of Corpus Christi. This was a new field for the missionary; and by 1760 the Fathers had penetrated across this plain to the Ucayali, and re-established the missions. Several missionaries lost their lives by the Cashibos Indians; and in 1767 the Indians of the Ucayali rose upon the missionaries, killed nine of them, and broke up their settlements. But not for this were they to be deterred. In 1790, another Father, with two others, again established these missions, of which there remain three at this time.

The difficulties of penetrating into these countries, where the path is to be broken for the first time, can only be conceived by one who has travelled over the roads already trodden. The broken and precipitous mountain track—the deep morass—the thick and tangled forest—the danger from Indians, wild beasts, and reptiles—the scarcity of provisions—the exposure to the almost appalling rains—and the navigation of the impetuous and rock-obstructed river, threatening at every moment shipwreck to the frail canoe—

form obstacles that might daunt any heart but that of the gold-hunter or the missionary.

The most remarkable voyage down the Amazon was made by a woman. Madame Godin des Odonnais, wife of one of the French commissioners who was sent to measure an arc of the meridian near Quito, started in 1769, from Rio Bamba, in Ecuador, to join her husband in Cayenne by the route of the Amazon. She embarked at Canelos, on the Borbonaza, with a company of eight persons, two, besides herself, being females. On the third day the Indians who conducted their canoe deserted: Another Indian, whom they found sick in a hovel near the bank, and employed as pilot, fell from the canoe in endeavoring to pick up the hat of one of the party, and was drowned.

The canoe, under their own management, soon capsized, and they lost their clothing and provisions. Three men of the party now started for Andoas, on the Pastaza, which they supposed themselves to be within five or six days of, and never returned. The party left behind, now consisting of the three females and two brothers of Madame Godin, lashed a few logs together and attempted again to navigate; but their frail vessel soon went to pieces by striking against the fallen trees in the river. They then attempted to journey on foot along the banks of the river, but finding the growth here too thick and tangled for them to make any way, they struck off into the forest in hopes of finding a less obstructed path.

They were soon lost: Despair took possession of them, and they perished miserably of hunger and exhaustion. Madame Godin, recovering from a swoon, which she supposes to have been of many hours' duration, took the shoes from her dead brother's feet and started to walk, she knew not whither. Her clothes were soon torn to rags, her body lacerated by her exertions in forcing her way through the tangled and thorny undergrowth, and she was kept constantly in a state of deadly terror by the howl of the tiger and the hiss of the serpent. It is wonderful that she preserved her reason. Eight terrible days and nights did she wander alone in the howling wilderness, supported by a few berries and birds' eggs. Providentially (one cannot say accidentally) she struck the river at a point where two Indians (a man and a woman) were just launching a canoe. They received her with kindness, furnished her with food, gave her a coarse cotton petticoat, which she preserved for years afterwards as a memorial of their goodness, and carried her in their canoe to Andoas, whence she found a passage down the river, and finally joined her husband. Her hair turned gray from suffering, and she could never hear the incidents of her voyage alluded to without a feeling of horror that bordered on insanity.

Chapter II

INTRODUCTORY

*Orders—Investigation of routes—River Beni—Cuzco route—
Preparations for the journey—The start*

ON THE FOURTH OF APRIL, 1851, Lieutenant Lardner Gibbon, of the Navy, arrived at Lima, and delivered me orders from the Navy Department, of which the following is a copy:

NAVY DEPARTMENT, *February 15, 1851.*

SIR: The department is about to confide to you a most important and delicate duty, which will call for the exercise of all those high qualities and attainments, on account of which you have been selected.

The government desires to be put in possession of certain information relating to the valley of the river Amazon, in which term is included the entire basin, or water-shed, drained by that river and its tributaries.

This desire extends not only to the present condition of that valley, with regard to the navigability of its streams; to the number and condition, both industrial and social, of its inhabitants, their trade and products; its climate, soil, and productions; but also to its capacities for cultivation, and to the character and extent of its undeveloped commercial resources, whether of the field, the forest, the river, or the mine.

You will, for the purpose of obtaining such information, proceed across the Cordillera, and explore the Amazon from its source to its mouth.

Passed Midshipman Lardner Gibbon, a prudent and intelligent officer, has been selected to accompany you on this service, and is instructed to report accordingly.

This, together with a few instruments, necessary for such an expedition, will be delivered to you by him.

Being joined by him, you will commence to make such arrangements as may be necessary for crossing the Andes and descending the Amazon; and having completed them, you will then proceed on your journey without further orders.

The route by which you may reach the Amazon River is left to your discretion. Whether you will descend the Ucayali, or the Huallaga, or any other of the Peruvian tributaries, or whether you will cross over into Bolivia, and, passing through the province of Yongas, embark on the Mamoré or Ytenes, or whether you will try the Beni or any other route to the Madeira, and thence to the Amazon, the state of the information which you have collected, under a former order, will enable you to decide more judiciously than it is possible for the department, with the meagre state of its information upon the subject, to do.

It is not desired that you should select any route by which you and your party would be exposed to savage hostility, beyond your means of defence and protection.

Neither is it desirable that your party should be so large, on the one hand, as to excite the suspicion of the people, or give offence to the authorities, of the country through which you may pass, nor so small, on the other, as to endanger its success.

You are, therefore, authorized to employ a cook, servant, guide, and interpreter, and to provide them with such arms as it is customary only for travellers generally, in that part of the world, to carry for their own protection. And these arms you will have returned to you at Pará.

The Navy Agent at Lima has been instructed to furnish, upon your requisition, the necessary articles for the outfit of yourself and party, and to honor your draft for a sum not exceeding five thousand dollars, to cover your expenses by the way. As these expenses will be mostly for mules and *arrieros,* boats and boats' crews, it is supposed that the sum named will be much more than sufficient. You will use of it only for the *necessary* expenses of the party.

The geographical situation and the commercial position of the Amazon indicate the future importance, to this country, of the free navigation of that river.

To enable the government to form a proper estimate as to the degree of that importance, present and prospective, is the object of your mission.

You will, therefore, avail yourself of the best sources of information that can be had in answer to any or all of the following questions:

What is the present condition of the silver mines of Peru, and Bolivia—their yield; how and by whom are they principally wrought?

What is the machinery used, whence obtained, and how transported?

Are mines of this metal, which are not worked, known to exist? What impulse would the free navigation of the Amazon give to the working of those mines? What are their capacities; and if the navigation of that river and its tributaries were open to commerce, what effect would it have in turning the stream of silver from those mines down these rivers? With what description of craft can they be navigated respectively?

What inducements are offered by the laws of Peru and Bolivia for emigrants to settle in the eastern provinces of those two republics, and what is the amount and character of the population already there? What are the productions? the value of the trade with them—of what articles does it consist, where manufactured, how introduced, and at what charges upon prime cost?

What are the staple productions for which the climate and soil of the valley of the Amazon, in different parts, are adapted? What is the state of tillage; of what class are the laborers; the value of a day's work; the yield per acre and per hand of the various staples, such as matté, coca and cocoa, sugar, rice, *cinchona,* hemp, cotton, India-rubber, coffee, balsams, drugs, spices, dyes, and ornamental woods; the season for planting and gathering; the price at the place of production, and at the principal commercial mart; the mode and means of transportation? with every other item of information that is calculated to interest a nautical and commercial people.

You will make such geographical and scientific observations by the way as may be consistent with the main object of the expedition, always bearing in mind that these are merely incidental, and that no part of the main objects of the expedition is to be interfered with by them.

It is desirable that you should bring home with you specimens or samples of the various articles of product from the Amazon River, together with such seeds or plants as might probably be introduced into this country with advantage.

Arriving at Pará, you will embark by the first opportunity for the United States, and report in person to this department.

Wishing you a pleasant journey and a safe return to your country and friends,

I am, respectfully, your obedient servant,

WILL. A. GRAHAM.

Lieut. WILLIAM L. HERNDON, *U.S. NAVY, Peru, or Bolivia.*

As the choice of route was thus left to my discretion, this, in connexion with the best and most efficient mode of carrying out my instructions, became an object of much consideration with me.

Upon my arrival in Lima, I immediately set to work to investigate routes. As I had some time previously received intimation of the intention of the department to issue such orders, whilst in Valparaiso and Santiago I had sought what information was to be had there, and conversed with many persons regarding the routes through Bolivia and the navigability of the Bolivian tributaries of the Amazon. Two interesting routes presented themselves through this country: one from Cochabamba, by the river Mamoré, and the other by the Beni (also a confluent of the Madeira), which seems nearly a *terra incognita.*

It was suggested that I should take the route of the Beni on account of the honor of discovery, and the addition I should make to geographical knowledge; and the ex-President of Bolivia strongly urged me to take one of the Bolivian rivers, but an unanswerable objection to this in my mind was that such a route would bring me into the Amazon very low down, and make the necessity of ascending that river to its sources; a work which would occupy years in its execution, and probably break down a much stronger man than I am.

A deputy in Congress from Cuzco in strong and earnest terms advocated the propriety of taking the Cuzco route. But this route had the same objections as that by the Bolivian tributaries; that is, it would bring me into the Amazon too low down. It is, however, a route of great importance, and well worth investigation. There is no doubt that there is a great unknown river in these parts. Every expedition made into this country brought back accounts of it, and represented it under various names as great and containing much water.

If there should be a navigable communication between this country and the Atlantic, the advantages to commerce would be enormous, and the *Brillante Porvenir,* or dazzling future of Cuzco, would be no dream. I judge, from the description of the country through which this "great river" flows, that it is not navigable. Yet I judge that there is a much nearer and easier communication with the Atlantic by this route, than by the passage of the Cordillera and the voyage around Cape Horn; and that the opening to trade of a country which produces, in abundance, gold, and the best quality of *cinchona,* would soon repay the courage, enterprise, and outlay of money which would be necessary to open, at most, but a short road, and to remove a few obstructions from a river.

I felt that, under my instructions requiring me to explore the Amazon from its source to its mouth, I could not neglect a third route, which I finally determined to take. It would enable me to form a judgment respecting the practicability of a transitable connexion between Lima and the navigable headwaters of the tributaries of the Amazon—would lead me through the richest and most productive mineral district of Peru—would put under my observation nearly all the course of the Amazon—and would enable me to gather information regarding the *Pampa del Sacramento,* or great plain, shut in between four great rivers, and concerning which the *Viagero Universal* says "that the two continents of America do not contain another country so favorably situated, or so fertile."

This last and most commonly used route to the Montaña is through the cities of Truxillo, Caxamarca, Chachapoyas, Moyobamba, &c. The Andes here break into many chains, sending off spurs in all directions, but none of any great height, so that there is a tolerably good mule road all the way to Moyobamba; and almost all articles of foreign manufacture are supplied by this route. The climate and productions of this country are, on account of its precipitous elevations, and, consequently, deep valleys, very various; and here the sugar-cane and the pine-apple may be seen growing by a spectator standing in the barley field and the potato patch.

This route crosses the Amazon, or rather the Marañon, where it is sixty yards wide, and rushes between mountains whose summits are hid in the clouds. This point is about three degrees north of its source, in Lake Lauricocha, but the river is nowhere navigable until Tomependa, whence it may be descended, but with great peril and difficulty, on rafts. There are twenty-seven *pongos,* or rapids, to pass, and the water rushes over these with frightful velocity. Four days of such navigation passes the last, and I am satisfied that an unbroken channel of at least eighteen feet in depth may be found thence to the Atlantic Ocean.

That the rains might be entirely over, and the roads on the mend in the Cordillera, I fixed upon the twentieth of May as the day of departure, and Mr. Gibbon and I set about making the necessary preparations. I engaged the services of Don Manuel Ijurra, a young Peruvian, who had made the voyage down the Amazon a few years before, as interpreter to the Indians; and the captain of a frigate was kind enough to give me a young master's mate from his ship, named Richards, besides supplying me with carbines, pistols, ammunition, and a tent. Another captain also offered me anything that the ship could supply, and furnished me with more arms, and fifteen hundred fathoms of the fishing-line now put on board ships for deep-sea soundings.

Our purchases were four saddle-mules, which, through the agency of Dr. Smith, we were fortunate enough to get young, sound, and well bitted (indispensable requisites), out of a drove just in from the mountains. We consulted the learned in such matters on the propriety of having them shod, and found the doctors disagreeing upon this subject very much. As they were from the mountains, and their hoofs were round, sound, and apparently as hard as iron, we decided not to shoe; and, I believe, did better than if we had followed a contrary course. We also purchased about a thousand yards of coarse cotton cloth, made in the mills at Lima, and put up for mountain travel in bales of half a mule-load; hatchets, knives, tinder-boxes, fish-hooks, beads, looking-glasses, cotton handkerchiefs, ribbons, and cheap trinkets, which we thought might take the fancy of the Indians, and purchase us services and food when money would not. These things were also put up in boxes of the same size and shape, and each equal to half a mule-load. Our trunks were arranged in the same way, so that they might be lashed one on each side of the mule's back, with an India-rubber bag, which carried our bedclothes, put on top in the space between them. This makes a compact and easily handled load; and every traveller in the Cordillera should take care to arrange his baggage in this way, and have, as far as possible, everything under lock and key, and in water-tight chests. Such small, incongruous articles as our pots and pans for cooking, our tent, and particularly the tent-pole, which was carried fore and aft above a cargo, and which, from its length, was poking into everything, and constantly getting awry, gave us more trouble than anything else.

Our bedding consisted of the saddle-cloths, a stout blanket, and anything else that could be packed in the India-rubber bag. An Englishman from New Holland, whom I met in Lima, gave me a coverlet made of the skins of a kind of raccoon, which served me many a good turn; and often, when in the cold of the Cordillera I wrapped myself in its warm folds, I felt a thrill of gratitude for the thoughtful kindness which had provided me with such a comfort. We purchased thick flannel shirts, *ponchos* of India-rubber, wool, and cotton, and had straw hats, covered with oil-cloth, and fitted with green veils, to protect our eyes from the painful affections which often occur by the sudden bursting out of the sunlight upon the masses of snow that lie forever upon the mountain tops.

We carried two small kegs—one containing brandy, for drinking, and the other the common rum of the country, called *Ron de Quemar,* for burning; also, some coarse knives, forks, spoons, tin cups, and plates. I did not carry, as I should have done, a few cases of preserved meat, sardines, cheese, &c., which would have given us a much more agreeable meal than we often got on the road; but

I did carry, in the India-rubber bags, quite a large quantity of biscuit, which I had baked in Lima, which served a very good purpose, and lasted us to Tarma.

We had the mules fitted with the heavy, deep-seated box saddles of Peru. I believe the English saddle would be much more comfortable, and probably as safe to the rider accustomed to it; but it would be almost impossible with these to preserve the skin of the mule from chafe. The Peruvian saddles rest entirely upon the ribs of the animal, which are protected by at least six yards of a coarse woollen fabric manufactured in the country, called *jerga,* and touch the back-bone nowhere. These saddles are a wooden box frame, stuffed thickly on the inside, and covered outwardly with buckskin. They are fitted with heavy, square, wooden stirrups, which are thought to preserve the legs from contact with projecting rocks, and, being lined with fur, to keep the feet warm. There is also a heavy breast-strap and crupper for steep ascents and descents; and a thick *pillon,* or mat, made of thrums of cotton, silk, or hair, is thrown over the saddle, to make the seat soft. The reins and head-stall of the bridle should be broad and strong, and the bit the coarse and powerful one of the country.

Our guns, in leathern cases, were slung to the crupper, and the pistols carried in holsters, made with large pockets, to carry powder-flasks, percussion caps, specimens that we might pick up on the road, &c. A small box of instruments for skinning birds and dissecting animals; a medicine chest, containing, among other things, some arsenical soap, for preserving skins; a few reams of coarse paper, for drying leaves and plants; chart paper, in a tin case; passports and other papers, also in a tin case; note-books, pencils, &c., completed our outfit. A chest was made, with compartments for the sextant, artificial horizon, boiling-point apparatus, camera lucida, and spy-glass. The chronometer was carried in the pocket, and the barometer, slung in a leathern case made for it, at the saddle-bow of Mr. Gibbon's mule.

Before leaving Lima I had several interviews with the President, who exhibited much interest in my mission; and the U.S. chargé d'affaires had presented me to the Minister of Peru, who caused to be issued to me the following passport and letter:

To the PREFECT OF THE DEPARTMENT OF AMAZONAS.

SIR: Wm. Lewis Herndon, lieutenant of the Navy of the United States, and Lardner Gibbon, passed midshipman of the same, commissioned by the goverment of that nation to make a scientific expedition in the eastern parts of Peru, accompanied by Henry Richards, Mauricio N., and Manuel Ijurra, as adjuncts to the expedition, direct themselves toward the department under your command in the discharge of their commission. As the expedition deserves, on account of its important object, the particular protection of the government, his Excellency the President commands me to advise you to afford them whatever resources and facilities they may need for the better discharge of their commission, taking care, likewise, that there shall be preserved to them the considerations that are their due.

The which I communicate to you for its punctual fulfilment.

God preserve you.

Given in Lima, the 13th of May, 1851.

On the fifteenth of May I engaged the services of an *arriero,* or muleteer. He engaged to furnish beasts to carry the party and its baggage from Lima to Tarma at ten dollars the head, stopping on the road wherever I pleased, and as long as I pleased, for that sum.

An ordinary train of baggage mules may be had on the same route for about seven dollars the head. The *arrieros* of Peru, as a class, have a very indifferent reputation for faithfulness and honesty, and those on the route (that from Lima to Cerro Pasco), to which my friend particularly belonged, are said to be the worst of their class. He was a thin, spare, dark Indian, of the Sierra or mountain land, about forty-five years of age, with keen, black eye, thin moustache, and deliberate in his speech and gesture. I thought I had seldom seen a worse face; but Mr. McCall said that he was rather better-looking than the generality of them. He managed to cheat me very soon after our acquaintance.

Arrieros, when they supply as many mules as I had engaged, always furnish a *peon,* or assistant, to help load and unload, and take care of the mules. Mine, taking advantage of my ignorance in these matters, said to me that his *peon* was *desanimado* (disheartened), was afraid of the *Piedra Parada*, or upright rock, where we were to cross the Cordillera, and had backed out; but that he himself could very well attend to the mules if I would be good enough to let him have the occasional assistance of my Indian servant. I unwarily promised, which was the cause of a good deal of difficulty; but when the old rascal complained of over-work and sickness on the road, I had an answer for him which always silenced him—that is, that it was his own cupidity and dishonesty which caused it, and that if he did not work and behave himself, I would discharge him without pay, and send back to Lima for another.

I directed him to bring the mules to the hotel door on the twentieth; but, upon his finding that this was Tuesday, he demurred, saying that it was an unlucky day, and that no *arriero* was willing to start on that day, but that Monday was lucky, and begged that I would be ready by then. This I could not do; so that on Wednesday, the twenty-first of May, we loaded up, though I had to cajole, and finally to bribe, the old fellow to take on all the baggage, which he represented to be too much for his beasts.

I did wrong to start, for the party was short of a servant allowed by my instructions. (I had not been able to get one in Lima, except at an unreasonable price, and depended upon getting one in some of the towns of the Sierra.) The *arriero* needed a *peon,* and the mules were overloaded. I would strongly advise all travellers in these parts to imitate the conduct of the Jesuits, whose first day's journey is to load their burden mules, saddle and mount their riding-mules; go twice round the patio or square, on the inside of their dwelling, to see that everything is prepared and fits properly; and then unload and wait for the morning. However, I foresaw a longer delay by unloading again than I was willing to make; and after a hard morning's work in drumming up the Peruvian part of the expedition (these people have not the slightest idea that a man will start on a journey on the day he proposes), the party, consisting of myself, Mr. Gibbon, Mr. Richards, Mr. Ijurra, Mauricio, an Indian of Chamicuros (a village on the Huallaga), and the *arriero,* Pablo Luis Arredondo, with seven burden-mules, defiled out by the Gate of Marvels and took the broad and beaten road that ascends the left bank of the Rímac.

CHAPTER III

❧

Passports—Means of defence—The road—Narrow pass—
Bridge—Tribute money—Dividing line between the Coast and
the Sierra—Varieties of the potato—Mines of Párac—Narrow
valley—Summit of the Cordillera—Reflections

WE WERE ACCOMPANIED for a mile or two on the road by our kind
friends and countrymen, who drew up at the cemetery to bid us
good-bye, one advising us to halt at the first place we could find
pasturage for the mules. The road we were to travel had reputation for robbers, and they desired to know how we were to defend
ourselves in case of attack, as we carried our guns in leather cases,
strapped to the crupper, and entirely out of reach for a sudden
emergency. Gibbon replied by showing his six-barrelled Colt, and
observed that Ijurra, Richards, and myself had each a pair of pistols at hand. As for Mauricio, he kept his pistols in his saddle-bags;
and I was satisfied, from some attempts that I had made to teach
Luis to shoot (though he was very ambitious and desirous to learn),
that it was dangerous to trust him with a pair, as he might as readily
fire into his friends as his enemies. With the comfortable observation from one of our friends that he never expected to see us again,
we shook hands and parted.

Our course lay about east-northeast over an apparently level and very stony road. To the right were the green cane and alfalfa fields, and on the left and behind, the vegetation afforded by the valley of the Rímac; but ahead all was barren, grim, and forbidding.

Just before sunset we stopped at the *hacienda* (estate, or farm, or settlement) of Santa Clara, and applied for pasturage. We were told by an old negro woman sitting on the ground at the door of the house that there was none; which was confirmed by two men who just then rode up, and who expressed their regret at not being able to accommodate us. It was remarkable to see such poverty and squalid wretchedness at nine miles from the great city of Lima; it was like passing in a moment from the most luxurious civilization into savage barbarity—from the garden to the desert. We rode on, about three miles further, to an *hacienda,* where we arrived at half past six P. M.

Before the mules could be unloaded it became very dark, so that the *arriero* and Mauricio had considerable trouble in driving them to the pasturage. Indeed some of them got away; I could hear them galloping furiously up and down the road, and I went to bed on a table in the only room in the house, with the comfortable reflection that I had balked at starting, and should have to return or send back to Lima to buy more mules.

Tormented with these reflections, and oppressed with the excitement and fatigue of the day, I could not sleep; but tossed "in restless ecstacy" for many a long hour, until just before daylight, when, as I was dropping to sleep, a couple of game cocks, tied by the leg in the room, commenced "their salutation to the morn," and screamed out their clarion notes within a yard of my ear. This was too much for me. I rushed out—to meet a heavenly morning, and old Luis, with the intelligence that the mules were "all right." I took off my upper clothes, and plunged head, neck, and shoulders into the water of a little mountain stream that rushed clear and cold as ice by the roadside in front of the house. Thus refreshed and invigorated, the appearance of affairs took a new aspect, and light-heartedness and hope came back as strong and fresh as in the days of boyhood.

The *mayordomo,* or steward of the estate, was a Chino (descendant of Indian and negro), and seemed an amiable and intelligent fellow. He gave us a supper of a thin soup (*caldo*) and *chupe. Chupe* is a universal article of diet in the Sierra. It is a broth, or soup, made generally of potatoes, cheese, and lard; sometimes meat is boiled in it. It is the last dish served at dinner at a gentleman's table before the dessert. Whilst we were eating it, the *mayordomo* was engaged in teaching the children of a neighbor the multiplication table and the catechism.

The house was built of *adobe,* or sun-dried bricks, and roofed with tiles. It had but one room, which was the general receptacle for all comers. A mud projection of two feet high and three wide stood out from the walls of the room all round, and served as a standing bed place for numbers. Others laid their blankets and *ponchos* and stretched themselves upon the floor; so that, with whites, Indians, negroes, trunks, packages, horse furniture, game cocks, and Guinea pigs, we had quite a caravansera appearance. The supper and bed that the steward had given us were gratuitous; he would accept no remuneration; and we got our breakfast of *chupe* and eggs at a *tambo,* or roadside inn, nearly opposite.

Though we commenced loading up soon after daylight, we did not get off until half past nine. Such delays were invariable, and this was owing to the want of a *peon* and another servant.

The height of Pacayar above the level of the sea is 1,346 feet.

MAY 22—Roads still good; valley gradually narrowing, and hills becoming higher, and more barren and rocky. We passed several squads of asses and llamas carrying potatoes and eggs, some of them as far as from Jauxa, to Lima. Soon the stream approached the hills so close that there was no longer room between them for road, and this had to be cut out of the side of the hill. It was very narrow, and seemed in some places to overhang the stream fifty feet below it.

Just as we were turning an angle of the road we met a man driving two horses before him, which immediately mingled in with our burden mules, and endangered their going over the precipice. Our *arriero* shouted to the man, and, spurring his horse through the mules, commenced driving back the horses of the other, who flourished his whip, and insisted upon passing. I expected to see a fight, and mischief happen, which would probably have fallen upon us, as the other had nothing to lose, when Ijurra called out to him, and represented that our cargoes were very valuable, and that if one were lost he should be held responsible; whereupon he desisted, drove his horses back, and suffered us to pass. This caused us to be more careful in our march, and I sent Gibbon, with Richards, ahead, to warn persons, or give us warning, in time to prevent a collision. The burden mules were driven by the *arriero* and the servant, in the middle; while Ijurra and I brought up the rear.

At two P.M. we stopped at the *tambo* of Yanacoto. I determined to stay here a day or two to get things shaken into their places, and obtain a new error and rate for the chronometer, which had stopped the day before, a few hours out of Lima, though we had not discovered it till this morning. I cared, however, very little for this, as I was satisfied that it would either stop again or so vary in its rate as to be worthless. No chronometer will stand the jar of mule

travel over these roads, especially if carried in the pocket, where
the momentum of the jar is parallel to the movement of the balance wheel of the watch. Were I to carry a chronometer on such a
journey again, I would have it placed in its box on a cushion on
the saddle-bow; and when I travelled in a canoe, where the motion is the other way, I would hang it up. We pitched the tent in
the valley before the road, and proceeded to make ourselves as
comfortable as possible.

MAY 23—Bathing before breakfast is, on this part of the route, both
healthful and pleasant. There seemed to be no cultivation in this
valley, which here is about half a mile wide. It is covered with
bushes, except close to the water's edge, where grow reeds and flags.
The bushes are dwarf willow, and a kind of locust called *Sangre
de Christo,* which bears a broad bean, containing four or five seeds,
and a pretty red flower, something like our crape myrtle. There is
also a bush, of some ten or twelve feet in height, called *Molle.* This
is the most common shrub of the country, and has a wider climatic
range than any other of this slope of the Andes. It has long, delicate leaves, like the acacia, and produces an immense quantity of
small red berries in large bunches. The leaves, when crushed, have
a strong aromatic smell; and many persons believe that it is certain
death to sleep under its shade.

The elevation of Yanacoto is 2,337 feet, a little more than one
thousand feet above Pacayar. The distance between them is about
ten miles, showing a rise to the mile of about one hundred feet,
which is very little greater than that between Callao and Lima.

MAY 24—Valley still narrowing; the hills becoming mountains,
mostly of granite; rock piled upon rock for hundreds of feet, and

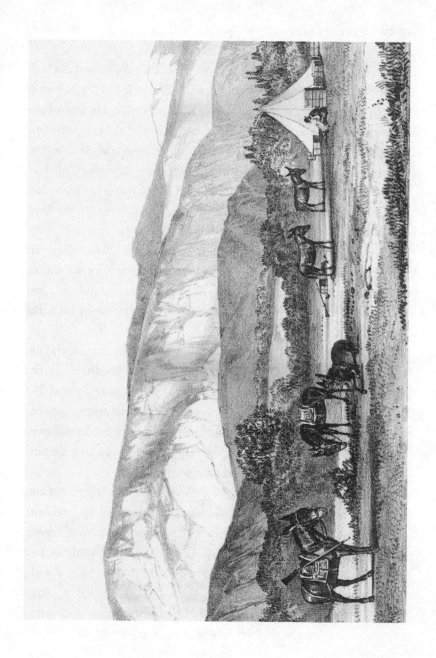

in every variety of shape; no vegetation, except where the hardy cactus finds aliment in the crevices of the rock.

About four and a half miles above Yanacoto we passed the little village of San Pedro Mama, where the first bridge is thrown over the Rímac. Heavy, rough stonework is built on each side of the river, into which are inserted massive pieces of timber, standing out a few feet from the face of the masonry, and hewn flat on top. On their ends are laid trunks of trees, crossing the river, and securely lashed. Athwart these are laid sticks of wood, of some two or three inches diameter, lashed down, and covered over with bundles of reeds, mud, and stones.

There is very little cultivation till near Cocachacra, where we saw well-tilled fields, green with alfalfa and Indian corn. We arrived at this place at half past five, and pitched the tent in a meadow near the river, and without the town, for the purpose of avoiding company and disagreeable curiosity.

Although we had seen fields of lucern before entering the village, we could get none for our mules after we got there; and to every inquiry for hay, fodder, or grain, the constant reply was *"No hay"* (there is none). Gibbon, however, persevered until someone told him, in an undertone, as if imparting a great secret, where a little corn was to be purchased, and he got a peck or two shelled. We were continually annoyed and put to inconvenience by the refusal of the people to sell to us. I think it arose from one of two causes, or probably both—either that money was of less value to them than the things we wanted, or they feared to have it known that they had possessions, lest the hand of authority should be laid upon them, and they be compelled to give up their property without payment.

Cocachacra is a village of about one hundred inhabitants, and at present the residence of the sub-prefect, or governor, of the province, which is that of Huarochiri. This province, according to the official almanac published yearly at Lima, has ninety miles of length from northwest to southeast, and seventy-two of breadth. There are 14,258 native inhabitants generally engaged in mining, cultivating potatoes, and raising cattle, or as muleteers. The houses, like all those of the Sierra, are built either of stone or *adobe,* and thatched with wheat or barley straw.

We called on the sub-prefect and exhibited our Peruvian passports, asking, at the same time, that he would give us some assistance in obtaining food for our beasts. This he seemed lukewarm about, and I did not press him, for I had made up my mind that as far as it was possible I would avoid appealing to authority for the purpose of obtaining supplies, and go without what I could not buy or beg. He had in the house the semi-yearly contribution of his province towards the support of the government, which he was to send to Lima next day. A gentleman suggested that he might be robbed that night; but he said that his guns were loaded (pointing to some muskets standing around the room), and that he might count upon assistance from our party, which seemed well armed.

Very little help he would have had from us. He had shown no disposition to oblige us, and moreover I had no notion of interfering in other people's quarrels, or preventing the people from taking back their money if they wanted it. We slept comfortably in the tent. Nights getting cool.

MAY 25—Started at ten A.M. Valley getting so narrow as not to allow room for the road, which is in many places cut from the rock on the side of the hill, very narrow, rough, and precipitous, rising and falling as it crosses the spurs of the hills. We passed on the road the ruins of an ancient Indian town; the houses had been small, and built of stone on terraces cut from the mountain side.

At two we passed through the village of Surco, the largest we have seen. It appears capable of holding five or six hundred people, but seemed deserted. We were told that the inhabitants were away over the hills, looking after their plantations and flocks, and that they returned at night. But if this is so, judging from the height of the mountains on each side of the village, I should say that half their time is lost in going and returning from their work.

Here we leave the district called the Coast, and enter upon that called the Sierra. There is *tertiana* below, but none above this. In his book, *Peru As It Is,* Dr. Smith, speaking of the climate of this district, says

> that it is neither winter nor summer, but one perpetual spring. It is out of the sphere of frosts, and exempted from the raw fogs and sultry heats of the coast. The atmospherical currents of mountain and coast meet here and neutralize each other; the extremes of both disappear; and the result is a delicious climate for the convalescent, whose tender organs require a gentle, uniform temperature, alike removed from the extremes of heat and cold, dryness and moisture. With this important fact the delicate inhabitants of Lima are perfectly acquainted; and they are accustomed to resort to the *cabezadas*, or headlands of valleys, where these verge on the joint air of mountain and coast, as, for example, Matucana, the favorite resting-place of phthiscal and hæmoptic individuals, who find themselves obliged to retire from the capital in order to recover health by visiting those celebrated sites of convalescence, Tarma and Juaxa.

We certainly had delicious weather, but did not stay long enough, of course, to pronounce authoritatively upon its general climate.

At five P.M., we arrived at the *chacra* of Moyoc. Here we pitched for the night, having travelled about fifteen miles, which is our usual day's journey. This is a most beautiful little dell, entirely and closely surrounded by mountains. The valley has widened out so as to give room for some narrow patches of corn and alfalfa. The Rímac, here a "babbling brook," rushes musically between its willow-fringed banks; and the lingering of the sunlight upon the snowy summits of the now not distant Cordillera, long after night had settled upon the valley, gave an effect to the scenery that was at once magical and enchanting.

The nights in the Cordillera at this season are very beautiful. The traveller feels that he is lifted above the impurities of the lower strata of the atmosphere, and is breathing air entirely free from taint. I was never tired of gazing into the glorious sky, which, less blue, I think, than ours, yet seemed palpable—a dome of steel lit up by the stars. The stars themselves sparkled with intense brilliancy. A small pocket spy-glass showed the satellites of Jupiter with distinctness; and Gibbon even declared on one occasion that he could see them with the naked eye. I could not, but my sight is bad at night. The temperature is now getting cool, and I slept cold last night, though with all my clothes on, and covered with two parts of a heavy blanket and a woollen *poncho*. The rays of the sun are very powerful in the day, until tempered by the southwest wind, which usually sets in about eleven o'clock in the morning.

The steward here, a nice old fellow with a pretty young wife, gave us, at a reasonable price, pasturage for the beasts and a capital *chupe*. The productions of the country are maize, alfalfa, and potatoes. We saw here, for the first time, a vegetable of the potato kind called *Oca*. It resembles in appearance the Jerusalem artichoke, though longer and slimmer; and boiled or roasted it is very

agreeable to the taste. Richards compared its flavor to that of green corn; I suggested pumpkin, and he allowed that it was between the two. Gibbon shot a pair of beautiful small wild ducks that were gambolling in the stream and shooting the rapids with the speed of an arrow.

MAY 26—Started at eleven, and passed the village of Matucana, a mile from Moyoc. This appears about the size of Surco, and is the capital of the province (still Huarochiri). Service was going on in the church; and Gibbon and Richards, who were far ahead, had time to go in and say their prayers.

The river is now reduced to a mountain torrent, raging in foam over the debris of the porphyritic cliffs, which overhang its bed for hundreds of feet in height. The valley still occasionally widens out and gives room for a little cultivation. Where this is the case it is generally bounded on one side or the other by cliffs of sandstone, in which innumerable parrots have perforated holes for nests; and the road at these places lies broad and level at their base. We crossed the river frequently on such bridges as I have described at San Pedro Mama, and arrived at San Mateo at half past five P.M., having travelled only twelve miles. The barometer shows a much greater ascent than we have yet made in one day's travel. We pitched in an old and abandoned alfalfa field above the town, and got supper from the postmaster.

MAY 27—San Mateo, a village about the size of Surco and Matucana, is situated on both sides of the Rímac, and at an elevation of 10,200 feet above the level of the sea. The men work the *chacras* of maize, potatoes, and beans; and the women do all the household work, besides carrying their meals to the workmen on the farms, over hills that would make a lazy man shudder even to look at. They live in poverty and filth, but seem happy enough. We saw the women winnowing the beans (which were gathered dry from the plant) by collecting them in pans made of large gourds, and flinging them into the air; and also sifting flour, which comes from the other side of the Cordillera, about Jauxa. The costume of the Serrana women is different from that of the women of the coast. It consists of a very narrow skirt and a body of coarse woollen cloth, generally blue, which comes from Lima, and is belted around the waist with a broad-figured woollen belt, woven by themselves. A woollen apron, with a figured border, is worn on the left side, hanging from the right shoulder by a strap; and in the cold of the morning and evening the shoulders are covered with a thick colored blanket, reaching to the hips. A high, broad-brimmed straw hat, with shoes of raw-hide, drawn with a string around the ankle, and no stockings, complete the costume. These people seem contented with what they have, and don't want money. It was with great difficulty we could persuade them to sell us anything, always denying that they had it. On our return from the mines at Párac (where Mr. Gibbon had been sick with chills and fever), he could not eat the *chupe,* which had, at first, been made with *charqui,* or jerked beef, but which had now dwindled down to cheese and potatoes. I made a speech to some curious loafers about the tent, in which I appealed to their pride and patriotism, telling them that I thought it strange that so large a town as San Mateo, belonging to so famous a country as Peru, could not furnish a sick stranger, who could eat nothing else, with a few eggs. Whereupon, a fellow went off and brought us a dozen, though he had just sworn by the Pope that there were no such things in the village.

MAY 28—Mr. Gibbon and I, guided by a boy, rode over to the *hacienda* of San Jose de Párac, leaving Richards and Ijurra in charge

of the camp. The ride occupied about three hours, over the worst roads, bordered by the highest cliffs and deepest ravines we had yet seen. The earth here shows her giant skeleton bare: Mountains, rather than rocks, of granite, rear their gray heads to the skies; and our proximity made these things more striking and sublime. We found, on the sides of the hills, short grass and small clover, with some fine cattle feeding; and, wherever the mountain afforded a level shelf, abundance of fine potatoes, which the people were then gathering.

I brought letters from my countryman in Lima, Mr. Prevost, the owner of the mines, to Don Torribio Malarin, the superintendent of the mines, who received us kindly, and entertained us with much hospitality. His house was comfortably heated with a stove, and the chamber furnished with a large four-post bedstead, and the biggest and heaviest bureau I had ever seen. I was somewhat surprised at the sight of these—

> *Not that the things were very rich or rare,*
> *I wonder'd how the devil they got there.*

They must have come up in pieces, for nothing so large could have been fastened on a mule's back, or passed entire in the narrow parts of the road.

The *hacienda* is situated near the head of a small valley, which debouches upon the road below San Mateo; the stream which drains it emptying into the Rímac there. It is a square, enclosed with one-story buildings, consisting of the mill for grinding the ore, the ovens for toasting it when ground, the workshops, store-houses, and dwelling-houses. It is managed by a superintendent and three *mayordomos,* and employs about forty working hands. These are Indians of the Sierra, strong, hardy-looking fellows, though generally low in stature, and stupid in expression. They are silent and patient, and, having coca enough to chew, will do an extraordinary quantity of work. They have their breakfast of caldo and *cancha* (toasted maize), and get to work by eight o'clock. At eleven they have a recess of half an hour, when they sit down near their place of work, chat lazily with each other, and chew coca, mixed with a little lime, which each one carries in a small gourd, putting it on the mass of coca leaves in his mouth with a wire pin attached to the stopper of the gourd that carries the lime. Some dexterity is necessary to do this properly without cauterizing the lips or tongue. They then go to work again until five, when they finish for the day, and dine off *chupe.* It has made me, with my tropical habit of life, shiver to see these fellows puddling with their naked legs a mass of mud and quicksilver in water at the temperature of 38 degrees Fahrenheit.

These Indians generally live in huts near the *hacienda,* and are supplied from its store-houses. They are kept in debt by the supplies; and by custom, though not by law, no one will employ an Indian who is in debt to his *patrón,* so that he is compelled to work on with no hope of getting free of the debt, except by running away to a distant part of the country where he is not known, which some do.

The diseases incident to this occupation are indigestion, called *empacho,* pleurisy, and sometimes the lungs seem affected with the fumes and dust of the ore; but, on the whole, it does not seem an unhealthy occupation.

The principal articles furnished from the store-house are maize, coca, mutton, *charqui,* rum, sugar, coffee, tea, chocolate, *chancaca* (cakes of brown sugar), soap, baize, cotton, and coarse linen cloths, woollen cloths, silk handkerchiefs, foreign *ponchos,* ribbons, silk sashes, &c., &c., which are supplied to the Indian at about 100 percent advance on their cost at Lima, and charged against his wages, which amount to half a dollar a day, with half a dollar more if he works at night.

The manner of getting the silver from the ore, or beneficiating it, as it is called in Peru, is this: The ore, after it is dug from the mine and brought to the surface, is broken into pieces about the size of an English walnut, and sent to the *hacienda,* in hide-bags, on the backs of llamas or mules. There it is reduced, by several grindings and siftings, to an impalpable powder. The mill consists of a horizontal water-wheel, carrying a vertical axis, which comes up through the floor of the mill. To the top of this axis is bolted a large cross-beam, and to the ends of the beam are slung heavy, rough stones, each about a ton weight. These stones are carried around nearly in contact with a concave bed of smoother and harder rock, built upon the floor of the mill. The ore is poured by the basket-full upon the bed, and the large hanging rocks grind it to powder, which pours out of holes made in the periphery of the bed. This is sifted through fine wire sieves, and the coarser parts are put in the mill again for re-grinding. The ground ore, or *harina,* is then mixed with salt and taken to the ovens and toasted.

The fuel used in these ovens is the dung of cattle, called *taquia*. After the *harina* is toasted, it is carried in hide-bags to the square enclosed in the buildings of the *hacienda,* and laid in piles of about six hundred pounds each. Ten of these piles are laid in a row, making a *caxon* of 6,250 pounds. The piles are then moistened with water, and quicksilver is sprinkled on them through a woollen cloth.

The mass is well mixed by treading with the feet and working with hoes. The pile is often examined to see that the amalgamation is going on well. In some conditions the mass is called hot; in others, cold. The state of heat is cured by adding a little lime and rotten dung; that of cold, by a little magistral or oxide of iron. It is then left to stand for eight or nine days, until the amalgamation is complete. It is then carried to an elevated platform of stone, and thrown, in small quantities at a time, into a well sunk in the middle of the platform; a stream of water is turned on, and four or five men trample and wash it with their feet.

The amalgam sinks to the bottom, and the mud and water are let off, by an aperture in the lower part of the well, into a smaller well below, where one man carries on the washing with his feet. More amalgam sinks to the bottom of this well, and the mud and water again flow off through a long wooden trough, into a pit, where the water percolates through the soil, leaving the mud to be again re-washed.

The water, which by this time is clear, is let off, and all the amalgam, called *pella,* is collected, put in hide-bags, and weighed. Two *caxons* are washed in a day. The *pella* is then put into conical bags of coarse linen, which are hung up, and the weight of the mass presses out a quantity of the quicksilver, which oozes through the interstices of the linen, and is caught in vessels below. The mass, now dry, and somewhat harder than putty, is carried to the ovens, where the remainder of the quicksilver is driven off by heat, and the residue is the *plata piña,* or pure silver. This is melted, run into bars, stamped according to the ley or quality of the silver, and sent to Lima, either for the mint or for exportation. The proportion of pure silver in the amalgam is about 22 percent.

MAY 29—Visited the mines. The road, or rather path, lay along the side of the mountain, and zigzagged up and down to turn precipices, now running near the banks of the little stream, and now many hundreds of feet above it. The ride was bad enough at this time—it must be frightful in the rainy season, though the superintendent says he sometimes travels it on horseback. This I am sure I should not do; and when these paths are slippery I would much prefer trusting to my own legs than to those of any other animal. Many persons suffer much in riding amongst these precipices and ravines. One of a party of English officers, who crossed the Cordillera at Valparaiso whilst I was there, had to return without crossing, because he could not bear the sight of the sheer descents.

The valley of Párac lies about east and west, and the veins of silver on the sides of the mountains east-northeast and west-southwest, thus crossing the valley diagonally. There are four mines belonging to the establishment, which employ about sixty workmen, though more could be employed to advantage. They are divided into two gangs for each mine: One party will go on duty at seven P.M. and work till five A.M., when they come out, rest two hours, and go on again till seven P.M. They are then relieved by the other party. This is very hard work, for the mines are very wet and cold. The getter-out of the ore wields, with one hand, a hammer of thirty pounds, and the carriers of the ore bear a burden of 150 pounds from the bottom of the shaft to the surface—a distance in this case of about a quarter of a mile, of a very steep and rough ascent. When I first met one of these men toiling up in the dark, I thought, from the dreadful groans I heard before I saw him, that someone was dying near me; but he does this *a purpose,* for when we met he had breath enough to give me a courteous salutation, and beg a paper cigar. Boys commence this work at eight years of age, and spend probably the greater part of their lives in the mine.

The mine that we visited has a perpendicular depth of 520 feet and penetrates the mountain at an angle from the horizon of about 25 degrees. The superintendent told us that he had instructed the workmen not to blast whilst we were in the mine, because the dreadful reverberation of sound often had an unhappy effect upon people not accustomed to it, which, as we were men who sometimes dealt in heavy artillery, we did not thank him for.

Returning from the mine we met a drove of llamas on their way from the *hacienda*. This is quite an imposing sight, especially when the drove is encountered suddenly at a turn of the road. The leader, which is always elected on account of his superior height, has his head decorated with tufts of colored woollen fringe, hung with little bells; and his extreme height (often six feet), gallant and graceful carriage, pointed ear, restless eye, and quivering lip, as he faces you for a moment, make him as striking an object as one can well conceive. Upon pressing on him he bounds aside, either up or down the cliff, and is followed by the herd scrambling over places that would be impassable for the mule or the ass.

They travel immense distances, but by short stages—not more than nine or ten miles per day. It is necessary, in long journeys, to have double the number required to carry the cargo, so as to give them relays. The burden of the llama is about 130 pounds; he will not carry more, and will be beat to death rather than move when he is overloaded or tired. The males only are worked; the females are kept for the breed. They appear gentle and docile, but when irritated they have a very savage look, and spit at the object of their anger with great venom. The spittle is said to be very acrid, and will raise blisters where it touches the skin. We saw none in the wild state. They are bred on the *haciendas* in great numbers. We had no opportunity of seeing the *guanaco* or *alpaca* (other varieties of the Peruvian sheep), though we now and then, in crossing the mountains, caught a glimpse of the wild and shy *vicuña*. These go in herds of ten or fifteen females, accompanied by one male, who is ever on the alert. On the approach of danger he gives warning by a shrill whistle, and his charge makes off with the speed of the wind. The wool of the *vicuña* is much finer and more valuable than that of the other species—it is maroon-colored. Were any care taken in the rearing of these wild sheep of Peru, the country might draw a great revenue from the sale of their wool.

JUNE 1—Found Richards sick and the muleteer growling at the delay; loaded up, and got off at eleven. At twelve the valley narrowed to a dell of about fifty feet in width; the stream occupying its whole breadth, with the exception of a narrow, but smooth and level mule-path on its right bank. This is a very remarkable place. On each side the rock of red porphyry rises perpendicularly for a full five hundred feet. In places it overhangs the stream and road. The traveller feels as if he were passing through some tunnel of the Titans. The upper exit from the dell is so steep that steps have been cut in the rock for the mule's feet; and the stream rushes down the rock-obstructed declivity in foaming fury, flinging clouds of white spray over the traveller, and rendering the path slippery and dangerous.

Passed Chiglla and Bella Vista, mining *haciendas.* The country is quite thickly settled, there being houses in sight all the way between these two places. The barley here does not give grain, but is cut for fodder. The alfalfa has given way to short, thin grass; and we begin to find difficulty in getting food for the beasts. We saw cabbages growing in the gardens of Chiglla, which is a straggling village of some three or four hundred inhabitants. Just after passing Chiglla the mountains looked low, giving the appearance of a rolling country, and were clothed with verdure to the top. Upon turning a corner of the road the snow-covered summits of the Cordillera were close before us, also looking low; and when the snow or verdure suffered the earth to be seen, this was of a deep pink color. We stopped at four at a *tambo,* where we pitched and bought barley straw (*alcaser*) at the rate of twelve and a half cents the armful, called *tercio,* which is just enough for one mule. The mercury in the barometer being below the scale, we had to cut away the brass casing in front, and mark the height of the column on the inside of the case with a pen-knife.

JUNE 2—Got off at half past ten. Road tolerably good, and not very precipitous. At twelve we arrived on a level with the lowest line of snow. We were marking the barometer, when a traveller rode up, who proved to be an old schoolmate of mine, whom I had not seen or even heard of since we were boys. The meeting at this place was an extraordinary and very agreeable occurrence. It was also fortunate for me, for my friend was head machinist at the mines of Morococha, and gave us a note to the administrator, which secured us a hospitable reception and an interesting day or two. Without this we should have been compelled to pass on, for pasturage here is very scant, and the people of the mines have to pay a high price for their barley straw, and are not willing to give it to every stray traveller. At two P.M. we arrived at the highest point of the road, called the pass of *Antarangra,* or copper rock. (The pass of the *Piedra Parada,* or standing rock, which passes by the mines of Yauli, crosses a few miles to our right.) Some scattering mosses lay on a hill-side above us; but Gibbon and I spurred our panting and trembling mules to the summit of the hill, and had nothing around us but snow, granite, and dark gray porphyry.

I was disappointed in the view from this place. The peaks of the Cordillera that were above us looked low, and presented the appearance of a hilly country, at home, on a winter-day; while the contrast between the snowy hills and the bright green of lower range, together with the view of the placid little lakes which lie so snug and still in their midst, gave an air of quiet beauty to the scene very distinct from the savage and desolate grandeur I had expected.

Gibbon, with the camera lucida, sketched the Cordillera. I expended a box of matches in boiling the snow for the atmospheric pressure; and poor Richards lay shivering on the ground, enveloped in our pillons, a martyr to the *veta*.

Veta is the sickness caused by the rarity of the atmosphere at these great elevations. The Indians call it *veta,* or vein, because they believe it is caused by veins of metal diffusing around a poisonous infection. It is a remarkable thing that, although this affection must be caused by absence of atmospheric pressure, yet in no case except this (and Richards was ill before) that I have known or read of has it been felt at the greatest elevation, but always at a point below this—sometimes on one side, sometimes on the other. The affection displays itself in a violent headache, with the veins of the head swollen and turgid, a difficulty of respiration, and cold extremities. The smell of garlic is said to alleviate the symptoms; and the *arrieros* generally anoint their cattle over the eyes, and on the forehead, with an unguent made of tallow, garlic, and wild marjoram, as a preventive, before attempting the ascent. I did not observe that our animals were affected, though they trembled and breathed hard, which, I think, was attributable to the steepness of the hill up which we rode. The barometer stood at 16.730, indicating an elevation of 16,044 feet. Water boiled at 182.5 degrees; temperature of the air, 43 degrees.

The road hence is cut along the flank of the mountain, at whose base lies a pretty little lake. The *hacienda* of Morococha is situated on the banks of a second, which communicates with it; and this again pours its waters, by a small and gentle stream, into a third, below.

Though not yet sixty miles from the sea, we had crossed the great "divide" which separates the waters of the Atlantic from those of the Pacific. The last steps of our mules had made a striking

change in our geographical relations; so suddenly and so quickly had we been cut off from all connexion with the Pacific, and placed upon waters that rippled and sparkled joyously as they danced by our feet to join the glad waves of the ocean that wash the shores of our own dear land. They whispered to me of home, and my heart went along with them. I thought of [brother-in-law and father of oceanography Matthew Fontaine] Maury, with his researches concerning the currents of the sea; and, recollecting the close physical connexion pointed out by him as existing between these—the waters of the Amazon and those of our own majestic Mississippi— I musingly dropped a bit of green moss, plucked from the hillside, upon the bosom of the placid lake of Morococha; and as it floated along I followed it, in imagination, down through the luxurious climes, the beautiful skies, and enchanting scenery of the tropics, to the mouth of the great river; thence across the Caribbean Sea, through the Yucatan pass, into the Gulf of Mexico; thence along the Gulf-stream; and so out upon the ocean, off the shores of the "Land of Flowers." Here I fancied it might meet with silent little messengers cast by the hands of sympathizing friends and countrymen high up on the head-waters of the Mississippi, or away in the "Far West," upon the distant fountains of the Missouri.

It was, indeed, but a bit of moss floating on the water; but as I mused, fancy awakened, and, stimulated by surrounding circumstances, had already converted it into a skiff manned by fairies, and bound upon a mission of high import, bearing messages of peace and good-will, telling of commerce and navigation, of settlement and civilization, of religious and political liberty, from the "King of Rivers" to the "Father of Waters"; and, possibly, meeting in the Florida pass, and "speaking," through a trumpet louder than the tempest, spirits sent down by the Naiads of Lake Itaska, with greetings to Morococha.

I was now, for the first time, fairly in the field of my operations. I had been sent to explore the Valley of the Amazon, to sound its streams, and to report as to their navigability. I was commanded to examine its fields, its forests, and its rivers, that I might gauge their capabilities, active and dormant, for trade and commerce with the States of Christendom, and make known to the spirit and enterprise of the age the resources which lie in concealment there, waiting for the touch of civilization and the breath of the steam-engine to give them animation, life, and palpable existence.

Before us lay this immense field, dressed in the robes of everlasting summer, and embracing an area of thousands upon thousands of square miles on which the footfall of civilized man had never been heard. Behind us towered, in forbidding grandeur, the crests and peaked summits of the Andes, clad in the garb of eternal winter. The contrast was striking, and the field inviting. But who were the laborers? Gibbon and I. We were all. The rest were not even gleaners. But it was well. The expedition had been planned and arranged at home with admirable judgment and consummate sagacity; for, had it been on a grand scale, commensurate with its importance, or even larger than it was, it would have broken down of its own weight.

Though the waters where I stood were bound on their way to meet the streams of our Northern Hemisphere, and to bring, for all the practical purposes of commerce and navigation, the mouth of the Amazon and the mouth of the Mississippi into one, and place it before our own doors; yet, from the head of navigation on one stream to the head of navigation on the other, the distance to be sailed could not be less than ten thousand miles. Vast, many, and great, doubtless, are the varieties of climates, soils, and productions within such a range. The importance to the world of settlement, cultivation, and commerce in the Valley of the Amazon cannot be over-estimated. With the climates of India, and of all the habitable portions of the earth, piled one above the other in quick succession, tillage and good husbandry here would transfer the productions of the East to this magnificent river basin, and place them within a few days' easy sail of Europe and the United States.

Only a few miles back we had first entered the famous mining district of Peru. A large portion of the silver which constitutes the circulation of the world was dug from the range of mountains upon which we are standing; and most of it came from that slope of them which is drained off into the Amazon. Is it possible for commerce and navigation up and down this majestic water-course and its beautiful tributaries to turn the flow of this silver stream from its western course to the Pacific, and conduct it with steamers down the Amazon to the United States, there to balance the stream of gold with which we are likely to be flooded from California and Australia?

Questions which I could not answer, and reflections which I could not keep back, crowded upon me. Oppressed with their weight, and the magnitude of the task before me, I turned slowly and sadly away, secretly lamenting my own want of ability, and sincerely regretting that the duty before me had not been assigned to abler and better hands.

Chapter IV

❧

*Mines of Morococha—A Yankee's house—Mountain
of Puy-puy—Splendid view—Lava stream—Chain bridge at
Oroya—Descent into the valley of Tarma—American
physician—Customs—Dress—Religious observances—Muleteers
and mules—General Otero—Farming in the Sierra—Road to
Chanchamayo—Perils of travel—Gold mines of Matichacra—
View of the Montaña—Fort San Ramon—Indians of
Chanchamayo—Cultivation*

WE ARRIVED AT Morococha at five P.M. This is a copper mining *hacienda,* belonging to some German brothers of Lima, who own, also, several silver mines of the neighborhood. The copper and silver of these mountains are intimately mixed; they are both got out by smelting, though this operation, as far as regarded the silver, had been abandoned, and they were now beginning the process of extracting the silver, by grinding and washing—such as I have described at Párac.

The copper ore is calcined in the open air, in piles consisting of alternate layers of ore and coal, which burn for a month. The ore thus calcined is taken to ovens, built of brick, and sufficient heat is employed to melt the copper, which runs off into moulds below. The copper in this state has about 50 percent of pure copper, the residue being silver, iron, &c., &c. There is a mine of fine coal eighteen miles from the *hacienda,* which yields an abundant supply. It is bituminous, but hard, and of great brilliancy. The *hacienda* employs about one hundred hands; more are desired, but they cannot be had at this time, because it is harvest, and the Indians are gathering the corn, barley, and beans of the valleys below. The director told me that the silver ore of this region was very rich.

The mining business of the *hacienda* is conducted by a director, an intelligent and gentlemanly young German; and its fiscal affairs and general business, by an administrator, a fine-looking young Spaniard, whose kindly courtesy we shall long remember. The engineer, or machinist, is my friend and schoolmate Shepherd, who seemed to be a "Jack of all trades"—blacksmith, carpenter, watch-maker, and doctor. His room was quite a curiosity, and bespoke plainly enough the American. I never saw so many different things gathered together in so small a place: shelves of fine standard books; a dispensary for physic; all manner of tools, from the sledge-hammer and the whip-saw to the delicate instruments of the watch-maker; parts of watches lying under bell-glasses; engravings hanging around the walls, with a great chart, setting forth directions for the treatment of all manner of diseases and accidents; horse furniture, saddle-bags, boots, shoes, and every variety of garment, from the heavy woollen *poncho* of the man to the more delicate cotton petticoat of the woman; for my friend has a pretty young Sierra wife, who took great pleasure in talking to me about the home and relations of my *paisano*. Shepherd's warm room and bed, with plenty of covering, was a princely luxury in that cold climate. These things are comparative, and I had not slept under a roof but twice since I left Lima. An old Englishman from the Isle of Guernsey, who seemed to be a sort of factotum, and knew and did everything, and who was unwearied in his kindness and attention to us, made up the sum of our pleasant acquaintances at Morococha. We had beef and mutton for dinner, with good butter and cheese; vegetables scarce; Gibbon not well; Richards very sick, and under treatment from Shepherd.

JUNE 3—We all went to see the Mountain of Puy-puy, said to be higher than Chimborazo. The place of view is about three miles from Morococha. We passed the openings of a copper and silver mine, and rode along a boggy country, where turf is cut for fuel. We saw many snipes, ducks, and other aquatic birds. This upset all my preconceived notions; I had no idea that I should see, at fifteen thousand feet above the level of the sea, anything that would remind me of duck-shooting in the marshes of the Rappahannock. To see the mountain, it was necessary to cross a range of hills, about seven or eight hundred feet in height. The road went up diagonally, but the ascent was the most toilsome operation I had ever undertaken. We were obliged to dismount, when about three fourths of the way up, and lead the mules; the path was muddy and slippery, and we had to stop to blow at every half-dozen steps. Gibbon declared that this was the only occasion in which he had ever found the big spurs of the country of any service; for when he slipped and fell, as we all frequently did, he said that he should inevitably have gone to the bottom had he not dug his spurs into the soil, and so held on. I think that I suffered more than any of the party. On arriving at the top, I was fairly exhausted; I thought my heart would break from my breast with its violent agitation, and I felt, for the first time, how painful it was

To breathe
The difficult air of the iced mountain's top.

I soon recovered, however, and was amply repaid by the splendor of the view. The lofty cone-shaped mountain, clad in its bril-

liant mantle from the top even to the cylindrical base upon which it rested, rose in solitary majesty from the plain beneath us; and when the sunlight, bursting from the clouds, rested upon its summit, it was beautiful, indeed. Gibbon almost froze taking a sketch of it; and the rest of us tired ourselves nearly to death endeavoring to get a shot at a herd of shy *vicuñas* that were seen feeding among the distant rocks. We had a fatiguing ride, and enjoyed a late dinner and a good night's rest.

JUNE 4—We took leave of our hospitable friends (whom I could no longer intrude our large party upon), and started at meridian, leaving Richards too sick to travel. We rode down the "Valley of the Lakes" in about an east-northeast direction. We travelled over a heavy rolling country; the southern sides of the hills clothed with verdure, and affording tolerable pasture; the northern sides bare and rocky—no trees or bushes. About nine miles from Morococha, we crossed a range of hills to the right, and entered the village of Pachachaca.

This is situated in a valley that comes down from Yauli. The stream of the Valley of the Lakes at this place joins with the larger and very serpentine stream of the Yauli Valley. This valley has a flat and apparently level floor of half a mile in width, affording a carriage-road of two or three miles in length. Pachachaca is a small village of two hundred inhabitants. The people seem more industrious than those of the villages on the other side. There are fine crops of barley here, and we saw cabbages, onions, peaches, and eggs in the shops. We were greater objects of curiosity in this place than we had been before. The people, I believe, took us for peddlers, and the woman from whom we got our supper and breakfast seemed offended because we would not sell her some candles, and importuned Gibbon for the sale of his straw hat. The men wore short woollen trousers, buttoned at the knee, together with, generally, two pair of long woollen stockings. The woollen articles of clothing are woven in this neighborhood, except the *ponchos,* which come from Tarma. Fuel is the *taquia,* or dried cattle manure. Gibbon and I had occasion afterwards to laugh at our fastidiousness in objecting to a mutton-chop broiled upon a coal of cow-dung.

JUNE 5—We travelled down the valley about east. At about one and a half mile we passed a very curious-looking place, where a small stream came out of a valley to the northward and westward, and spread itself over a flat table-rock, soft and calcareous. It poured over this rock in a sort of horse-shoe cataract, and then spread over an apparently convex surface of this same soft rock, about 250 yards wide, crossing the valley down which we were travelling. This rock sounded hollow under the feet of the mules, and I feared we should break through at every instant. I am confident it was but a thin crust; and, indeed, after crossing it, we observed a clear stream of water issuing from beneath it, and flowing into the road on the farther side. We saw another such place a little lower down, only the stream tumbled, in a variety of colored streaks, principally white, like salt, over the metallic-looking rock, into the rivulet below. I presume there must have been some volcano near here, and that this rock is lava, for it had all the appearance of having once been liquid.

The valley about two miles from Pachachaca is cut across by rocky hills. Here we turned to the northward and eastward. The country at first offered some pasturage, but became more barren as we advanced, only showing, now and then, some patches of barley. We travelled till noon on the left bank of the Yauli stream, when we crossed it by a natural bridge, at a little village of a few huts. At half past two, after a ride over a stony and dusty plain, bordered on each side by rocky mountains, we arrived at the bridge of Oroya. This is a chain suspension bridge, of about fifty yards in length, and two and a half in breadth, flung over the river of Jauxa, which is a tributary of the Ucayali. The Yauli stream, into which emptied the stream from the lakes at Morococha, joins this river here, and this is the connexion that I spoke of between those lakes, near the very summit of the Andes and the Atlantic Ocean.

The bridge consisted of four chains, of about a quarter of an inch diameter, stretched horizontally across the river from strong stone-work on each side. These are interlaced with thongs of hide; sticks of about one and a half inch in diameter are laid across them and lashed down, forming a floor. Two other chains are stretched across about four feet above these, and connected with them by thongs of hide; these serve for balustrades, and would prevent a mule from jumping off. The bridge was about fifty feet above the water when we passed. It seemed very light, and rocked and swayed under the motion of the mules in crossing it. The heavy cargoes are taken off and carried over on the shoulders of the bridge-keeper and his assistants. The toll is twelve and a half cents the mule; and the same, the cargo. The bridge-ward seemed astonished, and somewhat annoyed, when I told him that one of the cargoes, which he left on the mule, was the heaviest I had, being a box filled with bags of shot, balls, and powder, together with the specimens of ore and rocks we had collected.

The river at this place turns from its southern course and runs to the eastward, by the village of Oroya, where we camped. This village contains about one hundred inhabitants, though we saw only five or six men, most of the male inhabitants being away to the harvest on the plains above. The women seemed nearly all to be employed in spinning wool, holding the bundle of wool in the left hand and spinning it out by a hanging broach. Very few of them

spoke Spanish, but a corrupt Quichua, or language of the Incas. We bought barley straw for the mules, and got a beef *chupe,* with eggs and roasted potatoes, for ourselves. We saw some small trees within the deserted enclosures where houses had been, bearing a very fragrant flower, something resembling the heliotrope, but much larger, and tinged with a reddish color.

JUNE 6—Got under way at nine A.M., steering north-northeast, and making a considerable ascent for about two miles. We then rode over a plain, with rolling hills on each side, covered with a short grass, giving pasturage to large flocks of sheep and some cows. The road then rose again, taking our column of mercury in the barometer out of sight, till half past eleven, when we stood at the head of a ravine leading down to the valley of Tarma. The height of this spot above the level of the sea was 11,270 feet. We rode down this ravine, north, for three quarters of an hour, and at an angle to the horizon of full 30 degrees. When nearly at the foot, the plants and flowers familiar to us on the other side began to make their appearance, and in such quick succession that it seemed that an hour's ride carried us over many a mile of the tedious ascent to the westward of the mountains. First appeared the hardy little flowers of the heights above San Mateo; then, the barley; the alfalfa; the Indian corn; beans; turnips; shrubs, becoming bushes; bushes, trees; flowers growing larger and gayer in their colors (yellow predominating), till the pretty little city of Tarma, embosomed among the hills, and enveloped in its covering of willows and fruit trees, with its long lawns of alfalfa (the greenest of grasses) stretching out in front, broke upon our view. The ride of to-day was a long and tiresome one, being mostly a bone-shaking descent; and we hailed with pleasure the sight of the little town as a resting place, after the

tedious passage of the Cordillera, and felt that one of the inconve-
niences and perils of the expedition was safely and happily passed.

We arrived at four P.M., and rode straight to the house of a
gentleman to whom I brought a letter of introduction, which contained the modest request that he should place his house at my
disposal. This he acceded to without hesitation, removing his sick
wife, in spite of remonstrance, into another room, and giving us
his hall for our baggage, and his chamber for our sleeping room.
This I would not have acceded to, except that this is not his place
of residence, but a new house which he is constructing here and
which he is only staying at for a few days till his wife is able to travel
to their regular place of residence. There is no public house in the
town, and it is customary to take travellers in. When I (next morning) presented a letter of introduction from the Bishop of Eretria
to the Cura of Tarma, his first question was, "Where are you
lodged?" And when I told him, he seemed annoyed, and said that
I had not treated him properly in not coming to his house.

Tarma, a town of some seven thousand inhabitants, belonging to the province of Pasco and department of Junin, is beautifully situated in an amphitheatre of mountains, which are clothed
nearly to the top with waving fields of barley. The valley in front,
about half a mile wide, and two miles long, appears level, and is
covered with the greenest and richest pasturage. Its borders are
fringed with fruit trees; and the stream which waters it plunges,
in a beautiful little cataract, of some thirty feet in height, over a
ledge of rocks at the farther end. Its climate is delicious; and it is
the resort of sickly people from Lima and the cold and inclement
mining districts who find comfort and restoration in its pure atmosphere and mild and equable temperature. I was told, although
the district contains nearly twenty thousand inhabitants, and its
villages are close together, and easily accessible, that it could not,

of itself, support a physician. A young American physician, recently established in Tarma, gave me this account, but said that not even this had been sufficient to keep one here. I cannot vouch for this story. It has an apocryphal sound to me. I only know that it is a very healthy place, and that my medical friend is a person of repute there. When I proposed to carry him off with me, the ladies of my acquaintance raised a great outcry, and declared that they could not part with their *médico*. I am satisfied, though there are so few diseases, that a good-looking young graduate of medicine, who would go there with money enough to buy him a horse, might readily marry a pretty girl of influential family, and soon get a practice that would enrich him in ten years.

The houses of Tarma are built of *adobe,* and the better sort are whitewashed within and without, floored with gypsum and tiled. The doors of the house we are living in very much resemble "birds-eye maple." Some of the houses are partially papered, and carpeted with common Scotch carpeting.

Sunday is the great market-day, and the market-place is filled with country people, who come in to sell their manufactures of *ponchos,* blankets, shoes, hats (made of the *vicuña* wool), &c., and to buy coca, cotton goods, and *aguadiente,* as well as to attend mass and get drunk. It is quite a busy and animated scene. The men are generally dressed in tall straw hats, *ponchos,* breeches, buttoned at the knee, and long woollen stockings; the women, in a blue woollen skirt, tied around the waist, and open in front, to show a white cotton petticoat, the shoulders covered with a mantle consisting of two or three yards of gay-colored plush, called *Bayeta de Castilla,* or Spanish baize. Everything foreign in this country is called *de Casilla* (of Castile); as in Brazil, it is called *da Rainha* (of the Queen). The skirt of a lady of higher quality consists of a colored print, or mousseline. She rarely, unless dressed for company, takes the trouble to put on the body of her dress, which hangs down behind, and is covered with a gay shawl, passed around the bust, with the end thrown gracefully over the left shoulder. The hair, particularly on Sundays, is in perfect order; parted in the middle, and hanging down in two plaits behind. It is surmounted by a very neat, low-crowned straw hat, the crown being nearly covered with a broad ribbon; and she is always *bien calzada* (well shod). The women are generally large and well developed; not very pretty, but with amiable, frank, and agreeable manners; they have, almost invariably, a pleasant smile, with an open and engaging expression of countenance.

Religion flourishes in Tarma, and the Cura seems to have a busy time of it, though it is said he is cheated of half his rights in the way of marriage fees. I think that no day passed while we were here that there was not a *fiesta* of the church; for, although there are not more than twenty-five or thirty feast days in the year insisted upon by the church and the government, yet any piously disposed person may get up one when he pleases. A person, either from religious motives or ostentation, approaches the altar, and, kissing one of its appendages (I forget which), proclaims his intention of becoming *mayordomo* or superintendent of such and such a *fiesta*. This binds him and his heirs to all the expenses of the celebration, which, in the great functions in Lima, may be set down at no small matter. I am told that many a person impoverishes his family for years by paying the expenses of one of these festivals.

The *fiestas* in Tarma are generally celebrated with music, ringing of bells, firing of rockets, and dances of Indians. A dozen vagabonds are dressed in what is supposed to be the costume of the ancient Indians. This consists of a red blanket hanging from one shoulder, and a white one from the other, reaching nearly to the knee, and girded around the waist; the usual short blue breeches, with a white fringe at the knee; stockings of an indifferent color, and shoes or sandals of raw-hide, gathered over the toes with a draw-string, and tied around the ankles. The head-dress is a low-crowned, broad-brimmed round hat, made of wool, and surrounded with a circlet of dyed feathers of the ostrich.

Thus costumed, the party march through the streets, and stop every now and then to execute a sort of dance to the melancholy and monotonous music of a reed pipe, accompanied by a rude flat drum—both in the hands of the same performer. Each man has a stick or club, of hard wood, and a very small wooden or hide shield, which he strikes with the club at certain periods of the dance, making a low clattering in time with the music. They have also small bells, called *cascabeles,* attached to the knees and feet, which jingle in the dance. They and their company of Indians and Mestizos smell very bad on a near approach.

Connected with this there is a great deal of riot and drunkenness; and I felt annoyed that the church should patronize and encourage so demoralizing a procedure. The secular clergy of Peru, with a few honorable exceptions, have not a high character, if one is to believe the stories told of them by their own countrymen; and I had occasion to observe that the educated young men, as well of Chili as of Peru, generally spoke of them in terms of great contempt. I judge that the case is different with the clergy of the monastic orders, particularly the missionaries. Those I met with were evidently men of high character; and to their zeal, energy, and ability, Peru owes the conquest of by far the largest and richest part of the republic. It happens, unfortunately for the Peruvian character, that nearly all of these are foreigners—generally Spaniards and Italians.

JUNE 7—I suffered all day with violent pain in the head and limbs, from the ride of yesterday. These Peruvian saddles, though good for the beasts, and for riding up and down hill, stretch the legs so far apart as for a long time to give the unaccustomed rider severe pains in the muscles of the thighs; and I had to ride a large portion of the distance with my leg over the pommel, like a lady.

We paid off and parted with the *arriero,* Pablo Luis Arredondo. I did not find him so great a rascal as I expected; for, except the disposition to get all out of me he could (which was very natural), and an occasional growl (which was also to be expected), I had no reason to be dissatisfied with Luis. Ijurra was always quarreling with him; but I think Ijurra has the fault of his countrymen generally, and wants the temper and patience necessary to manage ignorant people. By soft words and some bribery, I got along well enough with the old fellow; and he loaded his mules beyond their usual cargoes, and drove them along very well. I was frequently astonished at the difficulties they surmounted, loaded as they were. The usual load is 260 pounds; and these animals of ours, with, I am sure, in some instances, a heavier load, and of a most incongruous and heterogeneous description, ascended hills and descended valleys which one would scarcely think an unloaded mule could travel over. Our riding mules were perfect treasures. Sure-footed, steady, strong, and patient, they bore us along easily and with comfort; and Gibbon says that he will part with his with tears, when we are compelled to give them up and take to the boats.

We had a visit from the Cura, and went to see the sub-prefect of the province, who promised me such assistance as I needed in my visit to Chanchamayo. Both of these gentlemen earnestly deprecated the idea of trusting myself and party among the Chunchos Indians on the other side of the river Chanchamayo, saying that they were hostile to the whites, and dangerous. The Cura promised to look out for a servant for us. We had visits, also, from several gentlemen of the town; all seemed much interested in my expedition to Chanchamayo, and hoped a favorable report.

JUNE 11—We rode about a league down the valley which leads to Chanchamayo, to the farm of a General Otero, to whom we brought letters. We found this farm a different sort of affair from anything we had hitherto seen in our travels. This is in a high state of cultivation, well enclosed with mud walls, and in beautiful order. The General—a good-looking, farmer-like old gentleman—met us with great cordiality, and showed us over the premises. He has a very large house, with all the necessary offices attached, which he built himself. Indeed, he said he had made the farm; for when he purchased it, it was a stony and desolate place, and he had expended much time, labor, and money on it. There were two gardens: one for vegetables and fruit, and one for flowers. They were both in fine order. The fruits were peaches of various kinds, apples, strawberries, almonds, and some few grapes. The flowers were principally roses, pinks, pansies, jessamines, and geraniums. There were a few exotics, under bell-glasses. Both fruit and flowers were of rather indifferent quality, but much better than one would expect to see in so elevated and cold a situation. The nights here, particularly in the early morning, are quite cold.

This is the harvest season, and the General was gathering his crop of maize. About twenty *peons,* or laborers, were bringing it in from the fields and throwing it down in piles in a large courtyard, while boys and women were engaged in "shucking" it. In one corner of the square, under a snug little shed attached to one of the barns, sat the General's three daughters, sewing, and probably superintending the shucking. They were fair, sweet-looking girls.

I cannot give a good idea of farming in this country, for want of information of the value of land, this depending so entirely on its situation and condition. The mountain sides are so steep, and the valleys so rocky, that I imagine there is no great deal of cultivable land in all this district, and therefore it is probably high. Quantities of barley are cultivated on the mountain sides, but the grain does not come to perfection, and it is generally cut green for fodder; though the General says that it is not good for that, the straw being coarse and hard. Potatoes are a good crop.

One of the principal articles of food of the laborers of this country is *cancha,* or toasted maize. They mix a little lime with the grains before putting them in the hot ashes, which makes them whiter and improves their flavor. It is really very sweet and good, and I liked it better than the green corn roasted, which is such a favorite dish with us. *Chicha,* a fermented liquor, is also made from Indian corn, and much drunk by all classes. The General gave us some that he had prepared and bottled himself. It was very good, rose-colored, and sparkled like champagne.

We visited the stables, which were very clean, and paved, and contained some ten or fifteen fine-looking young horses; and there were thirty or forty more, mares and colts, in a spacious corral or enclosure near, with an American farrier from Tarma attending to some of them. There is also a neat little chapel occupying a corner of the *patio,* with the inscription over the door, *Domus mea, domus orationis est.* The General's manners were exceedingly courteous and affable, and he possessed that suavity and gentleness of bearing that seems to me always to characterize the military man of high rank when in retirement. The whole establishment reminded me of one of our best-kept Virginia farms, where the owner had inherited the homestead of his father, and was in easy circumstances.

JUNE 14—Rode out to the southward, in the direction of Jauxa. This valley, which rises very rapidly, is thickly settled, and well cultivated. Road bad. Another valley debouches from this, about four miles above Tarma, to the southward and eastward, leading to the Montaña of Vitoc.

JUNE 15—Had a long visit from General Otero. The vivacious old gentleman discoursed very pleasantly. He said that it was difficult to get at the population of the town proper, the census being generally taken of the Doctrina, or district over which the Cura had religious jurisdiction; that this was about ten or twelve thousand, of which one-twelfth part were pure white, about one half Mestizos (descendants of whites and Indians), and the balance Indians, there being very few negroes. I asked him to account for the number of blind people we had noticed in the streets. He said that most of the blind people came from Jauxa, in which country much wheat and barley are produced; that they sifted these grains, and got rid of the chaff by throwing them up in the air, and he believed that the blindness arose from the irritation caused by the chaff and barbs flying into the eyes of the people who sifted.

He also said that he thought I should not attempt to cross the Chanchamayo amongst the Indians, for that I would not be able to defend myself against their attacks; but thought that, if I wished to descend the Ucayali, I had better take a more southern tributary, called the Pangoa; that there the Indians were not so much irritated against the whites, and that the river was known to be navigable for canoes, for he himself had known a friar who, in 1817, had descended it for the conversion of the Indians of the Ucayali, and had afterwards established a missionary station at Andamarca, where the Indians came at stated periods to be baptized and receive presents of hatchets, knives, beads, &c., but that, on the occasion of the war in 1824, the supplies had been stopped, and the Indians would come no more. He, as did the sub-prefect, liked my idea of ascending from the mouth of the Ucayali, with a properly equipped Indian force, and looking into the navigability of the Perené and Chanchamayo that way.

JUNE 16—We left Tarma for the Chanchamayo. This is the first time I have applied to authority for the means of locomotion. I did it inadvertently, and was sorry for it; for, though I would probably have been cheated in the price, yet I should not have been the cause of injustice and oppression. I had said to the sub-prefect, a few days before, that I wanted the means of transportation for some baggage to Chanchamayo, which he promised to furnish me. Yesterday I went to ask for it for to-day, and he referred me to the governor of the district, who was present, and who told me that he would have what I required—viz: two asses and a saddle-mule, with two *peons*—ready by to-morrow morning. Accordingly, this morning he sent for me, and presented to me the owner of the mule, the owner of the asses, and the two *peons*. The wages of these were to be four *reals,* or half a dollar, a day; and I paid each three dollars in advance. To the Governor I paid a dollar for each ass, and two for the mule, with the understanding that I was to pay as much more on my return. The *peons* were then lectured on their duties, and sent round to my house with an escort of half a dozen *alguaziles,* or constables, armed with sticks, to prevent their escaping or getting drunk before the start. The asses and mules were also sent round under a similar guard, so that my *patio* seemed filled with a clamorous multitude, who created such a confusion that I had to turn out all but my own people. I ordered these to load up; but they said that the owners of the asses had sent no *lassos,* or thongs, to bind on the burdens; and I soon discovered that there was a general unwillingness for the job, and that the governor had pressed the animals into the service against the will of the owners.

Strong efforts were made to get the mule away from me. The woman of the house, who, it appears, was a sister of the owner, advised me not to take it; and said that it was a bad, vicious animal, that would do me a mischief. I was surprised at this, as he looked particularly docile; and I directed my new servant (one recommended by the Cura, and who looked twice as vicious as the mule) to mount and ride him around the patio. The fellow grinned maliciously, and proved my judgment correct. Finding this would not do, the owner (who had put his sister up to making this attempt) then came forward, and said I must pay him half a dollar more, as the Governor had kept back that much of the price. This being "no go," he tried to steal away his mule while our backs were turned; but being prevented, he went off, got drunk in about fifteen minutes, and came back maudlin; embracing, kissing, and weeping over his mule, crying in piteous tones, *"Mi macho, mi macho"* (my mule, my mule). We shoved him aside and rode off, followed, I have no doubt, by the curses of the community.

This was all very annoying to me. I afterwards mentioned these circumstances to the Commandant of the fort at Chanchamayo, telling him how much I would prefer to pay double price and get voluntary service. He said that my sympathies were all thrown away upon these people, that I must go to the governors for the means of transportation, for that the Indians would not let me have their beasts at any price; and related instances of his having to use threats, and even force, to induce a sulky Indian to give him and his beast food and shelter when in the Cordillera, and the approach of night made it impossible to go on. Several travellers in these parts have also told me that they have been compelled to shoot the poultry of an Indian, who with a large stock, would refuse to sell at any price; but who, after the thing was done, would good-humoredly accept a fair value.

Ijurra also related instances of oppression and tyranny on the part of the governors, particularly in the province of Mainas, where commerce is carried on by transportation of the goods on the backs of Indians. A travelling merchant goes to the governor and says, "I have such and such a cargo; I want so many Indians to transport it." The governor, generally a white or Mestizo, sends for the *Curaca* (the lineal hereditary governor of the tribe of Indians of that district, who has great authority, and without whose assistance the whites probably could not govern at all), and orders him to have so many Indians detailed for a journey. The Curaca drums them up, directing them to toast their corn and prepare their *fiambre* (food for the road) for a journey of so many leagues; and they are taken from their occupations and sent off, for probably many days, at a pay of anything that the governor may direct.

It would seem that men could never improve under a system of such absolute slavery as this; yet to give them liberty is to abandon them and return them to a state of barbarity, shutting out all prospect of improvement; and the only hope seems to be in the justice and moderation of the rulers—a slim hope here.

We got off at noon, stopped at the *chacra* of General Otero, and received a letter of introduction to the commandant of the fort. When the old gentleman saw our new servant Mariano, he crossed himself most devoutly, and ejaculated *"Satanas!"* He then told us that this was a notoriously bad boy, whom nobody had been able to manage, but that we, being strangers and military men, might get along with him by strictness and severity; and he gave the boy a lecture upon his duties and the faithful performance of them.

A mile and a half beyond General Otero's is the town of Acobamba. I judge that it contains twelve or fifteen hundred inhabitants, but it is situated in a thickly settled district, and the Doctrina is said to be more populous than that of Tarma. Six more miles brought us to Palca, a straggling town of about one thousand inhabitants. We merely passed through and pitched the tent in an old corn-field, and slept delightfully. Tent-pegs for this country should be of iron. Although those we used were made of the hardest wood that could be found in Lima, we had used them all up by this time, beating their heads by driving them with a hatchet into the hard and stony ground.

The valley now narrows, and allows no room for cultivation. Though going down hill by the barometer, we were evidently crossing a chain of mountains, which the stream at the bottom of the valley has saved us the trouble of ascending and descending, by cleaving a way through for itself, and leaving the mountains on either hand towering thousands of feet above our heads. The ride was the wildest we have yet had; the road sometimes finding room along the borders of the river, and then ascending nearly to the top of the hills, and diminishing the foaming and thundering stream to a noiseless, silver thread. The ascents and descents were nearly precipitous, and the scene was rugged, wild, and grand beyond description.

We saw some miserable huts on the road, and met a few asses carrying reeds and poles from Chanchamayo. It seemed a providence that we did not meet these at certain parts of the road, where it is utterly impossible for two beasts to pass abreast, or for one to turn and retreat; and the only remedy is to tumble one off the precipice, or to drag him back by the tail until he reaches a place where the other can pass.

We met with a considerable fright in this way to-day. We were riding in single file along one of these narrow ascents, where the road is cut out of the mountain side, and the traveller has a perpendicular wall on one hand, and a sheer precipice of many hundreds of feet upon the other. Mr. Gibbon was riding ahead. Just as he was about to turn a sharp bend of the road the head of a bull peered round it, on the descent. When the bull came in full view he stopped, and we could see the heads of other cattle clustering over his quarters, and hear the shouts of the cattle-drivers, far behind, urging on their herd. I happened to be abreast of a slight natural excavation, or hollow, in the mountain side, and dismounting I put my shoulder against my mule's flank and pressed her into this friendly retreat; but I saw no escape for Gibbon, who had passed it. The bull, with lowered crest, and savage, sullen look, came slowly on, and actually got his head between the perpendicular rock and the neck of Gibbon's mule. I felt a thrill of agony, for I thought my companion's fate was sealed. But the sagacious beast on which he was mounted, pressing her haunches hard against the wall, gathered her feet close under her and turned as upon a pivot. This placed the bull on the outside (there was room to pass, though I did not believe it), and he rushed by at the gallop, followed in single file by the rest of the herd. I cannot describe the relief I experienced. Gibbon, who is as gallant and fearless as man can be, said, "It is of no use to attempt to disguise the fact—I was badly scared."

At two P.M., we arrived at a place called Matichacra, where there was a single hut, inhabited by a woman and her child, the husband having gone to Cerro Pasco to exhibit some specimens of gold ore which he had found here. The woman was afflicted with an eruption on her face, which she thought was caused by the metallic character of the earth around, particularly the antimonial. She took a knife, and, digging earth from the floor of her hut, washed it in a gourd, and showed us particles of metal like gold sticking to the bottom. I showed some of this earth to General Otero, who pronounced that there was no gold in it; but Lieuten-

ant Maury, who examined some that I brought home with a powerful magnifier, has declared that there was. The mountains have
an exceedingly metallic appearance, and the woman said that there
were still in the neighborhood traces of the mining operations of
the Spaniards.

About a mile and a half above Matichacra commenced the
steep regular descent of the mountain range, and from just above
it we could discern where the valley debouched upon an apparent
plain, though bounded and intersected by distant mountains, bearing and ranging in different directions. This place we judged to
be the Montaña. We stopped an hour at Matichacra (Gourd Farm,
from half a dozen gourd vines growing near the house), and made
a *chupe* with a leg of mutton we had bought the night before at
Palca. We saw a few patches of Indian corn on the side of the
mountain opposite, and the tops of the mountains are clad with
small trees. We passed on five miles further, and camped on a level
plat near the banks of the stream, with bushes and small trees growing around us.

JUNE 18—This was the longest and hardest day's ride. The road
was very bad; rocky and rough where it descended the river, and
steep and difficult where it ascended the mountain side. We
thought that the engineer who planned and constructed the road
had frequently "taken the bull by the horns," and selected the worst
places to run his road over; and that he would have done much
better had he occasionally have thrown a bridge across the stream,
and led the road along the flank of the mountains on the other side.
In seven and a half miles we arrived at the first *hacienda* where we
saw sugar-cane, *yucca,* pine-apples, and plantains. It had just been
opened, and nothing yet had been sold from it.

The road, by which we had descended the valley of Chancha-mayo, turned at this place sharp to the right, and faced the mountains that divide this valley from that of the Rio Seco. We were near the junction of the two valleys, but a rock had fallen from the hills above and blocked up the road on which we were travelling, so that we had to cross the mountain on our right and get into the other valley. The ascent was steep, and trying to man and beast. It is called the *Cuesta de Tangachuca,* or "Hill of take care of your hat," and is about three miles in length. The road, after passing through a thick forest, brought us out upon a bald eminence, the termination of the spur of the Andes that divides the two valleys. The rivers Seco and Chanchamayo unite at its base and flow off through a valley, rapidly widening out, covered with forests, and presenting an appearance entirely distinct from the rocky and stern sterility that characterizes the country above. This is the "Montaña" of which I had thought so much. I was woefully disappointed in its appearance. I had taken the impression that I should behold a boundless plain, alternating with forest and prairie, covered with waving grass, and with a broad and gentle river winding its serpentine course through it, between banks rich with the palm and plantain. In place of this, the view from the mountain top showed a country broken still into mountain and valley (though on a much smaller scale than above), shaggy with trees and undergrowth of every description, and watered by a small stream, still foaming and roaring over its rocky bed.

We descended the hill by a very circuitous and precipitous path, most of us on foot, though it may be ridden over, for Mr. Gibbon did ride over the worst parts of it, and only dismounted where a fallen tree made an obstruction that he could not pass. The descent brought us to the rocky bed of the Rio Seco, crossing which we were clear of the eastern chain of the Andes and in the Montaña of Chanchamayo.

A league from the crossing of the Rio Seco, we passed a bad and broken bridge that spans a small stream called Punta Yacu, coming down a valley from the southward, and halted at the first *hacienda* of the Montaña, where we camped for the night.

JUNE 19—Six miles of travel brought us to the fort of San Ramon. The road is a black mud bridle-path through the woods, much obstructed with the roots and branches of trees, but level. Comparatively few rocks are seen after leaving the *hacienda*. We were kindly received by the Commandant, a fine-looking young man, and his officers.

The fort is a stockade, embracing about six acres, armed with four brass four-pounders, and garrisoned with forty-eight men. It is situated at the junction of the rivers Chanchamayo and Tulumayo—the former about thirty and the latter forty yards wide—both shallow and obstructed with rocks. The current seemed about five or six miles the hour. A canoe, well managed, might shoot down the Tulumayo as far as we saw it.

The fort was constructed in 1847, under the direction of President Castilla, for the purpose of affording protection to the cultivators of the farms in its rear. It doubtless does this against the unwarlike Indians of this country; but I imagine that North American Indians, actuated by the feelings of hostility which these people constantly evince, would cross the rivers above the fort and sweep the plantations before the soldiers could reach them. The Indians have abandoned all idea of reconquering the territory they have lost, but are determined to dispute the passage of the rivers and any attempt at further conquest. They never show themselves now in person, but make their presence evident by occasionally setting

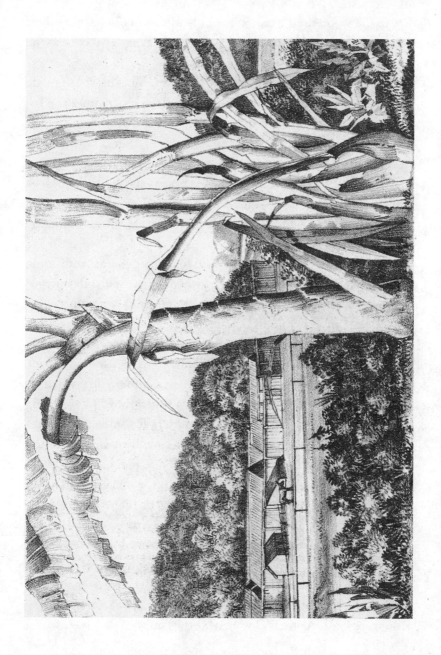

fire to the woods and grass on the hill-sides, and discharging their arrows at any incautious person who may wander too near the banks of the rivers.

The Commandant told us that many attempts had been made to establish friendly relations with them. In former times the Indians used to advance out of the forest, to the further bank of the river, and hold conversations and exchange presents with the officers of the post. They gave bows and arrows, rare birds and animals, and received in return, knives, beads, and looking-glasses. But these parleys always ended with expressions of defiance and insult towards the whites on the part of the Indians, and frequently with a flight of arrows.

He related to us that a year or two ago a general, with some officers, came to visit the fort, and wished to try their skill at negotiation. Accordingly, whilst they were at dinner, the sentinel reported that an Indian had made his appearance; whereupon the party rose from the table and went down to the river-side to have a talk. The Indian, after salutations, made signs for a looking-glass, which was thrown over to him; then, for a knife, with which he was also gratified. He then asked for a tinder-box. There being none at hand, Noel went up to his quarters for some. On his return, he met an officer coming up the bank, with an arrow through his arm; and shortly after, another, with one planted deep in his back, between the shoulders. It appears that, as soon as the Indian had received his presents, he drew his bow at the general. The party turned to fly; but a flight of arrows from the forest wounded the two officers; and the one who was shot in the back died of the wound eight days afterwards. These arrow-shots are of frequent occurrence, and several of the soldiers of the fort have been severely wounded. A number of arrows were discharged at some soldiers, who were washing their clothes near the banks of the river, whilst we were here. We picked them up, and theCommandant made us a present of them.

These arrows, as are the arrows of all the Indians I have met with, are so heavy that, at a greater distance than twenty or thirty yards, it is necessary to discharge them at an elevation, so that they shall describe a curve in the air; and it is wonderful to see with what precision the Indians will calculate the arc, and regulate the force so that the arrow shall fall upon the object. On the Amazon many fish and turtle are taken with bows and arrows. An Indian in a canoe discharges his arrow in the air. It describes a parabola, and lights upon the back of a fish, which the unpractised eye has not been able to see. The barb, with which the arrow is armed, ships on the end of it, and is held in its place by a cord which wraps around the shaft of the arrow, and is tied to its middle. The plunge of the fish shakes the arrow clear of the barb; the cord unwinds, and the arrow floats upon the water—an impediment to the fish, and a guide to the fisherman, who follows his arrow till the fish or turtle is dead. The motion of the arrow is so slow, and it is so readily seen in its course, that I imagine there would be no danger in the reception of single arrow-shots in front; for an abundance of time is allowed to step aside and avoid them. I have seen boys shooting at buzzards on the beach; and the arrow would alight upon the very spot where the bird had been sitting, some seconds after he had left it.

Whilst here, we visited the *haciendas* of the Brothers Santa Maria, Padre Saurez, and Zapatero—all, I believe, inhabitants of Tarma. That of the last seemed the largest, and the best order of any that I had yet seen. A description of the method of cultivating the staples of the country practised on this farm, will give an idea of the general system of farming in the Montaña.

Zapatero has about one hundred acres cleared, and most of it planted in cane, coca, *yucca,* pine-apples, plantains, coffee, and cot-

ton. The farm employs a *mayordomo,* or steward, and four resident
laborers. These are serfs, and cost the employer their support and
seven dollars a year each for their contribution to the government,
or poll tax. When more land is to be cleared, or the coca crop gathered, laborers are hired from the neighboring villages of Tarma,
Ocsabamba, or Palca, at nominal wages of half a dollar a day; but
their support is charged to them, at such prices as to swallow up
nearly all the wages. A sheep, for example, is charged to them at
three dollars: Its price in Tarma is one. The laborers who live on
the estate seem contented with their lot; they dwell in small, filthy
cane houses, with their wives and children; do very little work, and
eat *chalona* (or dried mutton), *charqui* (or jerked beef), *yucca,*
cancha, sweet potatoes, and beans; and drink *huarapo* (the fermented juice of the cane), and sometimes a glass of bad rum made
from it. They occasionally desert; but if they do this, they must
get some distance off, or custom, if not law, would return them as
debtors to their masters.

Sugar-cane is the most valuable and useful product of the
Montaña. The leaves of the cane, when green, serve for food for
the cattle; when dry, to make wrappings for the *chancaca* and sugar.
The crushed stalk is used as fuel for the oven. The hogs fatten on
the foam at the top of the boiling. From the first boiling is made
the *chancaca,* or brown sugar cake, which is eaten after dinner by
almost all classes, and in great quantities by the lower class.

Coca is a bush of about four feet high, producing a small light-
green leaf, which is the part used. The blossom is white, and the
fruit a small red berry. The leaf of this plant is to the Indian of Peru
what tobacco is to our laboring classes in the South—a luxury,
which has become a necessity. Supplied with an abundance of it,
he sometimes performs prodigies of labor, and can go without food
for several days. Without it, he is miserable and will not work. It

is said to be a powerful stimulant to the nervous system, and, like strong coffee or tea, to take away sleep; but, unlike tobacco and other stimulants, no one has known it to be injurious to the health. Von Tschudi thinks that an immoderate use of it is injurious, but that, taken in moderation, it is in no way detrimental to health; and that without it the Peruvian Indian, with his spare diet, would be incapable of going through the labor which he now performs. The coca plant he therefore considers as a great blessing to Peru.

He relates that an Indian, employed by him in digging, worked hard for five nights and days without intermission, except for two hours each night—and this without food. Immediately after the work the Indian accompanied him on a two days' journey of twenty-three leagues on foot, and then declared that he was ready to engage in the same amount of work, and go through it without food, if he were allowed an abundance of coca. This man was sixty-two years of age, and had never been sick in his life.

Coffee is propagated from suckers or slips, and it is necessary to protect the plants from the sun by cultivating the broad-leaved plantain among them till they have grown up to about four feet in height. No care, except an occasional cleaning about the roots, is taken of them here, and yet the finest coffee I have ever drunk was from this district. The bush grows to seven or eight feet in height, and is very beautiful in appearance. It has a small and very dark green leaf, pure white blossoms, and green, red, and dark purple fruit on it at the same time.

Cotton may be planted at any time. It does not grow on a bush or plant, as with us, but on a tree some eight or ten feet high. It gives its first crop in a year, and will continue to give for three years; after which the tree dries up, and it is necessary to replant. It bears cotton all the time, but it is not gathered during the rainy season. I could not ascertain how much cotton a tree will give in its lifetime, but, from the quantity of blossoms and bolls I saw on them, I should think its yield was great. The quality, particularly that of Chanchamayo, is very superior. It is the black-seed cotton, and when picked off leaves the seed perfectly bare and clean. An active man will pick one hundred pounds of cotton a day.

Yucca (cassava root), which is grown from the stalk of the plant, is planted at any time. It yields in nine months. The plant runs up to fifteen or twenty feet in height, with about the thickness of a man's wrist. It is difficult to distinguish this plant, or its fruit, from the *mandioc*. The *mandioc* is called in Peru *yucca brava,* or wild *yucca;* and this *yucca dulce,* or sweet *yucca.* This may be eaten raw; the juice of the other is a deadly poison. The *yucca* answers the same purpose in Peru that the *mandioc* does in Brazil. It is the general substitute for bread, and roasted or boiled is very pleasant to the taste. The most common drink of the Indians, called *masato,* is also made from the *yucca* by rasping the root to a white pulp, and then boiling it. During the boiling the Indian women take portions into their mouths, chew it, and spit into the pot. After it is sufficiently heated, it is put into large earthen jars, covered, and suffered to ferment. When used, it is taken out of the jar by the handful, mixed with water in a gourd, stirred with the fingers, and drunk. It is a disgusting beverage, and powerfully intoxicating.

Platanos—which is the general name for all kinds of plantains, or bananas—are the most common fruit of the country. The people eat them raw, roasted, boiled, baked, and fried. There can be no dinner without them, and a vile rum is also made of them. By the Indians the fruit is generally cut green and roasted. It is propagated from suckers or young bulbs, and gives fruit with such facility and abundance as to foster and minister to the laziness of the people, who won't work when they can get anything so good without it.

I have frequently thought that a governor would do a good act, and improve the condition, or at least the character, of the governed, who would set fire to, or grub up every *platanal* in his district, and thus compel the people to labor a little for their bread.

The only farming utensils used in Chanchamayo are short coarse sabres, with which weeds are cut up and holes dug in the earth in which to plant the seed.

This is not a good grazing country, though there were some cattle belonging to the fort which seemed in good condition. All the meat used is brought from Sierra. It seems difficult to propagate cattle in this country. All the calves are born dead, or die soon after birth with a goitre or swelling in the neck.

The houses on the *haciendas* are built of small, rough-hewn, upright posts, with rafters of the same forming the frame, which is filled in with wild cane (*caña brava*) and thatched with a species of narrow leafed palm, which is plaited over a long pole and laid athwart the rafters. The leaves lie, one set over the other, like shingles, and form an effectual protection against the rain and sun; though I should think the rain would beat in through the cane of the sides, as few of the houses are plastered. The Commandant of the fort was anxious to have his buildings tiled, as this palm thatch, when dry, is exceedingly inflammable; and he felt that the buildings of the fort were in constant danger from the not distant fires of the savages. Señor Zapatero thinks that the government may withdraw the troops from the fort at any time; but says that he has four swivels, which he means to mount around his house; and, as he has expended much labor and money on his *hacienda,* he will hold on to the last extremity, and not give up his property without a tussle.

It is a pity that there are not more like him, for many acres of fine land are lying uncultivated in Chanchamayo on account of this fear; and several of our Tarma friends offered us title deeds to large tracts of land there, because a feeling of insecurity regarding the stability of the government prevented them from expending time and money in the cultivation of them. Another such administration as that just closed under President Castilla will dissipate this apprehension; and then, if the Peruvian government would invite settlers, giving them the means of reaching there, and appropriating a very small sum for their maintenance till they could clear the forest and gather their first fruits, I have no doubt that fifty years would see settlements pushed to the navigable head waters of the Ucayali, and the colonists would find purchasers for the rich and varied products of their lands at their very doors.

JUNE 23—We started on the return to Tarma, accompanied by the Commandant and his servant. We walked up a part of the hill at Rio Seco. This is very hard work. I could not stand it more than half way, and made the mule carry me over the rest. It takes one hour to ascend, and an hour and a quarter to descend. Camped at Utcuyacu.

JUNE 24—Missing my saddle-bags, which had some money in them, we sent Mariano (our Tarma servant), accompanied by the servant of the Commandant, back to a place some distance the other side of the big hill, where the saddle-bags had been taken off to adjust the saddle. He started at six; we at eight, following our return track. We made the longest and hardest day's ride we had yet made, and were much surprised at being joined by the servants with the saddle-bags by nine P.M. They must have travelled at least thirty-six miles over these terrible roads, crossing the big hill twice, and ascending quite two thousand feet. Gibbon did not believe it. He thought—and with much probability—that the boy had hid the saddle-bags at Utcuyacu, and after we left there had produced them and followed in our track, persuading or bribing the soldier to keep the secret. The Commandant, however, thought his servant incorruptible, and that this was no great feat for these people.

One of our *peons* carried on his back, for a whole day (fifteen miles), a bundle of alfalfa that Gibbon could not lift with ease, and pronounced, upon trial, to be heavier than I am, or upwards of one hundred and twenty-five pounds.

JUNE 26—Discharged Mariano because we could not trust him. Though clever and active, he is neglectful and dishonest. We thought it rather hard that the Cura should have recommended him to us, as his character was notorious in the town. We believed that the Cura, with the people generally, was glad to get rid of him, and was disposed to palm him off on anybody.

We delighted the Tarma people with our favorable reports of the Chanchamayo, and they loaded us with civilities and kindness. They did not like the idea of my visiting the Montaña of Pozuzu and Mayro; and seemed to fear that I might find there a better communication with the Amazon.

Chapter V

Division of the party—Acobamba—Plain of Junin—
Preservation of potatoes—Cerro Pasco—Drainage of the mines

GIBBON AND I had long and earnest consultations about the
propriety of dividing the party; and I now determined to do so,
giving to him the task of exploring the Bolivian tributaries, while
I took the headwaters and main trunk of the Amazon. It was a
bold, almost a rash determination, for the party seemed small
enough as it was; and we might readily encounter difficulties on
our route which would require our united exertions to overcome.
I had many misgivings, and told Gibbon at first that it seemed
midsummer madness; but the prospect of covering such an extent of territory, of being enabled to give an account of countries
and rivers so little known, and the reflection that I need not abandon routes that I had looked upon with a longing eye were so
tempting that they overrode all objections; and we set about
making our preparations for the separation.

I furnished Mr. Gibbon with the following instructions:

TARMA, June 30, 1851.

SIR: From a careful perusal of my instruction from the Navy Department, it appears to be a matter of importance that as much of the great South American basin, drained by the Amazon and its tributaries, should be explored as the means placed at my disposal will allow; and having now arrived at a point where, if the party is kept together, some objects of much interest will have to be abandoned to secure others, I have determined to divide the party, and confide a portion of it to your direction.

You will, therefore, with Mr. Richards and a guide, proceed to Cuzco, and examine the country to the eastward of that place. It is said that a large and navigable river, called the Madre de Dios, has its source in the mountains of Carabaya, and may be approached at a navigable point by descending the Andes from Cuzco. Many arguments have been adduced to show that this river is the Purus, which is known to empty into the Amazon.

It is desirable that this should be determined; and you will make such inquiries in Cuzco as will enable you to decide whether it is practicable to descend this river. I am under the impression that its shores, near where you would be likely to embark, are inhabited by tribes of savage and warlike Indians, who have committed frequent depredations upon the *haciendas* established in the neighborhood. You will constantly bear in mind that your loss will deprive the government of the after-services expected of you in the prosecution of our important and interesting enterprise. You will therefore run no unnecessary risk, nor expose yourself or party to unreasonable danger from the attacks of these

savages. The inhabitants of Cuzco are said to be so much
interested in this discovery, that they may furnish you an
escort past the point of danger.

Should you find this route impracticable, you will
proceed south, to Puno, on the banks of the Lake Titicaca;
thence around the southern shores of this lake to La Paz, in
Bolivia; thence to Chohabamba; and, descending the
mountains in that neighborhood, embark upon the Mamoré,
and descend that river and the Madeira to the Amazon. You
will then ascend the Amazon to the Barra do Rio Negro,
and, making that your headquarters, make excursions for
the exploration of the main stream and adjacent tributaries,
until my arrival, or you hear from me.

You are already possessed of the views of the department regarding the objects of this expedition. A copy of its
instructions is herewith furnished you. You will follow them
as closely as possible.

Should you go into Bolivia, I would call your attention
to the *cascarilla,* or Peruvian bark, which is of better quality
in that country than elsewhere. Make yourself acquainted
with its history and present condition.

Wishing you success, I remain your obedient servant,
   WM. LEWIS HERNDON, Lieutenant U.S. Navy.

We divided the equipage, the *tocuyo,* or cotton cloth (which
we had not yet touched), the hatchets, the knives, the beads, the
mirrors, the arms and ammunition. I gave Gibbon $1,500 in money,
and all the instruments, except some thermometers and the boiling-
point apparatus, because I was to travel a route over which sex-
tants and chronometers had been already carried; and he might
go where these had never been. I directed him to hire a guide in

Tarma, and, so soon as Richards (who was still sick) should be able to travel, to start for Cuzco, and search for the headwaters of the Madre de Dios.

JULY 1—I started at noon with Ijurra and Mauricio, accompanied by Gibbon and the Commandant. A very pleasant gentleman this, and I shall long remember his kindness. Soon after, Gibbon and I lingered behind the company, and at the entrance of the valley of the Acobamba, which route I was to take, we shook hands and parted. I had deliberated long and painfully on the propriety of this separation; I felt that I was exposing him to unknown perils; and I knew that I was depriving myself of a pleasant companion and a most efficient auxiliary. My manhood, under the depressing influence of these feelings, fairly gave way, and I felt again that *hysterico passio,* that swelling of the heart and filling of the eyes that I have so often been called upon to endure in parting from my gallant and generous comrades of the Navy.

He returned to make the necessary arrangements for his expedition. We crossed the Chanchamayo by a stone bridge, and passed through the village of Acobamba. This town contains about fifteen hundred or two thousand inhabitants; but, like all the towns in the Sierra at this season, it appears deserted—no one in the streets, and most of the doors closed. The road is a steady and tolerably smooth ascent of the valley, which is narrow, pretty, and well cultivated. As usual, the hills facing the north are bare and rugged; those facing the south present more vegetation, but this is scant. Cactus and long clump grass run to within two thirds of the top, and then the rock shoots perpendicularly up in naked majesty.

Nine miles above Acobamba brought us to Palcamayo, a village of one thousand inhabitants, belonging to the Doctrina of Acobamba. A justice of the peace, a good-looking Indian, whom we encountered sitting at the door of a grog-shop in the plaza, conducted us to the house of the alcalde. We found this worthy drunk and asleep on the floor and were much annoyed with the attentions of another individual, who had a very dirty poultice on his jaws; this was his worship's secretary, who was in little better condition than his patron. Two drunken *regidores* came in to see us, and it seemed that all the magistracy of Palcamayo had been "on a spree." They required the money of us before they would get us or our cattle anything to eat.

It would be difficult to find a clearer sky and a purer atmosphere than we had here. The sky, at twilight, looked white or gray, rather than blue; and I thought it was cloudy until my eye fell upon the young moon, with edges as distinct and clear as if it were cut out of silver, and near at hand. The elevation of Palcamayo is 10,539 feet above the level of the sea.

JULY 2—Thermometer, at six A.M., 37; clear and calm. Three miles above Palcamayo we left the maize and alfalfa, and encountered potatoes and barley. The road a league above this point turns sharp to the westward, and ascends a steep and rugged *cuesta*. This brought us out upon a small plain, bounded by low hills, and dotted with small detached houses, built of stone and covered with conical roofs of straw. They were circular, and looked like beehives. The plain was covered with a short grass, and many tolerable-looking cattle and sheep were feeding on it. A small stream, coming from the westward, ran through its midst. The water had been carried by a canal half-way up the sides of the hills that bounded the plain to the northward, so as to enable the people to irrigate the whole plain. Where the water had broken through the canal, and spread itself over the side of the hill, it had frozen, and the boys were amusing themselves sliding down it.

At the western edge of the plain is the village of Cacas, of 250 or three hundred inhabitants. The people were celebrating the festival of St. Peter, for they are not particular about days. The church was lighted and decorated with all the frippery that could be mustered; and preparations were making for a great procession. There were two Indians, or Mestizos, dressed in some old-fashioned infantry uniform, with epaulets; flaming red sashes, tied in monstrous bows behind, and white gloves. (The cocked hats, for size and variegated plumage, beggar description.) These were evidently the military part of the procession; one was mounted on a little shaggy nag, with his sword hanging on the right-hand side; and the other was strutting about, nearly buried in his cocked hat, while just fourteen men were employed in caparisoning his horse. The drinking had already commenced; most of the population were getting drunk fast, and I have no doubt there was a grand row that night.

Drinking seems a very general vice amongst the inhabitants of these wet, cold, and highly elevated plains. The liquor is invariably the Pisco or Ica brandy, made in that province. It is pleasant to the taste and of good quality. In the Montaña we had often occasion to regret the exchange of this for new-made cane rum.

The hills that bound the plain on the west have two salt springs, from which the inhabitants of the village get their salt by evaporation. The hill over which we rode is called the Cuesta de la Veta, because travellers suffer from this sickness in passing it. As I had felt nothing of it, even at the Pass of Antarangra, I watched very closely for any symptoms of it here; but perceived none, though I sucked a cigar all the way to the top. The road to the top of the Cuesta is about three miles in length, and its ascent brought us to the historical plain of Junin, where Bolívar, on the sixth of August, 1824, gave the Spaniards a heavy and very nearly conclusive overthrow. Half an hour's ride over the plain brought into view the Western Cordillera, the Lake Chinchaycocha, and the pyramid erected by the prefect of the province to commemorate the battle. It stands off to the left of the road about a league, and is at the foot of a little hill, where the liberator stood to direct the fight; it is white, and seemed seventy or eighty feet high. Our day's ride of eighteen miles brought us to the town of Junin, where we took lodgings in the house of the governor; more drunken people there.

JULY 3—Junin is a village of one thousand inhabitants, situated about a mile and a half from the southern extremity of Lake Chinchaycocha, and 12,947 feet above the level of the sea. This lake is twenty miles long, in a northwest and southeast direction, and has an average breadth of about six miles. It is said to discharge its waters into the Amazon by the river of Jauxa, which we crossed at Oroya, and which is a tributary of the Ucayali.

The inhabitants of Junin, and the other towns of this plain, are herdsmen. They raise cattle for the supply of Cerro Pasco and Tarma, and mules for beasts of burden. Their houses are built of mud and straw; and they eat mutton and *macas* (a root of the potato kind, but looking, and when boiled tasting, more like a turnip). The people of these regions find it very difficult to procure vegetables, as *quinua* and barley will not grain, nor potatoes grow, in the wet soil and cold atmosphere of the plain. They therefore have to resort to means for preserving the potato and its varieties, which are got from the valleys of the Andes. These means are, generally, drying and freezing; and they make a variety of preparations from the potato in this way. The *macas* are simply exposed to the frost and sun for a number of days, and then put away in a dry room. The inhabitants make a sort of soup or sirup of them, the smell of which, Rivero says, "is a little disagreeable to people unaccustomed to it" (it is really very offensive); and it is the general opinion that it is a stimulant to reproduction.

The plain, about forty-five miles long, and from six to twelve broad, is generally wet, and in some places marshy. The soil is gravelly, with a light covering of mould, producing a short grass, scarcely adequate for the support of the flocks, which are indeed of small size, but sometimes fat and good. A great number of large beautiful waterfowl, including the scarlet flamingo and several varieties of snipe, frequent the banks of the lake and marshy places. The people cut their supply of fuel from the turf of the bogs, in the dry, and stack it up for use in the rainy season. There is said to be much thunder and lightning here at the commencement of the rainy season (about the first of October), and the lightning frequently falls on a hill about four miles to the eastward of the town, where the inhabitants say there is much loadstone. The plain is about thirteen thousand feet above the level of the sea.

The road onward from Junin runs not far from the banks of the lake. On the left we had the grand snow-covered domes and pinnacles of the Western Cordillera sleeping in the sunlight, while clouds and storm enveloped the Eastern. About two P.M., a breeze from the northward brought some of the storm down upon us. It snowed fast; the flakes were small and round, like hail, but soft and white. The thermometer, which was 54 at the commencement of the storm, fell, during its continuance of ten minutes, to 48. We found an overcoat very comfortable.

About fifteen miles from Junin we passed the village of Carhuamayo. Here I saw the only really pretty face I have met with in the Sierra, and bought a glass of *pisco* from it. The road between Junin and Carhuamayo is a broad and elevated one, built of stones

and earth by the Spaniards. Without this the plain would be impassable in the rainy season. Six miles further we stopped at the
tambo of Ninaccaca.

JULY 4—The village of Ninaccaca, of two or three hundred inhabitants, lies off to the right of the road, on which the *tambo* is situated, about half a mile. I would have gone there, but I was desirous
of sleeping in a *tambo,* for the purpose of testing the accounts of
other travellers who complain so bitterly of them. We were fortunate enough to have this *tambo* to ourselves, there being no other
travellers; and I had quite as comfortable a time as in the *alcalde*'s
home at Palcamayo, or in that of the governor of Junin. My bed is
generally made on the baggage in the middle of the floor, while
Ijurra takes to the mud-standing bed-places which are to be found
in every house. Last night I woke up, and finding him very un-
easy, I asked "if he had fleas up there." He replied, with the utmost *sang-froid,* and as if he were discussing some abstract
philosophical question with which he had no personal concern
whatever, that "this country was too cold for fleas, but that his bed-
place was full of lice." It made my blood run cold; but long before
I got out of the mouth of the Amazon I was effectually cured of
fastidiousness upon this or any similar subject.

    We were somewhat annoyed by the attentions of the master
of the house, who was very drunk. His wife told us next morning
that he came near killing her with his knife, and would infallibly
have beaten her, but that she told him "those strangers were soldiers, and would shoot him if he did." Her naïve way of telling how
she managed the man, and got off from the beating, was quite
amusing. The accent of these people is a sort of sliding drawl that
makes every voice alike.

Our route now approached the Western Cordillera fast. About three miles from the *tambo* the plain began to be broken into rolling hills. After crossing a range we stopped to breakfast at a collection of a few huts, where I was amused at an instance of the apathy of the people. A very common reply to the inquiry of the traveller if he can have such and such things is *"manam cancha"* (there is none; we haven't it). We rode up to the door of a hut, the mistress of which was sitting "knitting in the sun" at the back of it. She heard our horses' tread, and too lazy to change her position, without seeing us or ascertaining if we wanted anything, she screamed out *"manam cancha."* Ijurra abused her terribly; and we had our water boiled (which was all we wanted) at another hut.

Three miles from this, the country becomes more hilly and rocky, losing the character of Pampa. The passage of a low but abrupt chain of hills brings the traveller in view of Cerro Pasco. The view from this point is a most extraordinary one. I can compare it to nothing so fitly as the looking from the broken and rugged edges of a volcano into the crater beneath. The traveller sees small houses, built, without regard to regularity, on small hills, with mounds of earth and deep cavities in their very midst; and mud chimneys of ancient furnaces, contrasting strikingly with the more graceful funnel of the modern steam engine; the huge cross erected on the hill of Sta. Catalina, near the middle of the city, which his fancy may suppose placed there to guard, with its holy presence, the untold treasures beneath; two beautiful little lakes, only divided by a wide causeway at the southern extremity of the crater, and another embedded among the hills to the westward; hills (on one of which he stands) of five hundred feet in height, with bold white heads of rock, surrounding these; and the magnificent Cordillera from the right and left overlooking the whole.

These are the objects that strike the eye of the traveller at his first view. As he rides down the hill, he sees the earth open everywhere with the mouths of mines now abandoned; he is astonished at their number, and feels a sense of insecurity as if the whole might cave in at once and bury him quick. He rides into the narrow, ill-paved streets of the city, and, if he can divert his attention for a moment from the watching of his horse's footsteps, he will observe the motliest population to be met with anywhere out of the dominions of the Sultan. I believe that he may see, in a single ride through the city, men of all nations, and of almost every condition; and if he don't see plenty of drunken people, it will be a marvel.

I was delighted when we turned into the patio of the house of the sub-prefect of the province, and escaped the rude stare and drunken impertinence of the Indians, thronging the streets and doors of the grog-shops. This gentleman, whose kindness we had experienced at Tarma, gave us quarters in his house, and pressed us to make ourselves at home, to which his blunt, abrupt, and evidently sincere manners particularly invited.

After a wash, to which the coldness of the weather and the water by no means invited, I put on my uniform in honor of the day, and went out to see Mr. Jump, director of the machinery, and Mr. Fletcher, an *employé* of the Board of Miners to whom I brought letters of introduction from Lima. These gentlemen received me with great cordiality. Mr. Jump offered me a room in his house, and Mr. Fletcher handed me a number of letters from friends at home, at Lima, and at Santiago. These letters were cordial medicines to me; I had arrived cold, sick, and dispirited, and but for them should have passed the first night of mental and physical suffering that I had been called upon to endure since leaving Lima.

JULY 6—Rain nearly all night; I was cold and sick, and sat by the fire all day, trying to keep myself warm. The houses in Cerro Pasco are generally built of stones and mud, and covered in with tiles or straw; most of them have grates, with mud chimneys, and are plentifully supplied with good coal, both bituminous and hard. The sub-prefect says that if the place owes nothing else to the Pasco Peruvian Company, it owes it (at least) a debt of gratitude for the introduction of the grates. I found, however, very little comfort in them; for the houses are so open about the doors and windows that while my toes were burning, my back was freezing; and one has to be constantly twisting around, like a roasting turkey, to get anything of their benefit. My companion, Ijurra, whose fathers were rich miners and powerful men in these parts, had many visitors. The talk of the company was of nothing but the mines, and incessant was the complaining (which I have heard elsewhere) of the miseries and uncertainties of the miner's life. All seem to agree that it is a sort of gambling, in which most lose; but there is the same sort of feverish infatuation in it that there is in gaming with cards, and the unlucky player cannot but persevere, in the hope that the luck will change, and that the *boya* (striking the rich vein), like "the bullets and bragger oldest," will come at last.

I went out with Mr. Jump to look at the town. It was a most curious-looking place, entirely honey-combed, and having the mouths of mines (some two or three yards in diameter) gaping everywhere. From the top of the hill called Sta. Catalina, the best view is obtained of the whole. Vast pits, called *tajos,* surround this hill, from which many millions of silver have been taken; and the miners are still burrowing, like so many rabbits, in their bottoms and sides. I estimate that the *tajo* of Sta. Rosa is six hundred yards long, by four hundred broad and sixty deep; those of the

"Descubridora" and _____ are about half as large. The hill of Sta. Catalina is penetrated in every direction; and I should not be surprised if it were to cave in any day, and bury many in its ruins. The falling in of mines is of frequent occurrence; that of Mata-gente (kill people) caved in years ago, and buried three hundred persons; and four days ago a mine fell in and buried five; four have been recovered, but one is still incarcerated, and the people are now hard at work for him. The mines of Cerro Pasco were discovered in 1630, by an Indian making a fire on some stones and observing melted silver.

JULY 8—Visited the mines. We entered a mouth which seemed only a little larger than that of a common well, each of the party furnished with a tallow candle, shipped in an iron contrivance at the end of a staff. The descent was disagreeable, and, to the tyro, seemed dangerous; it was at an angle of at least 75 degrees from the horizontal line. The earth was moist, and the steps merely holes dug for the heels at irregular distances. I feared every moment that my boot-heel would slip, and that I should "come with a surge" upon my next in advance, sending him and myself into some gulf profound. I was heartily glad when we got upon the apparently level and broad bank of the great *socabon,* and had made up my mind that I would tempt Providence no more. But, reflecting that I should never, probably, visit the mines of Cerro Pasco again, I took courage and descended 110 feet further, by an even worse descent than the former, to the bottom of the pump shafts. A burly and muscular Cornishman, whom I at first took to be a Yankee, with a bit of candle stuck into a lump of mud in front of his hat, was superintending here, and growling at the laziness and inefficiency of his Indian subordinates. I should think that these pumps were not well attended to, so far from the eye of the master. All the metal work of the pumps is of copper. Iron is corroded very quickly, on account of the sulphuric acid and sulphates which the water of the mines holds in solution. The fish are said to have abandoned the lake of Quiulacocha, into which the waters are forced, on this account. The sides of the mines were covered in many places with beautiful sulphates of iron and copper.

Our exploration lasted about four hours; and we emerged at the *tajo* of Sta. Rosa, where, seated upon piles of silver ore, we partook of some bread and cheese, and a glass of *pisco,* which we found as welcome and as grateful as manna in the desert. This freshened us up, and we went to see the *boliches.* These are hand-mills, or rather foot-mills, for grinding ore; generally owned by Frenchmen or Italians, who grind the ore that is brought to them in small quantities by the workmen in the mines.

A *boliche* consists of a large flat stone laid on an elevated platform of rock or earth, and another, convex on its lower side, resting upon it. The grinder, standing upon this upper stone, spreads his feet apart, and gives it motion by the movement of his body. The bits of ore are placed between these stones, and a small stream of water from a barrel above mixes with the *harina,* and carries it off to a receptacle below. It may be imagined that, to draw any profit from so rude a contrivance as this, it is necessary that the ores ground by it should be of the richest kind.

The man who was buried by the falling in of one of the mines was got out yesterday. He seemed strong, though he had had no food for nearly seven days. He had lost the account of time, and thought he had been enclosed in the earth but three days.

JULY 9—Suffering to-day from an affection called *macolca,* which is incident to nearly everyone on his first visit to the mines. This is a painful soreness of the muscles, particularly on the front of the thigh. I could scarcely bear that my legs should be touched, and locomotion was anything but agreeable.

The town of Cerro Pasco is (by temperature of boiling water) 13,802 feet above the level of the sea. The population varies from six to fifteen thousand souls, according to the greater or less yield of the mines. Most of the adult part of this population are, of course, engaged in mining. This seems to be a calling that distorts much the moral perception, and engenders very confused ideas of right and wrong. The lust for money-making seems to have swallowed up all the finer feelings of the heart, and cut off all the amenities of society. There are no ladies—at least I saw none in society; and the men meet to discuss the mines, the probable price of quicksilver, and to slander and abuse each other. There seems to be no religion here even in form. The churches are mere barns, going to decay; and I saw no processions or religious ceremonies. One observer saw a procession in 1834, but I should doubt if there had been one of these contemptible mockeries since. Not that the people are getting better, but that their love of gain is swallowing up even their love of display.

I met with much kindness on the part of the gentlemen whose acquaintance I made, particularly on that of the sub-prefect, who lodged me in his house, and, by his frank and sincere manner, made me feel at home; and I do not say that men here are individually bad, but only speak of the philosophical fact that mining, as an occupation, has a tendency to debase men's characters, and destroy those sensibilities and affections that smooth and soften the rugged path of life. Moreover, I don't speak half so badly of them as they do of themselves; for one, if he were to seek it, might easily hear that every individual in the Cerro was a rascal.

The climate of this place is exceedingly uncomfortable, and I should suppose unhealthy. I could not sleep between sheets, but

preferred "the woollens," with an abundance of them. The mean temperature, during the months of July, August, and September, is at 44 degrees in the day, and 35 degrees at night. In these months there is an abundance of snow and hail, which lowers the thermometer considerably; and even without these it goes down to 30 degrees and 28 degrees in August. From the middle of October to the end of April the climate is insupportable from the rains, tempests, and lightnings, which almost every year cause damage. There is a period of fine weather from the middle of December to the middle of January, called, in the poetic language and religious turn of thought of the Spaniards, *El verano del niño,* or the summer of the child, from its happening about Christmas. The streams, which are fed from the rains of this country, invariably stop rising, and fall a little after this period. The temperature is so rigorous here that the hens do not hatch, nor the llamas procreate; and women, at the period of their confinement, are obliged to seek a more genial climate, or their offspring will not live.

Persons recently arrived, particularly if they have weak lungs, suffer from affections of the chest and difficulty breathing. The miners suffer paralysis from the sudden changes of temperature to which they are exposed in and out of the mines, and from inhaling the fumes of the mercury in the operation of distilling. Those who suffer in this way are called *azogados,* from *azogue* (quicksilver). The most common diseases are pleurisies, rheumatisms, and a putrid fever called *tabardillo.* Pleurisies are said to be cured by taking an infusion of *mullaca,* an herb which grows in the neighborhood. It has very small leaves, and gives a small, round red fruit.

There is no cultivation in this neighborhood, with the exception of a little barley, which gives no grain, but is cut for fodder.

The market, however, is well supplied from Huanuco, and the neighboring valleys. Expenses of living are great, particularly where articles of luxury from the coast are used.

JULY 12—I had a visit from an enthusiastic old gentleman, the Intendente of Pozuzu, who says that he is about to memorialize Congress for funds and assistance to carry on a work which he has himself commenced—that is, the opening of a road from the Cerro direct to Pozuzu, without taking the roundabout way by Huanuco. He says that when the road is opened from the Cerro to Pozuzu, and thence to Mayro (the head of navigation on the Pachitea), communication may be had and burdens carried between the Cerro and Mayro in four days; also, that roads may run to the southward from Pozuzu, over a plain, by which the commerce of foreign countries, coming up the Amazon, may reach Tarma, Jauxa, and all the towns of the Sierra.

This is the day-dream of the Peruvians of that district. They know the difficulties of the Cordillera passage, and look earnestly to the eastward for communication with the world, for between the Cerro and Mayro there is but one range of the Andes to pass to arrive at the Montaña (as is also the case between Tarma and Chanchamayo); whereas, by the route through Huanuco there are at least two, and these very broken, elevated, and rugged. I think that the Ucayali affords the best means of communication with the interior of Peru, and my impression is that it is best approached by the way of Chanchamayo. I hinted this, but my friend hooted at the idea; and I find the same jealousy in him that I found in the Tarma people. Both here and there they say it will be a great day for them when the Americans get near them with a steamer.

JULY 13—I had unfortunately selected a feast-day, and one, too, on which there was a regular bull fight (the first that had been seen in the Cerro), for my departure, and found great difficulty in getting off. The muleteers I had engaged were drunk at an early hour, and not making their appearance, I had to send the police after them. It is really curious to observe how entirely indifferent to the fulfilment of a promise these people are, and how very general the vice is. These muleteers had given me the strongest assurances that they would be at my door by daylight, and yet when they made the promise they had not the slightest idea of keeping it. The habit seems to be acquiesced in and borne with patience by even the true and promise-keeping English. My friend Mr. Jump did not sympathize in the least with my fretfulness, and seemed surprised that I expected to get off.

I desire to express my thanks to him, and the amiable members of his family, Mr. and Mrs. Biggs, for those kind attentions that cheer the heart and renew the energies of the worn wayfarer.

Chapter VI

Departure from Cerro Pasco—Mint at Quinua—Chinchao
Valley—Huallaga River

BY CAJOLING AND THREATS of appeal to the military (a small military force is stationed here as a police), we got our drunken vagabonds to "load up" and set off by half past one P.M. One of them gave us the slip at the outskirts of the town. The other wished to look him up, or at least to get the key of a *tambo* where two spare mules belonging to them were locked up, but we would not hear of it; and driving the loaded mules on, he was fain to follow. The deserter joined us at our stopping-place for the night, but on finding the condition of things, he had to return to the Cerro for his missing beasts.

Almost immediately on leaving the Cerro, and ascending the hills that encircled it on the north, we came in sight of the Eastern Andes, which is here a Cordillera, for it has many abrupt and snow-clad peaks. Close at hand, on the left, was a spot of marshy ground, which had some interest for us, as we were not to quit the waters which we saw trickling in tiny streams from it, until, swelled by many others, they pour themselves into the Atlantic by a mouth 180 miles broad. This is the source of the Huallaga, one of the head tributaries of the Amazon.

Seven miles in a north-northeast direction, and passing many *haciendas* for the grinding of ore, brought us to the village of Quinua. This village is just at the point where, leaving the sterility of the Cerro, we fall in with bushes and flowers.

Four miles further we stopped for the night at a *hacienda* called Chiquirin, which appears once to have been flourishing, but which is now nearly abandoned, being only tenanted by an old man to take care of the house. The bridge, which crossed the stream in front of the house, had had arched gateways at each end, and a respectable-looking church occupied one side of the *patio*. A field or two of barley is all the cultivation now about it. Indeed, there seemed little room for more, for the hills on each side now began to close in and present the appearance of mountains; and I have no doubt that, though still going down hill, we have begun to cross the second range of the Andes. We could get no supper at this place. I was tired enough to care little about it. Had Ijurra been with us, he would probably have found something; but he was absent, having dropped the compass on the road and ridden back to look for it. The height of Chiquirin, by boiling point, is 11,542 feet above the level of the sea.

JULY 14—We had a pleasant ride down the valley, which opens a little and gives room for some cultivation. There were pinks and hollyhocks in the little gardens adjoining the cottages; also cabbages, lettuce, and onions. We stopped to breakfast at Caxarmarquilla, a village of some eight or ten houses. At six miles further we passed a *hacienda*, where there were roses in bloom, and the flowering pea, with wheat on the hill-side, and a grist-mill; also, alfalfa and maize. Immediately afterwards, a valley from the south-ward and eastward joined the one I was travelling in, bringing its stream of water to swell the Huallaga. Gypsum crops out of the hills on the road-side, making the roads white. Houses here are whitewashed with it. We met continually mules laden with to-bacco, coca, and fruit, going from Huanuco and the Montaña beyond it to the Cerro. We stopped, at half past five, at San Rafael, an Indian town of some 250 souls, with a white lieutenant gover-nor, and put up at his house.

I had my bed made inside, instead of outside the house, which was a mistake, as I was "pigging in" with all the family; and from want of air, and villanous smell, expected to catch *tabardillo* before morning. The thermometer was at 62 degrees at seven P.M., and I imagine did not fall lower than 50 degrees during the night; so that I could very well have slept outside, and advise all travellers to do so, providing themselves with warm bed-clothing. Here I was joined by Ijurra, whom I was very glad to see, and the delinquent *arriero,* with his two mules. The height of San Rafael, by boiling point, is 8,551 feet above the level of the sea.

JULY 15—We got alfalfa for our mules, but it is now getting very scarce. The valley, after leaving San Rafael, is very narrow, and the road rises and falls along the bare flanks of the mountains. We shot at condors hovering over a dead mule, and saw a small hawk of variegated and pretty plumage, of a species which we had be-fore seen near Oroya. About ten miles from San Rafael we were crossing the highest part of the chain. An opening in the moun-tains to the right gave us a view of some splendid snow-clad peaks. After an hour's ride over a precipitous and broken path, rendered dangerous in some places by the sliding of the earth and soft rock from above upon it, we commenced a very sharp descent, which brought us, in fifteen minutes, to fruit-trees and a patch of sugar-cane on the banks of the stream. The sudden transition from rugged mountain peaks, where there was no cultivation, to a tropical vegetation, was marvellous. A few miles further on we crossed the boundary-line between the provinces of Pasco and Huanuco. The transition is agreeable, and I was glad to exchange the mining for the agricultural country. At half past four, we arrived at the town of Ambo, a village of one thousand inhabitants, situated at the junction of the rivers Huacar and Huallaga. The former stream comes down a ravine to the westward; each is about thirty-five yards broad, and, uniting, they pour their waters by the town with great velocity.

Two miles from Ambo, on the right or opposite bank of the river, is another very pretty little village, almost hidden in the luxuriant vegetation about it. The whole valley now becomes very beautiful. From the road on which we were travelling to the river's brink (a breadth of quarter of a mile), the land (which is a rich river bottom) is laid off into alternate fields of sugar-cane and alfalfa. The blended green and yellow of this growth, divided by willows, interspersed with fruit-trees, and broken into wavy lines by the serpentine course of the river, presented a gay and cheerful appearance, which, contrasting with the forbidding aspect of the rocks we had just left, filled us with pleasurable emotions, and indicated that we had exchanged a semi-barbarous for a civilized society. The only drawback with me was excessive fatigue. When Ijurra rode back to Cerro Pasco for the compass, he happened to be mounted on my mule. This gave her extra work; and the ride of to-day was a long one, so that the little beast by this time could barely put one foot before the other. There is scarcely anything more fatiguing than to ride a tired horse; and when I arrived (at five) at the hospitable gates of the *hacienda* of Quicacan, and with difficulty lifted myself out of the saddle, it was with the deep sigh which always accompanies relief from pain, and which was much more pleasurable than the sight of waving fields and babbling brooks.

The owner of the *hacienda*—an English gentleman, named Dyer, to whom I brought letters from Cerro Pasco—received me and my large party exactly as if it were a matter of course, and as if I had quite as much right to enter his house as I had to enter an inn. The patio was filled with horses, belonging to a large party from Huanuco bound to Lima, and every seat in the ample portico seemed filled. I was somewhat surprised at the size and appointments of the establishment. It looked like a little village of itself, with its offices and workshops. The dwelling—a large, substantial, though low building, with a corridor in front supported on massive arches, and having the spaces between the pillars enclosed with iron wire to serve for cages for numerous rare and pretty birds—occupied one side of the enclosed square; store-rooms occupied another; the sugar-house, another; and a chapel, the fourth. A bronze fountain, with an ample basin, decorated the centre. I was strongly reminded of the large farm-houses in some parts of Virginia; the same number of servants bustling about in each other's way; the children of the master and the servant all mixed up together; the same in the hospitable welcome to all comers; the same careless profusion. When I saw the servants dragging out mattresses and bed-clothing from some obscure room, and going with them to different parts of the house to make pallets for the visitors who intended to spend the night, I seemed carried back to my boyish days, and almost fancied that I was at a country wedding in Virginia. We dined at six in another spacious corridor, enclosed with glass, and looking out upon a garden rich with grape-vines and flowers. After dinner, the party broke up into groups for cards or conversation, which continued until ten o'clock brought tea and bed time.

I conversed with an intelligent and manly Frenchman, whose account of the seeking and gathering of Peruvian bark was exceedingly interesting; and I should judge that it is an occupation which involves much fatigue and exposure. I also had some talk with quite a pretty young woman, who had come from Quito by the way of the Pastaza, Marañon, and Huallaga Rivers. She said she was scared at the *malos pasos,* or rapids of the river, and never could relish monkey soup; but what gave her most uneasiness was the polite attention of the Huambisas Indians. She declared that this was frightful, and swore a good round oath, "*Caramba!* but they were mad for a white wife." Report here says that she prefers Yankee to Indian, and is about to bestow her hand upon a long countryman of ours, the head blacksmith, named Blake.

JULY 16—Dyer had put me into a wide "four-poster." None but a traveller in these parts can imagine the intense pleasure with which I took off my clothes and stretched my weary limbs between linen sheets, and laid my head upon a pillow with a frilled case to it. I could scarcely sleep for the enjoyment of the luxury. Rest, too, has renewed my beast; and the little black, which I thought last night was entirely done up, is this morning as lively as a filly.

We left Quicacan at noon, in company with Mr. Dyer and my French friend; stopped at three more *haciendas,* all belonging to Señor San Miguel, to whom I brought letters from Lima. All these, with another on the same road, belonged to a Colonel Lucar, of Huanuco, who gave them to his sons-in-law. Quicacan was the family mansion, and had been longest under cultivation. At half past four we arrived at Huanuco, and, presenting a letter to Colonel Lucar, from his son-in-law Dyer, we were kindly received, and lodgings appointed us in his spacious and commodious house.

JULY 17—Huanuco is one of the most ancient cities in Peru. It is prettily situated on the left bank of the Huanuco or Huallaga River, which is here about forty yards wide, and at this time (the dry season) about two feet deep in the channel. It, however, every two or three hundred yards, runs over rocks or a gravelly bed, which makes it entirely unnavigable, even for canoes, though when the river is up I believe articles are transported on it from *hacienda* to *hacienda* in small scows. A smaller stream, called the Higueros, empties into it just above the city.

The houses are built of *adobe,* with tile roofs, and almost all have large gardens attached to them—so that the city covers a good deal of ground without having many houses. The gardens are filled with vegetables and fruit-trees, and make delightful places of recreation during the warmer parts of the day.

The population numbers from four to five thousand. They seem to be a simple and primitive people; and, like all who have little to do, are much attached to religious ceremonies—there being no less than fifteen churches in the city, some of them quite large and handsome. The people are civil and respectful, and, save a curious stare now and then at my spectacles and red beard, are by no means offensive in their curiosity.

The trade of the place is with Cerro Pasco on the one hand, and the villages of the Huallaga on the other. It sends *chancaca,* tobacco, fruit, and vegetables to the Cerro, and receives foreign goods (mostly English) in return: broad-striped cassimere, such as gentlemen's trousers are made of; common silk handkerchiefs; silk hats; blue cloth drillings; narrow ribbon; cotton handkerchiefs; tolerable Scotch carpeting; *bayeta castilla* (a kind of serge or woollen cloth, with a long shag upon it, and of rich colors). In the market, beef and mutton from the province of Huamalies are found, as are

Indian corn, potatoes, salt from the coast at Huacho, sugar, generally from the coast (this in an eminently sugar country), and coffee. Very little meat is raised. I saw a small quantity of pork, with
plenty of tallow candles; and rotten potatoes for the consumption
of the Indians. Bread is good, but is generally made, in the best
houses, of American flour from Lima. Vegetables and fruit are
abundant and cheap. This is, par excellence, the country of the
celebrated *chirimoya*. I have seen this fruit in Huanuco quite twice
as large as it is generally seen in Lima, and of most delicious flavor. They have a custom here to cover the finest specimens with
gold leaf, and place them as a decoration on the altar of some patron Saint on his festival. The church afterwards sells them, and I
have seen several on Colonel Lucar's table.

This gentleman is probably the richest and most influential
man in Huanuco. He seems to have been the father of husbandry
in these parts, and is the very type of the old landed proprietor of
Virginia, who has lived always upon his estates, and attended personally to their cultivation. Seated at the head of his table, with his
hat on to keep the draught from his head—and which he would
insist upon removing unless I would wear mine—his chair surrounded by two or three little negro children, whom he fed with
bits from his plate; and attending with patience and kindness to
the clamorous wants of a pair of splendid peacocks, a couple of
small parrots of brilliant and variegated plumage, and a beautiful
and delicate monkey—I thought I had rarely seen a more perfect
pattern of the patriarch. His kind and affectionate manner to his
domestics (all slaves), and to his little grandchildren, a pair of
sprightly boys, who came in in the evening from the college, was
also very pleasing. There are thirty servants attached to the house,
large and small; and the family is reduced to the Colonel and his
lady (at present absent), and the boys.

The climate of Huanuco is very equable and very salubrious. There are no cases of affection of the chest which commence here; on the contrary, people with diseases caused by the inclemency of the weather about Cerro Pasco come to Huanuco to be cured. Dysentery and *tabardillo* are the commonest diseases; and I see many people (particularly women) with goitre. I saw a woman who had one that seemed to arise under each ear and encircle the throat like an inflated life-preserver. The affection is said to be owing to the impurity of the water, which is not fit to drink unless filtered. The lower class of people do not attend to this, and thus the disease is more general with them than with the higher classes. It is disagreeable to walk out in the middle of the day, on account of a strong northerly wind, which sets in at this season about noon, and lasts till dark, raising clouds of dust. The mornings and evenings are very pleasant, though the sun is hot for an hour or two before the breeze sets in. The height of Huanuco above the level of the sea is, by boiling point, 5,946 feet.

There is a college with about twenty-two "internal" and eighty day-scholars. Its income, derived from lands formerly belonging to convents, is $7,500 yearly. It has a fine set of chemical and other philosophical apparatus, with one thousand specimens of European minerals. These things were purchased in Europe, at a cost of $5,000; and the country owes them to the zeal for learning and exertions of Don Mariano Eduardo de Rivero, formerly prefect of the department, director general of the mines, and now consul general to the Netherlands, where he is said to be preparing a voluminous work on the antiquities of Peru. The Department of Junin owes much to its former prefect. He has founded schools, improved roads, built cemeteries, and, in short, whatever good thing I noticed on my route might generally be traced back to Rivero.

JULY 18—I called on the sub-prefect of the province, and delivered an official letter from the prefect of the department, whom I had visited at Cerro Pasco. He received me courteously, and promised me any assistance I might stand in need of.

People in Huanuco are fully alive to the importance of opening the navigation of the Huallaga to their city. They speak of it as a thing that would be of incalculable advantage to them, and their leaders and influential men have often urged them to be up and doing. But, although they cannot be stirred up to the undertaking themselves, they are jealous of the attempt by any other route.

Colonel Lucar showed me his *cuarto de habios,* or room where he keeps all his horse furniture. He has at least a dozen saddles of various patterns, with bridles, pillons, horse-cloths, holsters, and everything complete. Most of the bridles and stirrups are heavily plated with silver. People take great care of their horses in this country, and are generally good horsemen. There are one or two carriages and gigs in Huanuco, made in England.

JULY 22—Much to my annoyance our servant Mauricio deserted this morning. Ijurra accuses me of having spoiled him by indulgence; and I, on the other hand, think that he had disgusted him by tyranny. I imagine he went back to Lima. This was an intelligent young man, who gave me information about the Montaña. He said I would be amply protected in my contemplated voyage up the Ucayali with twenty-five Chasutinos (Indians of Chasuta), for they were a brave and hardy people; but that the Cocamas and Cocamillos, from about the mouth of the river, were great cowards, and would desert me on the first appearance of the savages—that they had so treated him. I rather suspect that the reason for Don Mauricio's shabby behavior was that we were getting into his own country, and that he had private reasons for desiring to avoid a visit home. He had asked me at Tarma to let him go with Gibbon.

Our *arriero* made his appearance at noon, instead of early in the morning, as he had promised; but we are now getting used to this. We did not ride our own mules, as they were sick and not in condition to travel, and the *arriero* supplied us with others. I got a horse, but did not derive much benefit from the exchange. Our course lay down the valley northeast, crossing the river soon after leaving the town by a rude bridge. We found the road good, but rocky, principally with the debris of quartz. Gold is occasionally found, but in small quantities, in the mountains bordering this valley. At six miles from Huanuco we passed the village of Sta. Maria del Valle. We stopped and took some fruit and *pisco* with the curate, to whom also I had a letter from Lima. Every traveller in this country should provide himself with letters of introduction. People, it is true, will receive him without them, but do not use that cordial and welcome manner which is so agreeable.

The Cura had some fifty or sixty new and well-bound books on shelves, and seemed a man superior to the generality of his class. He said that Valle was a poor place, producing only sugar-cane, which the inhabitants put to no other use than to make *huarapo* to drink; and that, if it were not for the neighborhood of Huanuco, he thought that he should starve. *Huarapo* is the fermented juice of the cane, and is a very pleasant drink of a hot day.

We saw a few sheep and goats after leaving the village. The trees were principally willow and fruit-trees, with here and there a cotton tree bearing indifferent staple. The mountains on the left, or Huanuco, side send down spurs towards the river, between which are pretty little valleys, not deep and narrow, but spread out like a fan. In each one of these there is situated a small village or a *hacienda,* presenting, with its fields of cane and alfalfa, and, higher

up, wheat, a very pretty appearance. It is not so on the right bank.
The small streams that flow into the river from this side come down
rugged ravines, with sides of soft rock and white earth, and are
generally very muddy. We stopped two miles beyond Valle at a
hacienda called Chullqui. Height of Chullqui, by boiling point,
5,626 feet above the level of the sea.

JULY 23—Course still northeast along the banks of the Huallaga.
Trees principally small acacias. At six miles from Chullqui we
crossed the river, turned to the north, and ascended a ravine (down
which flowed a small stream) to the village of Acomayo, a very
pleasantly situated village, of about three hundred inhabitants.
When the authorities are asked concerning the population of any
place, they always give the number of families. This place has seventy *casados,* or couples of married people; and I judge, from experience, that five to each family is a fair allowance. The water here
is very good, which was an agreeable change from the Huanuco
water; and the fruits, oranges, figs, guavas, and *chirimoyas* are of
good quality. I noticed, also, a tree bearing a large bell-shaped
flower, called *floripondio*. This is an old acquaintance of mine; it
gives out a delicious fragrance at night, which, accompanied, as I
have known it, by soft air, rich moon-light, and gentle company
makes bare existence a happiness.

About three miles up the Quebrada we turned to the northeast and commenced the ascent of the Cerro de Carpis. This is one
of a range of mountains running to the southward and eastward,
forming the left-hand side of the valley of Acomayo (looking down
the stream), and dividing the Sierra from the Montaña. The ascent is six miles long, and very tedious. I had no water to ascertain
its height by the boiling-point apparatus, but judge, from the great
descent to Cashi (a distance of four miles, and so steep that we

preferred to walk and lead our beasts), that the pass is a full eight thousand feet above the level of the sea; Cashi being 6,540 feet.

There is said to be a superb view of the Montaña from the summit of this hill, but the clouds (almost within reach of the hand) boiling up from the great deep below effectually cut it off, and we could see nothing. When we had got some distance down, and obtained a view through an opening in the thick growth of the mountain-side, we looked down upon the most rugged country I have ever seen. There seemed to be no order or regularity in the hills, which were thickly covered with forest; but the whole had the appearance of the surface of a vast boiling caldron suddenly stricken motionless. Just at the summit, and where the road turns to descend, hundreds of little wooden crosses were placed in the niches of the rock—votive offerings of the pious *arrieros,* either of gratitude for dangers passed, or for protection against dangers to come, in the ascent or descent of the mountain.

We walked down the descent, leading the beasts. The road was very rocky and muddy, and the mountain-side was clad with small trees and thick undergrowth. There were many creepers and parasitical plants, some of them very graceful and pretty. We stopped, at six, at a *tambo* called Cashi, built on a plat, about half-way down the mountain. We found our place of rest very agreeable; night clear, calm, and cold.

JULY 24—An hour's travel brought us to the bottom of the hill, where we encountered the Chinchao Valley coming down from the right. We crossed the stream that flowed through it, and travelled down the valley on its right bank, the road rising and falling on the sides of the hills. At seven miles from the *tambo* we passed the village of Chinchao, containing twelve houses and a church, with cotton, coffee, orange, and plantain trees scattered about the village. A pretty shrub, bearing a gay red flower, in appearance like our crepe myrtle, bordered the road-side. It is called San Juan, because it blooms about St. John's Day, the twenty-fourth of June. The cultivation of the coca commences here.

I brought a letter from the sub-prefect at Huanuco, for the Governor of Chinchao, but he was absent at his *chacra,* and not to be found. We then asked for the Lieutenant Governor; but though there seemed, from the general account, to be such a person, we could not find out exactly who he was, or where he lived. The *arriero* said he lived "a little lower down"; but at every house at which we called in our descent the reply still was *más abajo* (yet lower). At last we seemed to have treed him, and even the man's wife was produced; but after a little conversation it appeared that our friend was still *más abajo.* I was tired and hungry enough to wish he was—where he could not get any lower, for we had depended upon our letter for a breakfast. We continued our weary route, and at the next house (the best-looking we had seen) encountered a white woman, rather shrewish-looking, indeed, but still a woman, synonym everywhere for kindness. Ijurra civilly inquired if we could get a few eggs. I think our appearance, particularly the guns slung behind the saddles, bred mistrust, for we met with the invariable lie, *no hay* (haven't got any). I couldn't be baffled in this way; so, taking off my hat, and making my best bow, in my most insinuating tones I said "that we had something to eat in our saddle-bags, and would be very much obliged if La Señora would permit us to alight and take our breakfast there." She softened down at once, and said that if we had any tea she could give us some nice fresh milk to mix with it. We had no tea, but declared, with many thanks, that the milk would be very acceptable. Whereupon, it was put on to boil; and, moreover, a dozen fresh eggs, and boiled to perfection, were also produced. I enjoyed the breakfast very much, and was pluming myself on the effect of my fine address, when (alas for my vanity!) the lady, after looking at my companion for some time, said to him, "Arn't you *un tal* (a certain) Ijurra?" He said yes. "Then we are old playmates," said she. "Don't you recollect our play-ground, your old uncle's garden in Huanuco, and the apples you used to steal out of it to give me? I'm Mercedes Prado." Here was the solution to the enigma of our reception. Strange to say, the name awoke pleasant recollections in me also, and set before me the features of the gay and beautiful young girl whose quick repartee and merry laugh added so much to the charm of Valparaiso society.

The house of our hostess was very like a capsized ship, with the cut-water and upper part of the bows sawn off to make an entrance. It had a regular breast-hook made of saplings twisted together over the door, a kelson reaching from this to a very perfect stern frame, and, had the ribs been curved instead of straight, the likeness would have been exact. It was about fifty feet long, and made an airy and commodious residence. I was surprised to find that we were in the upper story of it, for we had entered from the ground without steps; but I afterwards discovered that we had entered from an esplanade cut in the side of the hill, levelled for the purpose of drying coca leaves, and that the lower story was at the bottom of the hill, the entrance facing the other way.

We went on our way rejoicing. The *arriero* had gone on ahead; and when we arrived at a *chacra,* called Atajo, at half past four, we found that he had unloaded the mules. I was quite angry at his stopping so soon, and ordered him to load up again; but finding that he went to work to do it, I let him off, cautioning him against unloading without orders. The means of living are getting very scarce. We could get nothing to eat, and had to draw upon our *charqui.* The people of the hut seem contented with a *chupe* made of lard, with *ullucas* and young onions. Nights still cool; elevation of Atajo, 3,910 feet.

JULY 25—The road from this place leaves the banks of the stream and ascends the hills on the right by a very steep and tedious ascent. After arriving at the summit, we turned northeast by north, and passed the *haciendas* called *Mesa Pata* (the top of the table) and Casapi, which seemed abandoned. The road hence is a very rough descent, and a mere path through the bushes; the earth white, like lime, with gypsum cropping out occasionally. Near night we stopped at Chihuangala, the last *hacienda* of the valley, and beyond which there is no mule-road. The *arrieros* left us to seek pasturage. This is our last dealing with this gentry. I was glad to dismount, for I was tired of riding; but in spite of the abuse that is generally heaped upon the *arrieros,* I think I have had little difficulty to complain of. They seem to be tolerably honest and faithful (when once on the road), and, with judicious treatment, one can get along with them very comfortably. It rained heavily all the latter part of the night.

JULY 26—At this place we were to await the Indians from Tingo Maria (a village at the head of canoe navigation on the Huallaga), to carry our luggage on. Ijurra had written from Huanuco to the governor of Tingo Maria, requesting him to send them to us at Chihuangala, sending the letter by one of Castillo's company who was returning.

We had hard commons here, our *charqui* beginning to decay. No eggs; no potatoes; nothing, in fact, but *yuccas* and bananas. There were turkeys, chickens, and a pig running about the *chacra;* but no entreaty, nor any reasonable offer of money, could induce the people to sell us one. I offered the *patrona* a dollar and a half for a half-grown turkey; but she said she must wait till her husband came in from his work, so that she might consult him. When he came, after long debate, it was decided that they would sell me a chicken for breakfast tomorrow. I tried hard to find out why they were so reluctant to sell, for they do not eat them themselves, but did not succeed. I believe it to be something like the miser-feeling of parting with property, the not being used to money, and also a dislike to kill what they have reared and seen grow up under their own eye.

Our *patrona* had six or seven children: one an infant, which, when she puts to sleep, she enwraps closely in a woollen cloth, and swathes tightly, over arms and all, with a broad thick band, so that it is perfectly stiff, and looks like a log of wood, or a roll of cloth. I asked why she did this, but could only get the reply that it was the "custom here." The young women of the country have very good features, and appear lively and good-tempered. Two daughters of the *patrona* came in on a visit to-day. I suppose they are out at work (probably as house servants) in some neighboring *hacienda*. They were dressed in red calicoes, always open in the back, and with the invariable shawl; and one of them had ruffles of cotton lace around the bottom of the sleeves, which did not reach to the elbow. The girls were nearly as dark as Indians, but I presume they had a mixture of white blood.

JULY 28—I walked, in company with Ijurra, about three miles to visit a Señor Martins, at his *hacienda* of Cocheros. We found this gentleman a clever and intelligent Portuguese, who had passed many years in this country. His wife is Doña Juana del Rio, a very lady-like person, in spite of her common country costume. It was quite surprising to see a Limeña, and one who had evidently lived in the first circles of that city, in this wild country, and in this rude though comfortable house. The floor was earth, and I saw no chairs. The lady sat in a hammock, and the men either on the mud benches around the sides of the room, or on a coarse wooden one alongside of a coarse table. Part of the house was curtained off into small bed-rooms. There was evident plenty, and great comparative comfort about the house; also, a fine lot of handsome, intelligent-looking children.

Nothing is sold from this valley but coca. Only sufficient coffee and sugar-cane are planted for the use of the inhabitants. Señor Martins gave us some very good *caçacha,* or rum made from the cane, and some tolerable pine-apples and plantains. A little cotton is cultivated, and a coarse cloth is woven by hand from it. Every old woman goes about her household avocations with a bunch of cotton in her hand, and a spindle hanging below. I was surprised not to see any wild animals, though I am told that there are deer, hares, tiger-cats, and animals of the mink kind, that occasionally run off with the poultry. There are not so many birds as I expected; those I have seen are generally of a gay and rich plumage. Insect life is very abundant, and nearly all sting or bite. The climate is very pleasant, though the sun is hot in mid-day. The diseases, which occur rarely, are cutaneous affections, *tabardillo,* and sometimes small-pox.

On our return from Cocheros we stopped at the house of a man who had, the day before, promised to sell us a fowl; with the usual want of good faith of these people, he now refused. Ijurra took the gun from my hand, and, before I was aware what he was about to do, shot a turkey. The man and his wife made a great outcry over it, and he was hurrying off, with furious gestures and menacing language, to report the matter to his *patrón,* when a few kind words, the helping myself to a chew of coca out of his *huallqui,* or leathern bag, in which it is carried, and the offer of a dollar and a half, which before he had indignantly spurned, changed his mood, and he smiled and expressed himself satisfied, now that the thing was done and it could not be helped. I had been often told by travellers that this was frequently necessary to get something to eat, but had always set my mind resolutely against any such injustice and oppression; and I expressed my opinion of the matter to Ijurra, and requested that the like should not occur again. The elevation of Chihuangala is 3,421 feet above the level of the sea.

JULY 30—At ten A.M., when we had begun to despair of the coming of our Indians, and Ijurra was about to start alone for Tingo Maria for the purpose of fetching them, they came shouting into the *chacra,* thirteen in number. They were young, slight, but muscular-looking fellows, all life and energy; and wanted to shoulder the trunks and be off at once. We, however, gave them some *charqui,* and set them to breakfast. At noon we started, and descended the valley of Chinchao in a north-northeast direction; the path steep and obstructed with bushes.

At about six miles from Chihuangala we arrived at the junction of the Chinchao River with the Huallaga, in a heavy shower of rain, with thunder and lightning. By leaving the Huallaga at Acomayo, below Huanuco, crossing a range of mountains at the Cerro de Carpis, striking the head of the valley of Chinchao, and descending it, we had cut off a great bend of the river, and now struck it again at the junction of the Chinchao. It is here some sixty yards wide, and the Chinchao thirty, both much obstructed with shoals and banks of gravel. The *peons* waded the Huallaga above the junction, and brought up a canoe from the *hacienda* of Chinchayvitoc, a few hundred yards below, and on the opposite side. We passed in the canoe, which the Indians managed very well. It was a great treat, after the tedious walk we had had, to feel the free, rapid motion of the boat as it glided down the stream. The stream seemed to run at the rate of five or six miles the hour; but, by keeping close in shore, two Indians could paddle the light canoe against it very well.

Our *peons* cooked our dinner of cheese and rice, and made us a good cup of coffee. These are lively, good-tempered fellows, and, properly treated, make good and serviceable travelling companions. Let them but be faithfully paid, a kind word now and then spoken to them, and their cargoes rather under than over the regular weight (eighty-seven and a half pounds), and they will serve faithfully and honestly, and go singing and chattering through the woods like so many monkeys. Above all, let them stop when they wish, and don't attempt to hurry them.

There is much moisture in the atmosphere, and I find it almost impossible to keep the guns in serviceable order.

We met at this place some Indians carrying tobacco from Tocache and Saposoa (towns of the Huallaga) to Huanuco. Enterprising men have frequently tried to establish a trade along this river, carrying down cotton goods, knives, hatchets, beads, &c., and getting return-cargoes of tobacco, rice, straw hats, rare birds, and animals; but the difficulties of the route seem to have baffled enterprise. About two and a half years ago Vicente Cevallos made a large venture. He carried down thirty-five trunks or packages of goods, and the people of the river still talk of his articles of luxury; but in passing one of the *malos pasos,* or rapids of the river, his boat capsized, and he lost everything.

The Indians here had blue limestone, which they were burning to mix with their coca.

JULY 31—I bathed in the river before starting. This is wrong in so humid an atmosphere. I became chilled, and did not get over it for some hours. A native traveller in these parts will not even wash his face and hands before the sun is well up. Soon after starting we crossed a small stream, and ascended a hill that overlooks the falls of Cayumba, beyond which canoes cannot ascend. I did not see the falls, but am told that there is no cascade of height, but rather a considerably inclined plain, much obstructed by drift.

The ascent of the hill was very tedious, and I should complain of the fatigue but for shame's sake; for there were Indians along, young and rather small men, who were carrying a burden of nearly one hundred pounds on their back. Their manner of carrying cargoes is to have a sort of cotton satchel, of open work, with a broad stout strap to it. The end of the trunk or package, which is placed on end, is put into the bag, and the Indian, sitting down with his back to it, passes the strap over his forehead, and then, with a lift from another, rises to his feet, and, bending forward, brings the weight upon the muscles of his neck and back. A bit of blanket, or old cotton cloth, protects the skin of the back from chafe. The traveller in these parts should be as lightly clad and carry as little weight as possible, for the path is very steep and muddy. I had been thoughtless enough to wear my heavy Sierra clothes, and to load myself with a gun of a greater weight, I believe, than a standard musket—and so had occasion to envy Ijurra his light rig of nankeen trousers and cotton shirt, long but light staff, and twilled cotton "Jeffersons."

The descent of this hill, which is nearly as tedious as the ascent, brought us to the banks of the river opposite the *mal-paso* of Palma. This is the first rapid I have seen, and it looked formidable enough. The river, obstructed in its rapid course, breaks into waves, which dash with thundering violence against the rocks, and rush between them in sluices of dazzling velocity. Cargoes must always be landed at this place, and carried around. The canoe, thus lightened, under skilful and practical management, may shoot the rapid; but this should not be attempted where it can be avoided. By prudence, these *malos pasos* (the dread of travellers) are stripped of all danger; but the Indians sometimes get drunk and insist upon the attempt, and thus these places have become the graves of many.

Nearly all the *malos pasos* are at the mouth of a tributary. These, in the floods, bring down quantities of drift, with heavy boulders, which, thrown crosswise into the stream, lodge and form the obstructions. Little labor would be required to clear away the rocks, and make the river passable for canoes at least, if not for light-draught steamboats.

The trees of the forest are large, tall, and without branches for a great distance up. Ijurra pointed out one to me, of smooth bark, about four feet diameter near the ground, and which ran up sixty or seventy feet without a branch. He said that it was so hard that it resisted all attacks of the axe; and, to get it down, it was necessary to remove the earth and set fire to the roots; and that, suffered to lie in the water for a long time, it turned to stone of so hard a character, that, like flint, it would strike fire from steel. Unfortunately for the accuracy of the statement, we next day saw gigantic trees of this species that had been felled with an axe. The wood is, however, very hard and heavy—too much so for any practical use here. The tree is called *capirona*. It has a smooth bark, which it is continually changing. The old bark is a very pretty light-red; the new, a pea-green.

At half past four P.M., we arrived at the Cave, a place where a huge rock, projecting from the hill-side, made a shelter which would cover and protect from dew or rain about a dozen persons. The Indian who carried my bag of bedding wished to make my bed there; but I decided that it was too damp, and made him spread it out on the shingle by the river brink. The largest part of the cargo had not arrived, and I feared that we were without drink or cigars, which would have been a great deprivation to us after the fatigue of the day. The rice and cheese were on hand; and, to our great delight, Ijurra found in his saddle-bags a bottle of sherry-brandy that Mr. Jump had insisted upon our taking from Cerro Pasco, and which I had forgotten. A tin-pan of hot boiled rice flavored with cheese, a teacup of the brandy, and half a dozen paper cigars made us very comfortable; and, lulled by the rustling of the leaves and the roar of the river, we slept in spite of the ants and other insects that left the mark of their bites upon our carcasses.

I saw here, for the first time, the *luciernago,* or fire-fly, of this country. It is, unlike ours, a species of beetle, carrying two white lights in its eyes (or, rather, in the places where the eyes of insects generally are), and a red light between the scales of the belly—so that it reminded me something of the ocean steamers. It has the power of softening the light of the eyes until it becomes very faint; but upon irritating it, by passing the finger over the eyes, the light becomes very bright and sparkling. They are sometimes carried to Lima (enclosed in an apartment cut into a sugar-cane), where the ladies, at balls or theatres, put them in their hair for ornament.

AUGUST 1—We started, without breakfast, at a quarter to seven, thinking that we were near Tingo Maria. But it was ten miles distant, and I was weary enough ere we arrived. My principal source of annoyance was having inadvertedly asked how far we were off from our destination. I would advise no traveller to do this; he is sure to be disappointed, and when he is told (as he will certainly be) that he is near, the miles appear doubly long. The Indians take no account of time or distance. They stop when they get tired, and arrive when God pleases. They live on plantains—roasted, boiled, and fried; and in the way of food, a *yucca* is their greatest good.

Talking with a young Indian, who had a light load, and kept up with me very well, I was struck with the comparative value of things. A Londoner, who has been absent for some time from his favorite city, and subjected to some privations on that account, could not have spoken of the elegances and comforts of London with more enthusiasm than my companion spoke of Pueblo Viejo, a settlement of half a dozen Indians, which we were approaching. "There are plantains," said he; "there are *yuccas;* there is everything"—(*Hay platanos, hay yuccas, hay todo*)—and I really expected to be surprised and pleased when I arrived at Pueblo Viejo. The town, in fact, consisted of a single hut, with a plantain grove, a small patch of *yuccas,* and another of sugar-cane. In several places near by, people were felling the trees and forming *chacras.* The road lay sometimes across and sometimes along these huge trees; and I envied the bare feet and firm step of my companion, feeling that my tired legs and muddy boots might, at any moment, play me a slippery trick, and cost me a broken leg or sprained ankle.

At eleven we arrived at Juana del Rio, a settlement of five or six houses, on the right bank of the river. The houses were all shut up, and nobody seemed to be at home. Here we crossed the river (one hundred yards broad, smooth, and deep), and walked down the left bank about half a mile to the pueblo of San Antonio del Tingo Maria. *Tingo* is the Indian term for the junction of two rivers, the Monzon emptying into the Huallaga just above this. The Governor, an intelligent and modest young man, a former friend of Ijurra, welcomed us cordially and gave us a capital breakfast of chicken broth.

Chapter VII

*Itinerary—Tingo Maria—Vampires—Blow-guns—Canoe
navigation—Shooting monkeys—Salt hills of Pilluana*

THE FOLLOWING TABLE gives the distance between Lima and the
head of canoe navigation on the Huallaga River:

From Lima to Chaclacayo . . . . 18 miles
    "   " to Santa Ana 10   "
    "   " to Surco 18   "
    "   " to San Mateo 18   "
    "   " to Acchahuarcu 13   "
    "   " to Morococha 12   "
    "   " to Oroya 17   "
    "   " to Tarma 16   "
    "   " to Palcamayo 15   "
    "   " to Junin 18   "
    "   " to Carhuamayo 15   "
    "   " to Cerro Pasco 20   "
    "   " to Caxamarquilla 15   "

```
  "      "    to San Rafael . . . . . . . . . . . . . . . . . . . . 15    "
  "      "    to Ambo . . . . . . . . . . . . . . . . . . . . . . . . 20    "
  "      "    to Huanuco . . . . . . . . . . . . . . . . . . . . . 15    "
  "      "    to Acomayo . . . . . . . . . . . . . . . . . . . . . 14    "
  "      "    to Chinchao . . . . . . . . . . . . . . . . . . . . 16    "
  "      "    to Chihuangala . . . . . . . . . . . . . . . . . 20    "
  "      "    to La Cueva . . . . . . . . . . . . . . . . . . . . 20    "
  "      "    to Tingo Maria . . . . . . . . . . . . . . . . . 10    "
                                                        ───
                                                        335    "
```

This distance of 335 miles may be shortened twenty-eight by going direct from Lima to Cerro Pasco. (We passed round by Tarma.) The traveller will find that the distance is divided in the table into days' journeys nearly. Thus it will cost him, with loaded mules, twenty-one days to reach the head of canoe navigation on the Huallaga by this route, and nineteen by the other. The last thirty miles between Chihuangala and Tingo Maria are travelled on foot, though there would be no difficulty in opening a mule-road.

The passage of the Cordillera at the season of the year when we crossed is neither very tedious nor laborious. In fact, we enjoyed much the magnificent scenery; we were pleased with the manners and habits of a primitive people, and we met hospitality and kindness everywhere. In the season of the rains, however, the passage must be both difficult and dangerous.

AUGUST 2—Tingo Maria is a prettily situated village, of forty-eight able-bodied men, and an entire population of 188. This includes those who are settled at Juana del Rio and the houses within a mile or two.

The *pueblo* is situated in a plain on the left bank of the river, which is about six miles in length, and three miles in its broadest part, where the mountains back of it recede in a semi-circle from the river. The height above the level of the sea is 2,260 feet. The woods are stocked with game—such as *pumas,* or American tigers; deer; *peccary,* or wild hog; *ronsoco,* or river hog; monkeys, &c. For birds— are several varieties of *curassoow,* a large bird, something like a turkey, but with, generally, a red bill, a crest, and shining blue-black plumage; a delicate *pava del monte,* or wild turkey; a great variety of parrots; with large, black, wild ducks, and cormorants. There are also rattlesnakes and vipers. But even with all these, I would advise no traveller to trust to his gun for support. The woods are so thick and tangled with undergrowth that no one but an Indian can penetrate them, and no eyes but those of an Indian could see the game. Even he only hunts from necessity, and will rarely venture into the thick forest alone, for fear of the tiger or the viper. There are also good and delicate fish in the river, but in no great abundance.

The inhabitants are of a tribe called Cholones, which was once large and powerful. I like their character better than that of any Indians whom I afterwards met with. They are good-tempered, cheerful, and sober, and by far the largest and finest-looking of the aborigines that I have encountered. They are obedient to the church and attentive to her ceremonies; and are more advanced than common in civilization, using no paint as an ornament, but only staining their arms and legs with the juice of a fruit called *huitoc,* that gives a dark blue dye, as a protection against the sand-flies, which are abundant, and a great nuisance. The place is generally very healthy. The common diseases are lymphatic swellings of the body and limbs (supposed to be caused by exposure to the great humidity of the atmosphere while fishing at night), and *sarna* (a cutaneous affection, which covers the body with sores, making the patient a loathsome object). These sores dry up and come off in scabs, leaving blotches on the skin, so that an Indian is frequently seen quite mottled. I imagine it is caused by want of cleanliness, and the bites of the sand-flies. They take, as a remedy, the dried root of a small tree called *sarnango,* grated and mixed with water. It is said to have a powerfully intoxicating and stupefying effect, and to cause the skin to peel off.

Ijurra shot a large bat, of the vampire species, measuring about two feet across the extended wings. This is a very disgusting-looking animal, though its fur is very delicate, and of a glossy, rich maroon color. Its mouth is amply provided with teeth, looking like that of a miniature tiger. It has two long and sharp tusks in the front part of each jaw, with two smaller teeth, like those of a hare or sheep, between the tusks of the upper jaw, and four (much smaller) between those of the lower. There are also teeth back of the tusks, extending far back into the mouth. The nostrils seem fitted as a suction apparatus. Above them is a triangular, cartilaginous snout, nearly half an inch long, and a quarter broad at the base; and below them is a semi-circular flap, of nearly the same breadth, but not so long. I suppose these might be placed over the puncture made by the teeth, and the air underneath exhausted by the nostrils, thus making them a very perfect cupping-glass. I never heard it doubted, until my return home, that these animals were blood-suckers; but a distinguished naturalist tells me that no one has ever seen them engaged in the operation, and that he has made repeated attempts for that purpose, but without success.

On one occasion, when a companion had lost a good deal of blood, the doors and windows of the house in which his party was lying were closed, and a number of these bats, that were clinging to the roof, killed; but none of them were found gorged, or with any signs of having been engaged in blood-sucking. I also observed no apparatus proper for making a delicate puncture. The tusks are quite as large as those of a rat, and, if used in the ordinary manner, would make four wounds at once, producing, I should think, quite sufficient pain to awaken the most profound sleeper. Never having heard this doubt, it did not occur to me to ask the Indians if they had ever seen the bat sucking, or to examine the wounds of the horses that I had seen bleeding from this supposed cause.

Once, I found my blanket spotted with blood, and supposed that the bat (having gorged himself on the horses outside) had flown into the house, and, fastening himself to the thatch over me, had disgorged upon my covering and then flown out. There was no great quantity of blood, there being but five or six stains on the blanket, such as would have been made by large drops. I presumed, likewise, from the feet of the drops being scattered irregularly over a small surface, that the bat had been hanging by his feet to the thatch, and swinging about. The discovery of the drops produced a sensation of deep disgust; and I have frequently been unable to sleep for fear of the filthy beast. Every traveller in these countries should learn to sleep with body and head enveloped in a blanket, as the Indians do.

I saw here, for the first time, the blow-gun of the Indians, called, by the Spaniards, *cerbatana;* by the Portuguese of the river, *gravatana* (a corruption, I imagine, of the former, as I find no such Portuguese word); and by the Indians, *pucuna.* It is made of any long, straight piece of wood, generally of a species of palm called *chonta*—a heavy, elastic wood, of which bows, clubs, and spears are also made. The pole or staff, about eight feet in length, and two inches diameter near the mouth end (tapering down to half an inch at the extremity), is divided longitudinally; a canal is hollowed out along the centre of each part, which is well smoothed and polished by rubbing with fine sand and wood. The two parts are then brought together; nicely woolled with twine; and the whole covered with wax, mixed with some resin of the forest, to make it hard. A couple of boar's teeth are fitted on each side of the mouth end, and one of the curved front teeth of a small animal resembling a cross between a squirrel and a hare is placed on top for a sight. The arrow is made of any light wood, generally the wild cane, or the middle fibre of a species of palm-leaf, which is about a foot in length, and of the thickness of an ordinary lucifer match. The end of the arrow, which is placed next to the mouth, is wrapped with a light, delicate sort of wild cotton, which grows in a pod upon a large tree, and is called *huimba;* and the other end, very sharply pointed, is dipped in a vegetable poison prepared from the juice of the creeper, called *bejuco de ambihuasca,* mixed with *aji,* or strong red pepper, *barbasco, sarnango,* and whatever substances the Indians know to be deleterious.

The marksman, when using his *pucuna,* instead of stretching out the left hand along the body of the tube, places it to his mouth by grasping it, with both hands together, close to the mouth-piece, in such a manner that it requires considerable strength in the arms to hold it out at all, much less steadily. If a practiced marksman, he will kill a small bird at thirty or forty paces. In an experiment that I saw, the Indian held the *pucuna* horizontally, and the arrow blown from it stuck in the ground at thirty-eight paces. Commonly the Indian has quite an affection for his gun, and many superstitious notions about it. I could not persuade one to shoot a very pretty black and yellow bird for me because it was a carrion bird; and the Indian said that it would deteriorate and make useless all the poison in his gourd. Neither will he discharge his *pucuna* at a snake, for fear of the gun being made crooked like the reptile; and a fowling piece or rifle that has once been discharged at an alligator is considered entirely worthless. A round gourd, with a hole in it for the *huimba,* and a joint of the *caña brava* as a quiver, completes the hunting apparatus.

AUGUST 3—Went to church. The congregation—men, women, and children—numbered about fifty; the service was conducted by the Governor, assisted by the *alcalde.* A little naked, bow-legged Indian child, of two or three years, and Ijurra's pointer puppy, which he had brought all the way from Lima on his saddle-bow, worried the congregation with their tricks and gambols; but altogether they were attentive to their prayers, and devout. I enjoyed exceedingly the public worship of God with these rude children of the forest; and, although they probably understood little of what they were about, I thought I could see its humanizing and fraternizing effect upon all.

At night we had a ball at the Governor's house. The *alcalde,* who was a trump, produced his fiddle; another had a rude sort of guitar, or banjo; and under the excitement of his music, and the *aguadiente* of the Governor, who had had his cane ground in anticipation of our arrival, we danced till eleven o'clock. The custom of the dance requires that a gentleman should choose a lady and dance with her, in the middle of the floor, till she gives over (the company around clapping their hands in time to the music, and cheering the dancers with *vivas* at any particular display of agility or spirit in the dance). He then presents his partner with a glass of grog, leads her to a seat, and chooses another. When he tires there is a general drink, and the lady has the choice. The Señor Commandante was in considerable request; and a fat old lady, who would not dance with anybody else, nearly killed me. The Governor discharged our guns several times, and let off some rockets that we had brought from Huanuco; and I doubt if Tingo Maria had ever witnessed such a brilliant affair before.

AUGUST 4—I waked up with pain in the legs and headache from dancing, and found our men and canoes ready for embarkation. After breakfast the Governor and his wife (though I grievously fear that there had been no intervention of the priest in the matter of the union), together with several of our partners of the previous night, accompanied us to the port. After loading the canoes the Governor made a short address to the canoe-men, telling them that we "were no common persons; that they were to have a special care of us: to be very obedient, &c., and that he would put up daily prayers for their safe return"; whereupon, after a glass all round, from a bottle brought down specially by our hostess, and a hearty embrace of the Governor, his lady, and my fat friend of the night before, we embarked and shoved off; the boatmen blowing their horns as we drifted rapidly down with the current of the river, and the party on shore waving their hats and shouting their adieus.

We had two canoes, the largest about forty feet long, by two and a half broad; hollowed out from a single log, and manned each by five men and a boy. They are conducted by a *puntero,* or bowman, who looks out for rocks or sunken trees ahead; a *popero,* or steersman, who stands on a little platform at the stern of the boat and guides her motions; and the *bogas,* or rowers, who stand up to paddle, having one foot in the bottom of the boat and the other on the gunwale. When the river was smooth and free from obstructions, we drifted with the current; the men sitting on the trunks and boxes, chatting and laughing with each other; but, as we approached a *mal-paso,* their serious looks, and the firm position in which each one planted himself at his post, showed that work was to be done. I felt a little nervous at first; but when we had fairly entered the pass, the rapid gesture of the *puntero,* indicating the channel; the elegant and graceful position of the *popero,* giving the boat a broad sheer with the sweep of his long paddle; the desperate exertions of the *bogas;* the railroad rush of the canoe; and the wild, triumphant, screaming laugh of the Indians, as we shot past the danger, made a scene that was much too exciting to admit of any other emotion than that of admiration.

We passed many of these to-day, and were well soaked by the canoes taking in water on each side; some of them were mere smooth declivities—inclined planes of gravel, with only three or four inches of water on them, so that the men had to get overboard, keep the canoes head on, and drag them down. The average velocity of the river here is three and a half miles to the hour, but when it dashes down one of these declivities, it must be much more. The breadth of the river is a constantly varying quantity, probably never over 150 yards, and never under thirty; banks low, and covered with trees, bushes, and wild cane. There were hills on each side, some distance from the bank, but now and then coming down to it. It is almost impossible to estimate the distance travelled with any degree of accuracy. The force of the current is very variable, and the Indians very irregular in their manner of rowing—sometimes paddling half an hour with great vigor, and then suffering the boat to drift with the tide. Averaging the current at three and a half miles the hour, and the rowing at one and a half, with nine hours of actual travel, we have forty-five miles for a day's journey at this season. I have estimated the number of travelling hours at nine, for we get off generally at five A.M., and stop at five P.M. We spend two hours for breakfast, in the middle of the day, and another hour is lost at the shallows of the river, or stopping to get a shot at an animal or bird.

At half past five we camped on the beach. The first business of the boatmen, when the canoe is secured, is to go off to the woods and cut stakes and palm branches to make a house for the *patrón*. By sticking long poles in the sand, chopping them half in two, about five feet above the ground, and bending the upper parts together, they make, in a few minutes, the frame of a little shanty, which, thickly thatched with palm leaves, will keep off the dew or an ordinary rain. Some bring the drift-wood that is lying about the beach and make a fire; the provisions are cooked and eaten; the bedding laid down upon the leaves that cover the floor of the shanty; the *mosquito* nettings spread; and, after a cup of coffee, a glass of grog, and a cigar (if they are to be had), everybody retires for the night by eight o'clock. The Indians sleep around the hut, each under his narrow cotton *mosquito* curtain, which glisten in the moon-light like so many tomb-stones. This was pleasant enough when provisions were plenty and the weather good; but when there was no coffee or brandy, the cigars had given out, and there was a slim allowance of only salt fish and plantains, with one of those nights of heavy rain that are frequent upon the Marañón, I could not help calling to mind, with some bitterness of spirit, the comforts of the ship-of-war that I had left, to say nothing of the luxuries of home.

AUGUST 6—Started at eight. River seventy yards broad, nine feet deep, pebbly bottom; current three miles per hour. We find in some places, where hills come down to the river, as much as thirty feet of depth. There are some quite high hills on the right-hand side, that might be called mountains; they run north and south. I was surprised that we saw no animals all day, but only river birds— such as black ducks, cormorants, and king-fishers; also many parrots of various kinds and brilliant plumage, but they always kept out of shot. We camped at half past five, tired and low-spirited, having had nothing to eat all day but a little rice boiled with cheese early in the morning. My wrists were sore and painful from sun-burn, and the sand-flies were very troublesome. Heavy clouds, with thunder and lightning, in the northwest. In the night, fresh breeze from that quarter. We heard tigers and monkeys during the night, and saw the tiger-tracks near the camp next morning.

AUGUST 6—Soon after starting we saw a fine doe coming down to-wards the river. We steered in, and got within about eighty yards of her, when Ijurra and I fired together, the guns loaded with a couple of rifle-balls each. The animal stood quite still for a few minutes, and then walked slowly off towards the bushes. I gave my gun, loaded with three rifle-balls, to the *puntero,* who got a close shot, but without effect. One of the balls, a little flattened, was picked up close to where the deer stood. These circumstances made the Indians doubt if she were a deer; and I judge, from their ges-tures and exclamations, that they thought it was some evil spirit that was ball-proof. I imagine that the ball was flattened either by passing through the branch of a brush or striking some particu-larly hard bone of the animal, or it might have been jammed in the gun by the other balls.

These Indians have very keen senses, and see and hear things that are inaudible and invisible to us. Our canoe-men this morn-ing commenced paddling with great vigor. I asked the cause, and they said that they heard monkeys ahead. I think we must have paddled a mile before I heard the sound they spoke of. When we came up to them, we found a gang of large red monkeys in some tall trees on the river-side, making a noise like the grunting of a herd of enraged hogs. We landed, and in a few minutes I found myself beating my way through the thick undergrowth, and hunt-ing monkeys with as much excitement as I had ever hunted squirrels when a boy. I had no balls with me, and my No. 3 shot only served to sting them from their elevated position in the tops of the trees, and bring them within reach of the *pucunas* of the Indians. They got two and I one, after firing about a dozen shots into him. I never saw animals so tenacious of life; this one was, as the Indians expressed it, bathed in shot (*bañado en municion*). These monkeys were about the size of a common terrier-dog, and were clad with a long, soft, maroon-colored hair; they are called *cotomonos*, from a large goitre (*coto*) under the jaw. This is an apparatus of thin bone in the wind-pipe, by means of which they make their peculiar noise. The male, called *curaca* (which is also the appellation of the chief of a tribe of Indians), has a long red beard. They are called *guariba* in Brazil, where they are said to be black as well as red; and I believe they are of the species commonly called howling monkeys.

It is scarcely worth while to say that the Indians use parts of this animal for the cure of diseases, for I know no substance that could possibly be used as a remedial agent that they do not use for that purpose. The mother carries the young upon her back until it is able to go alone. If the dam dies, the sire takes charge. There are vast numbers in all the course of the river, and no day passes to the traveller that they are not heard or seen.

When I arrived at the beach with my game, I found that the Indians had made a fire and were roasting theirs. They did not take the trouble to skin and clean the animal, but simply put him in the fire, and, when well scorched, took him off and cut pieces from the fleshy parts with a knife; if these were not sufficiently well done, they roasted them farther on little stakes stuck up before the fire. I tried to eat a piece, but it was so tough that my teeth would make no impression upon it. The one I killed was *enciente,* the fœtus about double the size of a wharf-rat. I wished to preserve it, but it was too large for any bottles I had; whereupon the Indians roasted and ate it without ceremony.

We also saw to-day several river hogs, and had an animated chase after one, which we encountered on the river-side, immediately opposite a nearly precipitous bank of loose earth, which crumbled under his feet so that he could not climb it. He hesitated to take the water in face of the canoes, so that we thought we had him; but after a little play up and down the river-side, he broke his way through the line of his adversaries, capsizing two Indians as he went, and took to the water. This animal is amphibious, about the size of a half-grown hog, and reminded me, in his appearance and movements, of the rhinoceros. He is also red, and I thought it remarkable that the only animals we had seen—the deer, the monkeys, and the hog—should be all of this color. It is called *ronsoco* here, and *capiuara* in Brazil.

We also heard the barking of dogs on the right, or *Infidel,* side of the river, in contradistinction to the other, which is called *La parse de la cristiandad,* supposed to be the dogs of the Cashibos Indians of the Pachitea.

Parrots and other birds were also more numerous than before.

We found the river to-day much choked with islands, shoals, and grounded drift-wood; camped at half past five, and supped upon monkey soup. The monkey, as it regards toughness, was monkey still; but the liver, of which I ate nearly the whole, was tender and good. Jocko, however, had his revenge, for I nearly perished of nightmare. Some devil, with arms as nervous as the monkey's, had me by the throat, and, staring on me with his cold, cruel eye, expressed his determination to hold on to the death. I thought it hard to die by the grasp of this fiend on the banks of the strange river, and so early in my course; and upon making a desperate effort, and shaking him off, I found that I had forgotten to take off my cravat, which was choking me within an inch of my life.

AUGUST 7—We got off at half past eight; at a quarter to ten passed the port of Uchiza. This is a village nine miles from the river. The port itself, like that of Tingo Maria, is a shed for the accommodation of canoes and passengers. Nearly all the towns on the river are built six or eight miles from the banks, on account of the overflow of the country when the river is full. Some hill on the bank is generally selected as the port, and a road is made thence to the town. This hill is sometimes forty feet out of water, and sometimes covered, and the whole land between it and the town overflowed. At a quarter past ten we passed the Quebrada, or ravine of Huinagua, on the right. A small stream comes down this ravine, the water of which is salt. The people of Uchiza ascend it—a day's journey—to a salt hill, where they supply themselves with this indispensable article. At twenty minutes past eleven we passed another; and at one P.M. another, where the people of Tocache get their salt. It is a day's journey from Tocache to the mouth of the Quebrada, and another to the salt hills.

To-day presented a remarkable contrast to yesterday for sportsmen. We did not see a single animal, and very few birds; even parrots, generally so plentiful, were scarce to-day. It was a day of work; the men paddled well, and we must have made seventy miles. On approaching Tocache, which was their last stage with us, the Indians almost deafened me with the noise of their horns. These horns are generally made of pieces of wood hollowed out thin, joined together, wrapped with twine, and coated with wax. They are shaped like a blunderbuss, and are about four feet long; the mouth-piece is of reed, and the sound deep and mellow. The Indians always make a great noise on approaching any place, to indicate that they come as friends. They fancy that they might otherwise be attacked, as hostile parties always move silently.

We arrived at five. I was wearied with the monotonous day's journey and the heat of the sun, and anticipated the arrival with pleasure, thinking that we were going to stop at a large village and get something good to eat; but I was grievously disappointed. We arrived only at the port, which was, as usual, a shed on a hill, the village being nine miles off. There was nothing to eat here, so we determined to start inland and see what we could pick up. A rapid walk of an hour and a quarter brought us to Lamasillo, which I had been told was a pueblo of whites, but which we found to be but a single house with a *platanal* attached to it. There were other houses near, but none within sight. I had been under the impression that *pueblo* meant a village, but I think now it signifies any settled country, though the houses may be miles apart. With much persuasion we induced the people of the house to sell us a couple of bottles of *aguadiente* and a pair of chickens. The Governor of the district had been at this place within the hour, but was gone to Tocache, which we understood to be two *coceadas* further on, or about the same distance that we had come over from the port to this place. Distance is frequently estimated by the time that a man will occupy in taking a chew of coca. From the distance between the port and Lamasillo, it appears that a chew of coca is about three fourths of a league, or thirty-seven and a half minutes.

We walked back by moon-light, and had a fowl cooked forthwith; which, as we had had nothing but a little monkey soup early in the morning, we devoured more like tigers than Christian men.

We made our beds in the canoes under the shed, and, tired as we were, slept comfortably enough. It seems a merciful dispensation of Providence that the sand-flies go to bed at the same time with the people; otherwise I think one could not live in this country. We have not yet been troubled with *musquitoes.* The sand-flies are here called *mosquitos,* the diminutive of *mosca,* a fly; our *musquitoes* are called *sancudos.* The sand-flies are very troublesome in the day, and one cannot write or eat in any comfort. Everybody's hands in this country are nearly black from the effects of their bite, which leaves a little round black spot, that lasts for weeks. It is much better to bear the sting than to irritate the part by scratching or rubbing.

AUGUST 8—I sent Ijurra to Tocache to communicate with the Governor, while I spent the day in writing up my journal, and drying the equipage that had been wetted in the journey. In the afternoon I walked into the woods with an Indian, for the purpose of seeing him kill a bird or animal with his *pucuna.* I admired the stealthy and noiseless manner with which he moved through the woods, occasionally casting a wondering and reproachful glance at me as I would catch my foot in a creeper and pitch into the bushes with sufficient noise to alarm all the game within a mile round. At last he pointed out to me a toucan, called by the Spaniards *predicador,* or preacher, sitting on a branch of a tree out of the reach of his gun. I fired and brought him down with a broken wing. The Indian started into the bushes after him; but, finding him running, he came back to me for his *pucuna,* which he had left behind. In a few minutes he brought the bird to me with an arrow sticking in his throat. The bird was dead in two minutes after I saw it, and probably in two and a half minutes from the time it was struck. The Indian said that his poison was good, but that it was in a manner ejected by the flow of blood, which covered the bird's breast, and which showed that a large blood-vessel of the neck had been pierced. I do not know if his reasoning were good or not.

Ijurra returned at eight, tired, and in a bad humor. He reported that he had hunted the Governor from place to place all day; had come up with him at last and obtained the promise that we should have canoes and men to prosecute our journey. My companion, who has been sub-prefect or governor of the whole province which we are now in (Mainas), and who has appointed and removed these governors of districts at pleasure, finds it difficult to sue where he had formerly commanded. He consequently generally quarrels with those in authority; and I have to put myself to some trouble, and draw largely upon my *bon homie* to reconcile the differences, and cool down the heats, which his impatience and irritability often occasion. He, however, did good service to the cause, by purchasing a hog and some chickens, which were to appear to-morrow.

AUGUST 9—We had people to work killing and salting our hog. We had difficulty in getting someone to undertake this office, but the man from whom we purchased the hog stood our friend, and brought down his family from Lamasillo to do the needful. We had very little benefit from our experiment in this way. We paid eight dollars for the hog, twenty-five cents for salt, twenty-five cents to Don Isidro, who brought him down to the port, and fifty cents to the same gentleman for butchering him. The wife and children of the owner took their pay for salting and smoking out of the hog himself. Our friends going up stream (according to Ijurra) stole half, and what was left spoiled before we could eat it.

Everybody is a Don in this country. Our Indian boatmen, at least the Poperos, are Dons; and much ceremonious courtesy is necessary in intercourse with them. I have to treat the governors of the districts with all manner of ceremony; when, while he exacts this, and will get sulky, and afford me no facilities without it, he will entertain the proposition to go along with me as my servant.

I had a note from the Governor, not written but signed by himself, requesting to know how many men I wanted, and saying that he hoped to see us in the *pueblo* early to-morrow. We excused ourselves from going to the town, and requested him to send the men down to the port for their pay. This he would not do, but insisted that we should pay at least at Lamasillo. We always pay in advance, and the boatmen generally leave their cotton cloth, in which they are nearly always paid, with their wives. These have preferred their pay partly in money.

AUGUST 10—The party for Huanuco got off this morning, and left the shed to Ijurra and me. Whilst bathing in the river, I saw an animal swimming down the stream towards me, which I took to be a fox or cat. I threw stones at it, and it swam to the other side of the river and took to the forest. Very soon after, a dog, who was evidently in chase, came swimming down, and missing the chase from the river, swam round in circles for some minutes before giving it up. This animal, from my description, was pronounced to be an *ounce,* or tiger-cat. It is called *tigre* throughout all this country, but is never so large or ferocious as the African tiger. They are rather spotted like the leopard, than striped like the tiger. They are said, when hungry, to be sufficiently dangerous, and no one cares to bring them to bay without good dogs and a good gun.

We talked so much about tigers and their carrying off people whilst asleep, that I, after going to bed, became nervous; and every sound near the shed made me grasp the handles of my pistols. After midnight I was lulled to sleep by the melancholy notes of a bird called *Alma Perdida,* or lost soul. Its wild and wailing cry from the depths of the forest seemed, indeed, as sad and despairing as that of one without hope.

AUGUST 11—Ijurra went to Lamasillo to pay the boatmen, some of them having come down to the port to carry up the cotton cloth. This left me entirely alone. The sense of loneliness, and the perfect stillness of the great forest, caused me to realize in all its force the truth of Campbell's fine line—

> *The solitude of earth that overawes.*

It was strange, when the scratch of my pen on the paper ceased, to hear absolutely no sound. I felt so much the want of society that I tried to make a friend of the lithe, cunning-looking lizard that ran along the canoe at my side, and that now and then stopped, raised up his head, and looked at me, seemingly in wonder.

I could see no traces of the height of the river in the *crecido,* or full; but, from a mark pointed out by one of the Indians, I judged that the river has here a perpendicular rise and fall of thirty feet.

The hill on which the port of Tocache is situated is about thirty feet above the present level of the river, and by boiling point is 1,579 feet above the level of the sea.

A canoe arrived from Juan Juy, and a party of two from Saposoa by land. These are towns further down the river. Each party had its *litakas* (hide trunks), containing straw hats, rice, tobacco, and *tocuyo Iistado,* a striped cotton cloth, much used in Huanuco for "tickings." It is astonishing to see how far this generally lazy people will travel for a dollar.

AUGUST 12—Had a visit from the Governor last night. He is a little, bare-footed Mestizo, dressed in the short frock and trousers of the Indians. He seemed disposed to do all in his power to facilitate us and forward us on our journey. I asked him about the tigers. He said he had known three instances of their having attacked men in the night; two of them were much injured, and one died.

Our boatmen made their appearance at ten A.M., accompanied by their wives, bringing *masato* for the voyage. The women carry their children (lashed flat on the back to a frame of reeds) by a strap around the brow, as they do any other burden. The urchins look comfortable and contented, and for all the world like young monkeys.

The Indians of this district are Ibitos. They are less civilized than the Cholones of Tingo Maria, and are the first whose faces I have seen regularly painted. They seem to have no fixed pattern, but each man paints according to his fancy; using, however, only two colors—the blue of Huitoc and the red Achote.

We started at twelve with two canoes and twelve men; river fifty yards broad, eighteen feet deep, and with three miles an hour current; a stream called the Tocache empties into it about half a mile below the port. It forces its way through five channels, over a bank of stones and sand. It is doubtless a fine large-looking river when at high water. The country is hilly on the right and flat on the left-hand side. At three P.M. we entered a more hilly country, and began to encounter again the *malos pasos;* passed the Rio Grande de Meshuglla, which comes in on the left in the same manner as the Tocache, and soon after, the port of Pisana; no houses at the port; saw an old white man on the beach, who was a cripple, and said he had been bedridden for nine years. He begged us for needles, or fish-hooks, or anything we had. We gave him a dollar. He is the first beggar for charity's sake that I recollected to have seen since leaving Lima. There are beggars enough, but they ask for presents, or, offering to buy some article, expect that it shall be given to them.

The river is now entirely broken up by islands and rapids. In passing one of these, we came very near being capsized. Rounding suddenly the lower end of an island, we met the full force of the current from the other side, which, striking us on the beam, nearly rolled the canoe over. The men, in their fright, threw themselves on the upper gunwale of the boat which gave us a heel the other way, and we very nearly filled. Had the *popero* fallen from his post (and he tottered fearfully), we should probably have been lost; but by great exertions he got the boat's head down stream, and we shot safely by rocks that threatened destruction.

At six we arrived at the port of Balsayacu. The *pueblo,* which I found, as usual, to consist of one house, was a pleasant walk of half a mile from the port. We slept there, instead of at the beach; and it was well that we did, for it rained heavily all night. The only inhabitants of the *rancho* seemed to be two little girls; but I found in the morning that one of them had an infant, though she did not appear to be more than twelve or thirteen years of age. I suppose there are more houses in the neighborhood; but, as I have before said, a *pueblo* is merely a settlement, and may extend over leagues.

AUGUST 13—Last night Ijurra struck with a fire-brand one of the boatmen, who was drunk, and disposed to be insolent, and blackened and burned his face. The man—a powerful Indian, of full six feet in height—bore it like a corrected child in a blubbering and sulky sort of manner. This morning he has the paint washed off his face, and looks as humble as a dog; though I observed a few hours afterwards that he was painted up again, and had resumed the usual gay and good-tempered manner of his tribe.

Between ten and eleven we passed the *mal-paso* of Mataglla, just below the mouth of the river of the same name, which comes in on the left, clear and cool into the Huallaga. This *mal-paso* is the worst that I have yet encountered. We dared not attempt it under oar, and the canoe was let down along the shore, stern foremost, by a rope from its bows, and guided between the rocks by the *popero*—sometimes with his paddle, and sometimes overboard, up to his middle in water. I am told that *balsas* pass in mid-channel, but I am sure a canoe would be capsized and filled. The *mal-paso* is a quarter of a mile long, and an effectual bar, except perhaps at high water, to navigation for any thing but a canoe or *balsa*.

The river to-day averages one hundred yards in breadth, eighteen feet of depth, and with four miles of current. Its borders are hilly, and it runs straighter and more directly to the north than before.

At one P.M. we arrived at the port of Sion. As our Tocache men were to leave us here, we had all the baggage taken up to the town. The walk is a pleasant one, over a level road of fine sand, well shaded with large trees. Ijurra, who went up before me, met the priest of Saposoa (who is on the annual visit to his parish) going south; and the governor of the district going north to Pachiza, the capital. This last left orders that we should be well received; and the Lieutenant Governor of the *pueblo* lodged us in the *convento,* or priest's house, and appointed us a cook and a servant.

I slept comfortably on the Padre's bedstead, enclosed with matting to keep off the bats. The people appear to make much of the visit of their priest. I saw in the corner of the *sala,* or hall of the house, a sort of rude palanquin, which I understood to have been constructed to carry his reverence back and forth, between the city and port.

AUGUST 14—We employed the morning in cleaning the arms and drying the equipage. Had a visit from some ladies, pretty Mestizas (descendants of white and Indian), who examined the contents of our open trunks with curiosity and delight. They refrained, however, from asking for anything until they saw some *chancaca* with which we were about to sweeten our morning coffee, when they could contain themselves no longer, but requested a bit. This seems an article of great request, for no sooner had the news spread that we had it, than the *alcalde* brought us an egg to exchange for some; and even the Lieutenant Governor also expressed his desire for a little. We refused the dignitaries, though we had given some to the ladies; for we had but enough for two or three cups more. Their wants, however, were not confined to sugar. They asked, without scruple, after a while, for anything they saw; and the Lieutenant wanted a little sewing cotton, and some of the soap we brought to wash ourselves with, to take for physic. These things we could more easily part with, and I had no objection to give him some, and also to regale his wife with a pair of pinchbeck earrings. There is nothing made or cultivated here for sale. They raise a few fowls and some *yuccas* and plantains for their own use; and it was well that we brought our own provisions along, or we might have starved.

I do not wonder at the indifference of the people to attempt to better their condition. The power of the governor to take them from their labor and send them on journeys of weeks' duration, with any passing merchant or traveller, would have this effect.

The town appears to have been once in a better condition than it is now. There are remains of a garden attached to the convent, and also of instruments of husbandry and manufacture—such as rude mortars, hollowed out from the trunk of a tree, for beating (with pestles) the husk from rice, and a press for putting into shape the crude wax gathered from the hollow trees by the Indians, used by the friars "lang syne"—all now seem going to decay. The people are lazy and indifferent. They cultivate plantains sufficient to give them to eat, and *yuccas* enough to make *masato* to get drunk on; and this seems all they need. Most of their time is spent in sleeping, drinking, and dancing. Yesterday they were dancing all day, having a feast preparatory to going to work to clear ground, and make a *chacra* for our "Lady of something," which the priest, in his recent visit, had commanded (the produce of this *chacra* is doubtless for the benefit of the church or its ministers); and I have no doubt that the Indians will have another feast when the job is done.

The dance was a simple affair so far as figure was concerned— the women whirling round in the centre, and the men (who were also the musicians) trotting around them in a circle. The music was made by rude drums, and fifes of reed, and it was quite amusing to see the *alcalde,* a large, painted, grave-looking Indian, trotting round like a dog on a tread mill, with a penny whistle at his mouth. I am told that they will dance in this way as long as there is drink, if it reach to a month. I myself have heard their music—the last thing at night as I was going to bed, and the first thing in the morning as I was getting up—for days at a time. The tune never changes, and seems to be the same everywhere in the Montaña. It is a monotonous tapping of the drum, very like our naval beat to quarters.

We embarked at the Caño port, and dropped down the Caño, a mile and a half to the river. We found the river deep and winding, and running, generally, between high cliffs of a white rock.

We passed the *mal-paso* of Shapiama, and, with fifteen minutes' interval, those of Savolayacu and Cachihuanushca. In the first two the canoes were let down with ropes, and we shot the last under oar, which I was surprised at, as I had heard that it was one of the worst on the river. *Malos pasos,* however, which are formidable when the river is full, are comparatively safe when it is low.

After passing the last we found the hills lower, the country more open, and the river wider and with a gentler flow. The average depth to-day in the smooth parts is thirty feet; current, three miles.

About sunset we arrived at Challuayacu, a settlement of twenty houses. All the inhabitants, except those of one house, were absent. We were told that they had been disobedient in some matter to the governor of the district, and that he had come upon them with a force and carried them off prisoners to Juan Juy, a large town further down the river, where authority might be brought to bear upon them. Two small horses, in tolerable condition, wandered about among the deserted houses of the village. There being no one to take care of them, I fancy the bats will soon bleed them to death.

AUGUST 16—Lovely morning. On stepping out of the house my attention was attracted by a spider's web covering the whole of a large lemon-tree nearly. The tree was oval and well shaped, and the web was thrown over it in the most artistic manner, and with the finest effect. Broad, flat cords were stretched out, like the cords of a tent, from its circumference to the neighboring bushes; and it looked as if some genie of the lamp, at the command of its master, had exhausted taste and skill to cover with this delicate drapery the rich-looking fruit beneath. I think the web would have measured a full ten yards in diameter.

At noon we arrived at the mouth of the Huayabamba, which is one hundred yards wide, has six feet water, and a beautiful pebbly bottom. A quarter of an hour's drag of the canoe along the right bank brought us to the village of Lupuna, the port of Pachiza. It contains fifteen houses and about seventy-five inhabitants. A little rice is grown, but the staple production is cotton, which seemed to be abundant. This may be called a manufacturing place, for almost every woman was engaged in spinning, and many balls of cotton-thread were hanging from the rafters of each house. A woman, spinning with diligence all day, will make four of these balls. These weigh a pound, and are worth twenty-five cents. They are very generally used as currency, there being little money in the country. I saw some English prints, which were worth thirty-seven and a half cents the yard, and are paid for in hats, wax, or these balls of cotton.

We had a visit from the Governor of Pachiza. I asked him why he had carried away prisoners nearly all the population of Challuayacu. He merely said that they had been rebellious, and resisted his authority, and therefore he had taken them to Juan Juy, where they could be secured and punished. I thought it a pity that a thriving settlement should be broken up, very probably on account of some personal quarrel.

After we had retired to our mats beneath the shed for the night, I asked the Governor if he knew a bird called *El alma perdida*. He did not know it by that name, and requested a description. I whistled an imitation of its notes; whereupon, an old crone, stretched on a mat near us, commenced, with animated tones and gestures, a story in the Inca language, which, translated, ran somehow thus:

An Indian and his wife went out from the village to work their *chacra,* carrying their infant with them. The woman went to the spring to get water, leaving the man in charge of the child, with many cautions to take good care of it. When she arrived at the spring she found it dried up, and went further to look for another. The husband, alarmed at her long absence, left the child and went in search. When they returned the child was gone; and to their repeated cries, as they wandered through the woods in search, they could get no response save the wailing cry of this little bird, heard for the first time, whose notes their anxious and excited imagination "syllabled" into pa-pa, ma-ma (the present Quichua name of the bird). I suppose the Spaniards heard this story, and, with that religious poetic turn of thought which seems peculiar to this people, called the bird "The lost soul."

The circumstances under which the story was told—the beautiful, still, starlight night—the deep, dark forest around—the faint-red glimmering of the fire, flickering upon the old woman's gray hair and earnest face as she poured forth the guttural tones of the language of a people now passed away—gave it a sufficiently romantic interest to an imaginative man. The old woman was a small romance in herself. I had looked at her with interest as she cooked our supper. She wore a costume that is sometimes, though not often, seen in this country. The body, or upper part of the dress, which was black, consisted of two parts—one coming up from the waist behind and covering the back, the other in front, covering the breast; the two tied together over each shoulder with strings, leaving her lank sides and long skinny arms perfectly bare.

AUGUST 17—We procured a canoe sufficiently large to carry all our baggage (we had hitherto had two), with eight *peons*. We found hills now on both sides of the river, which a little below Lupuna has 120 yards of breadth and thirty feet of depth. We passed a small raft, with a house built of cane and palm upon it, containing an image of the Virgin, which was bound up the river seeking contributions. The people buy a step towards Heaven in this way with their little balls of cotton.

We stopped for the night at Juan Comas, a small village situated on a bluff of light sandy soil, on the left bank. The hills on the other side are much more bare than is common, having only a few small trees and scattering bushes on them. We were quite objects of curiosity, and most of the people of the village came in to see us; one man, a strapping fellow, came in, and after a brief but courteous salutation to me, turned to one of the women, and drove her out of the house with kicks and curses. He followed her, and I soon after heard the sound of blows and the cries of a woman; I suppose the fellow was either jealous, or the lady had neglected some household duty to gratify her curiosity.

AUGUST 18—Just below Juan Comas the river has one hundred yards of width and forty-two feet of depth. This part of the river is called the "well" of Juan Comas; it is half a mile in length, and the current runs but one and a quarter mile the hour. The hills terminate just below this, and we have the country flat on both sides. We passed some rocky hills on the right-hand side, in one of which is a cave called *Puma huasi,* or Tiger house. It is said to be very extensive. Soon after we passed the mouth of the river Hunanza, a small stream coming in on the Infidel side of the river. Our *popero* says that the Infidels dwell near here, and the people of Tarapoto go a short distance up this river to capture the young Indians and take them home as slaves. I believe this story, for I found servants of this class in Tarapoto, who were bought and sold as slaves. Slavery is prohibited by the laws of Peru, but this system is tolerated on the plea that the Infidel is christianized and his condition bettered by it.

It is very easy for only a few white men, armed with guns, to rob the savages of their children; for these rarely live in villages, but in families of at most three or four huts, and widely separated from each other. They never assemble except for the purpose of war; and then the sound of a horn, from settlement to settlement, brings them together. They are also a timid people, and will not face the white man's gun.

It is possible that the story of the *popero* is not true, and that the whites may buy the children of the Indians; but if so, I imagine that the advantages of the bargain are all on one side.

The hills of Pilluana, which we now soon passed, have their base immediately upon the river, on the right-hand side. They are about three hundred feet in height, and stretch along the banks of the river for a quarter of a mile. The salt shows like frost upon the red earth at a distance; but seen nearer the heavy rains seem to have washed away the loose earth and left nearly the pure salt standing in innumerable cone-shaped pinnacles, so that the broken sides of the hills look like what drawings represent of the crater of a volcano, or the bottom of a geyser. Where the hills have been excavated, beautiful stalactites of perfectly pure salt hang from the roof in many varieties of shapes. There are much higher hills back of these that appear also to contain salt, so that there seems a supply here for all people and for all time.

We passed the mouth of the river Mayo, that comes in on the left between moderately high hills, and five minutes after arrived at Shapaja, one of the ports of Tarapoto. The river, just above the junction of the Mayo, narrows to forty yards, has thirty and thirty-six feet of depth, and increases much in velocity. This is preparatory to its rush over the Pongo, a strait of forty-five miles in length, where the river is confined between high hills, is much broken with *malos pasos,* and has its last considerable declivity.

Shapaja has twenty houses, mostly concealed in the high groves of plantains which surround them. Nearly all the men were away fishing, but the women (as always) received us kindly, and cooked our supper for us.

Chapter VIII

⁀⌣⁀

*Pongo of Chasuta—Chasuta—Sta. Cruz—Antonio, the
Paraguá—Laguna—Mouth of the Huallaga*

AUGUST 19—We started in company with a man who, with his
peons, was carrying fish that he had taken and salted below Chasuta
to Tarapoto. A smart walk of five hours (the latter part of it very
quick, to avoid the rain that threatened us) brought us to the town.
The road crossed a range of hills in the forest for about half the
distance. The ascent and descent of these hills were tedious, because light showers of rain had moistened the surface of the hard-
baked earth and made it as slippery as soap. For the other half of
the distance the road ran over a plain covered with high, reedy
grass, and some bushes; there was a short clump-grass underneath
that would afford capital pasturage. The distance between Shapaja
and Tarapoto I judge to be fifteen miles, and the direction west-
erly, although I could not tell exactly, on account of the winding
of the road.

Tarapoto—which is situated upon a moderate eminence near
the western edge of the plain before spoken of, and surrounded

by hills, which are mountains in the west—is by far the largest town I have seen since leaving Huanuco. The district numbers six thousand inhabitants.

There is little or no money in this country. *Tocuyo,* wax from the Ucayali, and balls of cotton thread are used in its place. The English goods that come from the interior sell in Tarapoto for four times their cost in Lima: For example, a yard of printed calico, which costs in Lima twelve and a half cents, sells in this place for either a pound of wax, four yards of *tocuyo,* or two pounds of cotton thread.

I suppose there is a little money obtained for these articles in Huanuco and Chachapoyas, or left here by travelling strangers. But if so, it falls into the hands of the traders and is hoarded away. These traders are either Moyobambinos (inhabitants of Moyobamba), or foreigners of Spain, France, and Portugal. The Moyobambinos are the Jews of the country, and will compass sea and land to make a dollar. I met with them everywhere on the river, and I think that I did not enter an Indian village without finding a Moyobambino domiciliated and trading with the inhabitants. They are a thin, spare, sickly-looking people, of a very dark complexion, but seem capable of undergoing great hardship and fatigue, for they carry their cargoes to marts hundreds of leagues distant by roads or river that present innumerable difficulties.

They bear a bad character on the river, and are said to cheat and oppress the Indians; so that when I could not get a *yucca* for my supper without paying for it in advance, I vented my spleen by abusing a Moyobambino, who had treated the people so badly that they distrusted everybody. But I have had reason, once or twice, for abusing other people besides Moyobambinos on this account; for the Governor of Tarapoto hesitated about trusting me with a canoe to descend the river, because a person representing himself as a countryman of mine had run off with one some years before.

I met at this place my countryman Hacket, whom I had heard spoken so highly of in Cerro Pasco and Huanuco. He is employed in making copper kettles (called *pailas*) for distilling, and in all kinds of blacksmith and foundry work. He seems settled in this country for life, and has adopted the habits and manners of the people. Poor fellow—how rejoiced he was to see the face and hear the speech of a countryman!

The people have no idea of comfort in their domestic relations; the houses are of mud, thatched with palm, and have uneven dirt floors. The furniture consists of a grass hammock, a standing bed-place, a coarse table, and a stool or two. The Governor of this populous district wore no shoes, and appeared to live pretty much like the rest of them.

August 20 we spent at Tarapoto, waiting for the *peons*. The Governor preferred that I should pay them in money, which I much doubt if the *peons* ever saw. He will probably keep the money and give them *tocuyo* and wax. I paid $1.50 for the canoe to carry me as far as Chasuta, a distance of about six hours down, with probably twenty-four to return (that is, twenty-four working hours); fifty cents to each *peon;* and a dollar to pay the people to haul the canoe up the bank and place it under the shed at Shapaja on its return.

The men who carried us from Tocache to Sion preferred half their pay in money; in all other cases I have paid in cotton cloth, valued at twenty-five cents the yard (its cost in Lima was twelve and a half cents). The amount of pay, generally fixed by the governor, is a yard per man per day, and about the same for the canoe.

An American circus company passed through Tarapoto a few months ago; they had come from the Pacific coast, and were bound down the Amazon. This beats the Moyobambinos for determined energy in making dollars. I imagine that the adventure did not pay, for I encountered traces of them, in broken-down horses, at several of the villages on the river. They floated their horses down on rafts.

I spoke with an active and intelligent young Spanish trader, named Morey, about the feasibility of a steamboat enterprise upon these rivers, bringing American goods and taking return-cargoes of coffee, tobacco, straw hats, hammocks, and sarsaparilla to the ports of Brazil on the river. He thought that it could not fail to enrich anyone who would attempt it; but that the difficulty lay in the fact that my proposed steamer would never get as far as this, for my goods would be bought up and paid for in return-cargoes long before she reached Peru. He thought, too, that the Brazilians along the river had money which they would be glad to exchange for comforts and luxuries.

Were I to engage in any scheme of colonization for the purpose of evolving the resources of the Valley of the Amazon, I think I should direct the attention of settlers to this district of Tarapoto. It combines more advantages than any other I know; it is healthy, fertile, and free from the torment of *musquitoes* and sand-flies. Wheat may be had from the high lands above it; cattle thrive well; and its coffee, tobacco, sugar-cane, rice, and maize are of fine quality. It is true that vessels cannot come up to Shapaja, the port of the town of Tarapoto; but a good road may be made from this town eighteen miles to Chasuta, to which vessels of five feet draught may come at the lowest stage of the river, and any draught at high water. Tarapoto is situated on an elevated plain twenty miles in diameter and is seventy miles from Moyobamba, the capital of the province, a city of seven thousand inhabitants.

I saw here very fine fields of Indian corn. The stalk grows quite as high as on our best bottom-lands in Virginia, and the ears were full, and of good grain. It may be planted at any time, and it yields in three months, thus giving four crops a year. A considerable quantity of tobacco is also cultivated in the neighborhood of Tarapoto.

AUGUST 21—We started for Juan Guerra on horseback, in company with a large fishing-party, got up by the Padre for his own profit; he seemed to carry nearly the whole town with him. The mounted party consisted of eight. There were two ladies along, whose company added to the gaiety and pleasure of the canter through the woods. Used as I had become by my travels in various parts of the world to the free and easy, I must confess that I was a little startled to see these ladies, when we arrived at Juan Guerra, denude themselves to a silk handkerchief around the loins, and bathe in the river within forty yards, and in full sight of all the men.

Arrived at Juan Guerra, we embarked upon the Cumbasa, which empties into the Mayo. Half an hour's dragging of the canoe over the shoals, and between the fallen trees on this stream, and one and a half hour's navigation on the Mayo, carried us to its mouth, which is only a quarter of a mile above Shapaja, and then shoved off to join the priest, who was to camp on a beach above.

The fishing-party of the Padre was a large affair. They had four or five canoes, and a large quantity of *barbasco*. The manner of fishing is to close up the mouth of a *caño* of the river with a network made of reeds, and then, mashing the *barbasco* root to a pulp, throw it into the water. This turns the water white, and poisons it, so that the fish soon commence rising to the surface dead, and are taken into the canoes with small tridents. Almost at the moment of throwing the *barbasco* into the water, the smaller fish rise to the surface and die in two or three minutes; the larger fish survive longer, and, therefore, a successful fishing of this sort is a matter of half a day, or till the canoes are filled.

When we left Shapaja for Tarapoto, we placed our trunks, several without locks, in charge of the women who lived in the shed where we slept; and, although they knew that the trunks contained handkerchiefs, red cotton cloth, beads, scissors, &c. (things which they most desire), we missed nothing on our return.

AUGUST 22—Two miles below Shapaja is the *mal-paso* of Estero. A point of rocks, stretching out from a little stream that enters on the left, makes this rapid, which is considered a very dangerous one. The stream, rushing against these rocks, is deflected to a point of rocks that makes out into the river a little lower down on the other side; this turns it aside again, and the waves mingle and boil below. The canoe was unloaded, and conducted by *sogas,* or ropes of vine, over and between the rocks on the left-hand side. It took an hour to unload, pass the canoe, and load up again. Three miles further is the *mal-paso* of *Canoa Yacu* (canoe water), from many canoes having been wrecked here. This is by far the most formidable rapid I have seen. There is a small perpendicular fall on each side, and a shoot of 20 degrees declivity in the middle, down which the water rushes with a velocity of at least ten miles the hour. The shoot looks tempting, and one is disposed to try the rush; but there are rocks below, over which the water dashes up some two or three feet in height, and I think no boat could shoot out of the force of the stream so as to avoid these rocks.

The river both here and at Estero is not more than thirty yards wide. The average velocity of the current through the Pongo is six miles the hour. It took one hour and a half to pass this obstruction. Two miles further down we shot the *mal-paso* of Matijuelo under oar; and immediately after, that of Chumia, where the canoe was let down as before, but without unloading. It took half an hour to do this. A quarter of an hour afterwards we passed the rapid of Vaquero; and at two P.M. arrived at Chasuta. We were kindly welcomed and hospitably entertained by the Cura, Don Sebastian Castro.

The *vaca marina* (sea cow) of the Spaniards, and *peixe boy* (fish ox) of the Portuguese (also found in our Florida streams, and there called *manatee*), is found in great numbers on the Amazon and its principal tributaries. It is an animal averaging, when full grown, about nine feet in length and six in circumference. It has much the appearance of a large seal, with a smooth skin, dark on the back, a dirty white on the belly, and thinly sprinkled with coarse hairs. The eyes and ears (or rather, holes for hearing) are very small. The mouth is also small, though it looks large on the outside, on account of a very thick and wide upper lip, which is shaped like that of an ox. In the one I examined, which was a young female, I could discover neither tongue nor teeth, but a thick, rough, and hard, fleshy cushion attached to both upper and lower jaws, which seemed to me very well adapted to masticating the grass which grows upon the banks of the river, and which is its principal food. The tail is broad and flat, and is placed horizontally. This, with two large fins far in advance, and very near the jaws, enables it to move in the water with considerable rapidity. It is not able to leave the water; but in feeding it gets near the shore and raises its head out. It is, when feeding, most often taken by the Indians. The flesh, salted or dried, is a good substitute for pork. It is put up in large jars in its own fat, and is called *michira*.

Chasuta is an Indian village of twelve hundred inhabitants, situated on a plain elevated about twenty-five feet above the present level of the river. It is frequently covered in the full, and the people take their canoes into their houses and live in them. The diseases, as all along the river, are pleurisy, *tarbardillo,* and *sarna.* The small-pox sometimes makes its appearance, but does little damage. It is a very healthy place, and few die.

The Indians of Chasuta are a gentle, quiet race; very docile, and very obedient to their priest, always saluting him by kneeling and kissing his hand. They are tolerably good boatmen, but excel as hunters. Like all the Indians, they are much addicted to drink. I have noticed that the Indians of this country are reluctant to shed blood, and seem to have a horror of its sight. I have known them to turn away to avoid killing a chicken, when it was presented to one for that purpose. The Indian whom Ijurra struck did not com-plain of the pain of the blow, but, bitterly and repeatedly, that "his blood had been shed." They eat *musquitoes* that they catch on their bodies, with the idea of restoring the blood which the insect has abstracted.

The Padre told me that the fee for a marriage was four pounds of wax, which was the perquisite of the sacristan; for a burial, two, which went to the sexton; and that he was regaled with a fowl for a christening. He complained of the want of salary, or fees; and said that it was impossible for a clergyman to live unless he engaged in trade. Every year the governor appoints twelve men to serve him. It is an office of distinction, and the Indians crave it. They are called Fiscales. They work the Padre's *chacra* and *trapiche;* fish for him; hunt for him (the fishermen and hunters are called *mitayos;* this is a remnant of an oppressive old Spanish law called *mita,* by which certain services, particularly in the mines, were exacted of the In-dians); do his washing; wait upon his table; and carry on for him his traffic on the river, by which he gains his salt fish and the means to buy crockery for his table.

I bought wax of the curate to pay for the canoes and boatmen to Yurimaguas. The men desired money, and I told the curate that he had better let me pay them in money, as to be familiar with its use would tend to civilize them. But he said that they did not know its value, and would only hoard it up or use it as ornaments. I don't know what else he will do with it, for certainly it never circulates. I have not seen a dollar since I left Huanuco, except those that were in my own hands. That the Indians have no idea of its value is evident. I bought a *pucuna* of one. He desired money, and his first demand was four dollars, which I refused to give. He then said six *reals* (seventy-five cents). I gave him a dollar, which I thought would pay him for the time and labor necessary to make another.

As we were now clear of the dangers of the river, and were to be more exposed to sun and rain, we had coverings made of hoop-poles, and thatched with palm, fitted to the canoe. The one over the stern, for the accommodation of the *patrón,* covers about six feet of it, and makes a good den to retreat to in bad weather. It is called by the Indians *parmacari.* The one fitted over the cargo, in the body of the boat, is called *armayari.* It is narrower than the other, allowing room for the Indians to sit and paddle on each side of it.

AUGUST 25—We left Chasuta in company with two canoes, one belonging to a Portuguese, resident of Tarapoto, carrying a cargo to Nauta; and the other manned by the Fiscales, and carrying the Padre's little venture of salt. We passed the salt hills of Callana Yacu, where the people of Chasuta and the Indians of Ucayali and Marañon get their salt. Soon after, we passed between cliffs of dark-red rocks, where the river deepened to forty-two feet. On one of these rocks, appearing like a gigantic boulder of porphyry, were cut rude figures of saints and crosses, with letters which are said to express "The leap of the Traitor Aguirre"; but they were too much worn by time and weather for me to make them out. We camped on the right bank of the river, having passed the country of the Infidels.

AUGUST 26—Being in company with Antonio, the Portuguese, who knows how to arrange matters, we get a cup of coffee at the peep of day and are off by half past five A.M. At five miles of distance we passed the lower extremity of the Pongo, which commences at Shapaja. *Pongo* is an Indian word, and is applied to designate the place where a river breaks through a range of hills, and where navigation is of course obstructed by rocks and rapids. The place where the Marañón breaks its way through the last chain of hills that obstructs its course is called the Pongo de Manseriche.

After passing the Pongo, we entered upon a low, flat country, where the river spreads out very wide, and is obstructed by islands and sandbanks. This is the deposit from the Pongo. In the channel where we passed, I found a scant five feet of water. This shoal water is but for a short distance, and the soundings soon deepened to twelve and eighteen feet. Small pebbly islands are forming in the river, and much drift-wood from above lodges on them. After having stopped two hours to breakfast, we passed the mouth of the Chipurana, which is about twenty yards wide.

River now two hundred yards wide, free from obstruction, with a gentle current, and between eighteen and twenty-four feet of depth. We saw turtle-tracks in the sand to-day for the first time; camped on the beach.

AUGUST 27—Saw flesh-colored porpoises; also a small seal, which looked like a fur-seal; got turtle-eggs. The turtles crawl out upon the beach during the night, deposit their eggs, and retreat before dawn, leaving, however, broad tracks in the sand, by which their deposits are discovered. We must have got upwards of a thousand;

I counted 150 taken from one hole. Since we have passed the Pongo we have encountered no stones; the beaches are all of sand.

AUGUST 28—Arrived at Yurimaguas. This little village, situated upon a hill immediately upon the banks of the river, and numbering 250 inhabitants, now appears almost entirely deserted. We could procure neither *peons* nor canoes. The men were away in the forest collecting wax for a *fiesta,* ordered by the curate; and the sub-prefect of the province, who had been gold-hunting up the Santiago, had taken all the canoes up the Cachiyacu with him on his return to Moyobamba. I was told that his expedition for gold up the Santiago, which consisted of a force of eighty armed men, had been a failure; that they got no gold, and had lost five of their company by the attacks of the Huambisas and other savages of the Santiago. This may not be true. The sub-prefect (I was told) said that the expedition had accomplished its purpose, which was simply to open friendly communications with the savages, with a view to further operations.

With great difficulty, and by paying double, I persuaded our Chasutinos to take us on to Sta. Cruz, where I was assured I could be accommodated both with boats and men. We could buy nothing at Yurimaguas but a few bunches of plantains and some salt fish out of a passing boat.

We left Yurimaguas after breakfasting. Half a mile below the village is the mouth of the Cachiyacu. This river is the general route between Moyobamba and the ports of the Amazon.

We met several canoes going up the river for salt; canoes passing each other on the river speak at a great distance apart. The Indians use a sing-song tone that is heard and understood very far, without seeming to call for much exertion of the voice. Every year at this season the Indians of the Marañón and Ucayali make a voyage up the Huallaga for their supply of salt. They travel slowly, and support themselves by hunting, fishing, and robbing plantain patches on their way.

About eight miles below Yurimaguas, an island with extensive sand-flats occupies nearly the whole of the middle of the river. We passed to the right, and I found but a scant six feet of water. The *popero* said there was less on the other side; but Antonio, the Portuguese, passed there, and said there was more. He did not sound, however. We tried an experiment to ascertain the speed of the canoe at full oar, and I was surprised to find that six men could not paddle it faster than two miles the hour; ours is, however, a very heavy and clumsy canoe. We have had frequent races with Antonio and the Fiscales, and were always beaten. It was a pretty sight to see the boat of the latter, though laden with salt to the water's edge, dance by us; and, although beaten, we could not sometimes refrain (as their *puntero,* a tall, painted Indian, would toss his paddle in the air with a triumphant gesture as he passed) from giving a hurrah for the servants of the church.

AUGUST 29—We met a canoe of Conibos Indians, one man and two women, from the Ucayali, going up for salt. We bought (with beads) some turtle-eggs, and proposed to buy a monkey they had; but one of the women clasped the little beast in her arms, and set up a great outcry lest the man should sell it. The man wore a long, brown cotton gown, with a hole in the neck for the head to go through, and short, wide sleeves. He had on his arm a bracelet of monkey's teeth; and the women had white beads hanging from the septum of the nose. Their dress was a cotton petticoat tied round the waist, and all were filthy.

We are now getting into the lake country, and hence to the mouth of the Amazon, lakes of various sizes, and at irregular distances, border the rivers. They all communicate with the rivers by channels, which are commonly dry in the dry season. They are the resort of immense numbers of waterfowl, particularly cranes and cormorants; and the Indians, at the proper season, take many fish and turtles from them.

Many of these lakes are, according to the traditions of the Indians, guarded by an immense serpent, which is able to raise such a tempest in the lake as to swamp their canoes, when it immediately swallows the people. It is called in the *"Lengua Inga" Yacu Mama,* or mother of the waters; and the Indians never enter a lake with which they are not familiar that they do not set up an obstreperous clamor with their horns, which the snake is said to answer; thus giving them warning of its presence.

I never saw the animal myself, but will give a description of it written by Father Manuel Castrucci de Vernazza, in an account of his mission to the Givaros and Zaparos of the river Pastaza, made in 1845:

> The wonderful nature of this animal—its figure, its size, and other circumstances—enchains attention, and causes man to reflect upon the majestic and infinite power and wisdom of the Supreme Creator. The sight alone of this monster confounds, intimidates, and infuses respect into the heart of the boldest man. He never seeks or follows the victims upon which he feeds; but, so great is the force of his inspiration, that he draws in with his breath whatever quadruped or bird may pass him, within from twenty to fifty yards of distance, according to its size. That which I killed from my canoe upon the Pastaza (with five shots of a fowling piece) had two yards of thickness and fifteen yards of length; but the Indians of this region have assured me that there are animals of this kind here of three or

four yards diameter, and from thirty to forty long. These swallow entire hogs, stags, tigers, and men, with the greatest facility; but, by the mercy of Providence, it moves and turns itself very slowly, on account of its extreme weight. When moving, it appears a thick log of wood covered with scales, and dragged slowly along the ground, leaving a track so large that men may see it at a distance and avoid its dangerous ambush.

The good father says that he observed "that the blood of this animal flowed in jets (*salia á chorros*), and in enormous abundance. The prejudice of the Indians in respect to this species of great snakes (believing it to be the devil in figure of a serpent) deprived me of the acquisition of the dried skin, though I offered a large gratification for it."

It is almost impossible to doubt a story told with this minuteness of detail. Doubtless the padre met with, and killed the boa-constrictor; but two yards of thickness is scarcely credible. He writes it *dos varas de grosor*. (*Grosor* is thickness.) I thought the father might have meant two yards in circumference, but he afterwards says that the Indians reported them of three and four yards in diameter (*de diametro*.)

We had a fresh squall of wind and rain from the northward and eastward. The Portuguese, who is a careful and timid navigator, and whose motions we follow because he is a capital caterer and has a wife along to cook for us, pulled in for the beach, and we camped for the night.

Seventy miles below Yurimaguas is Sta. Cruz. This is an Indian village of a tribe called Aquanos, containing 350 inhabitants. The Lieutenant Governor is the only white man in it. The women go naked down to their hips, and the children entirely so. I was quite an object of curiosity and fear to them; and they seemed never tired of examining my spectacles. The *pueblo* is situated on an eminence, as most of the villages of this country are, to avoid inundation. It has a small stream running by it, which empties into the river at the port, and is navigable in the rainy season for loaded canoes. The *convento* is the most respectable-looking house on the river. It is divided into apartments, has ceilings, and is plastered, inside and out, with a white clay. There was a portico in the rear, and it looked altogether as if it had been designed and built by a person who had some taste and some idea of personal comfort.

I obtained at this place the sap of a large tree called *catao,* which is said to be very poisonous. It appears to be acrid, and acts like a powerful caustic. The man who chopped the bark, to let the sap run, always turned away his face as he struck, for fear of its getting into his eyes. The Indians employ it for the purpose of curing old dull sores. The tree is generally very large; has a smooth bark, but with knots on it bearing short thorns. The leaf is nearly circular; it is called in Brazil *assacu,* and is there thought to be a remedy for leprosy. We gathered also some leaves and root of a running plant called *guaco,* which, steeped in spirits, and applied internally and externally, is said to be an antidote to the bite of a snake. I think it probable that this may be a fancy of the Indians, originating from the fact that the leaf has something the appearance and color of a snake-skin. There is a great abundance of it all over the Montaña.

We found difficulty in getting canoes at this place. The only one that would accommodate ourselves and baggage belonged to the church, and, like its mistress in Peru, it was in rather a dilapidated condition. We bargained for it with the *curaca* (chief of the Indians, and second in authority to the Lieutenant Governor); but when the Lieutenant returned from his *chacra,* where he had been setting out plantains, he refused to let us have it, on the ground that it wanted repairs. We were, therefore, obliged to take two small ones that would barely carry the trunks and boxes, and embark ourselves in the canoe of the Portuguese.

We have found this man, Don Antonio da Costa Viana, and his family, quite a treasure to us on the road. He is a stout, active little fellow, about fifty years of age, with piercing black eyes, long black curls, a face burned almost to negro blackness by the sun, deeply pitted with the small-pox, and with a nose that, as Ijurra tells him, would make a cut-water for a frigate. He is called *paraguá* (a species of parrot), from his incessant talk; and he brags that he is "as well known on the river as a dog." He has a *chacra* of sugar-cane and tobacco, with a *trapiche,* at Tarapoto. He sells the spirits that he makes for *tocuyo,* and carries the *tocuyo,* tobacco, and *chancaca* to Nauta, selling or rather exchanging as he goes. His canoe is fifty feet long and three broad, and carries a cargo which he values at $500; that is, five hundred in *efectos*—$250 in money. It is well fitted with *armayari* and *parmacari,* and carries six *peons*— Antonio, himself, his wife, and his adopted daughter, a child of ten years; besides affording room for the calls of hospitality. My friend is perfect master of all around him (a little tyrannical, perhaps, to his family); knows all the reaches and beaches of the river, and every tree and shrub that grows upon its banks. He is intelligent, active, and obliging; always busy; now twisting fishing-lines of the fibres of a palm called *chambira;* now hunting turtle-eggs, robbing plantain-fields, or making me cigars of tobacco-leaves given me by the priest of Chasuta. Every beach is a house for him; his *peons* build his *rancho* and spread his *musquito* curtain; his wife and child cook his supper. His mess of salt fish, turtle-eggs, and plantains is a feast for him; and his gourd of coffee, and pipe afterwards, a luxury that a king might envy. He is always well and happy. I imagine he has picked up and hoarded away, to keep him in his old age, or to leave his wife when he dies, some few of the dollars that are floating about here; and, in short, I don't know a more enviable person. It is true Doña Antonio gets drunk occasionally; but he licks her if she is troublesome, and it seems to give him very little concern.

I sometimes twit him with the immorality of robbing the poor Indians of their plantains; but he defends himself by saying, "That to take plantains is not to steal; to take a knife, or a hatchet, or an article of clothing, is; but plantains, not. Everybody on the river does it. It is necessary to have them, and he is perfectly willing to pay for them, if he could find the owners and they would sell them." The old rascal is very religious too; he has, hanging under the *parmacari* of his boat, a silver Crucifix and a wooden St. Anthony. He thinks a priest next of kin to a saint, and a saint perfection. He said to me, as his wife was combing her hair in the canoe, "A bald woman, Don Luis, must be a very ugly thing: not so a bald man, because St. Peter, you know, was bald"; and I verily believe that, although he is very vain of his black curls, were he to lose them, he would find consolation in the reflection that he had made an approach, in appearance at least, towards his great exemplar.

We shoved off from Sta. Cruz at sunset, and camped on the beach a mile lower down. It is very well to do this, for the canoemen are taken away from the temptation of the villages, and are sober and ready for an early start next morning.

SEPTEMBER 1—Heavy clouds and rains both to the northward and eastward and southward and westward, with an occasional spit at us; but we set the rain at defiance under the palm-thatched roof of Antonio. At half past three P.M. we arrived at Laguna. This town, the principal one of the district and the residence of the Governor, is one and a half mile from the port. The walk is a pleasant one through the forest at this season, but is probably mud to the knees in the rains. It contains 1,044 inhabitants; and the productions of the neighborhood are wax, sarsaparilla, copal, copaiba, and salt fish. I have seen all these in the hands of the Indians, but in small quantities, there being so little demand for them.

The Cocamillas, who form the largest part of the population of Laguna, are lazy and drunken. They are capital boatmen, however, when they have no liquor; and I had more comfort with them than with any other Indians except those of Tingo Maria.

SEPTEMBER 2—Waiting for boats and boatmen. There are no large canoes, and we are again compelled to take two. I was surprised at this as I was led to believe—and I thought it probable—that the nearer we got to the Marañón the larger we should find the boats, and the means of navigation more complete. But I have met with nothing but misstatements in my whole course. The impression I received in Lima of the Montaña was that it was a country abounding not only with the necessaries, but with the luxuries of life, so far as eating was concerned. Yet I am now satisfied that if one hundred men were to start without provisions, on the route I have travelled, the half must inevitably perish for want of food. Of meat there is almost none; and even salt fish, *yuccas,* and plantains are scarce, and often not to be had; game is shy; and the fish, of which there are a great number, do not readily take the hook; of fruit I have seen literally none edible since leaving Huanuco.

At Chasuta I was assured that I should find at Yurimaguas every facility for the prosecution of my journey; yet I could get neither a boat nor a man, and had to persuade my Chasuta boatmen to carry me on to Sta. Cruz, where the Yurimaguas people said there would be no further difficulty. At Sta. Cruz I could get but two small and rotten canoes, with three men to each, for Laguna, which, being the great port of the river, could in the estimation of the people at Sta. Cruz, furnish me with the means of crossing the Atlantic if necessary. I had been always assured that I could get at Laguna one hundred Cocamillas, if I wanted them, as a force to enter among the savages of the Ucayali; but here, too, I could with difficulty get six men and two small canoes to pass me on to Nauta, which I expected to find, from the description of the people above, a small New York. Had it not been that Señor Cauper, at that place, had just then a boat unemployed, which he was willing to sell, I should have had to abandon my expedition up the Ucayali, and build me a raft to float down the Marañón.

We found at the port of Laguna two travelling merchants, a Portuguese, and a Brazilian. They had four large boats of about eight tons each, and two or three canoes. Their cargo consisted of iron, steel, iron implements, crockery-ware, wine, brandy, copper kettles, coarse, short swords (a very common implement of the Indians), guns, ammunition, salt fish, &c., which they expected to exchange in Moyobamba and Chachapoyas for straw hats, *tocuyo,* sugar, coffee, and money. They were also buying up all the sarsaparilla they could find, and dispatching it back in canoes. They invited us to breakfast off roast pig, and I thought that I never tasted anything better than the *farinha,* which I saw for the first time.

Farinha is a general substitute for bread in all the course of the Amazon below the Brazilian frontier. It is used by all classes, and in immense quantities by the Indians and laborers. Our boatmen in Brazil were always contented with plenty of salt fish and *farinha.* Every two or three hours of the day, whilst travelling, they would stop rowing, pour a little water upon a large gourd-full of *farinha,* and pass around the mass (which they called *pirào*) as if it were a delicacy.

SEPTEMBER 3—Our boatmen came down to the port at eight A.M. They were accompanied, as usual, by their wives, carrying their bedding, their jars of *masato,* and even their paddles; for these fellows are too lazy, when on shore, to do a hand's turn; though when embarked they work freely (these Cocamillas), and are gay, cheerful, ready, and obedient. The dress of the women is nothing more than a piece of cotton cloth, generally dark brown in color, wrapped around the loins and reaching to the knee. I was struck with the appearance of one, the only pretty Indian girl I have seen. She appeared to be about thirteen years of age, and was the wife of one of our boatmen. It was amusing to see the slavish respect with which she waited upon the young savage (himself about nineteen), and the lordly indifference with which he received her attentions. She was as straight as an arrow, delicately and elegantly formed, and had a free, wild, Indian look, that was quite taking.

We got off at a quarter past nine, the merchants at the same time, and the Padre also returns to-day to Yurimaguas; so that we make a haul upon the population of Laguna, and carry off about seventy of its inhabitants. Twenty-five miles below Laguna, we arrived at the mouth of the Huallaga. Several islands occupy the middle of it. The channel runs near the left bank. Near the middle of the river we had nine feet; passing towards the left bank we suddenly fell into forty-five feet. The Huallaga, just above the island, is 350 yards wide; the Amazon, at the junction, five hundred. The water of both rivers is very muddy and filthy, particularly that of the former, which for some distance within the mouth is covered with a glutinous scum, that I take to be the excrement of fish, probably that of porpoises.

The Huallaga, from Tingo Maria, the head of canoe navigation, to Chasuta (from which point to its mouth it is navigable for a draught of five feet at the lowest stage of the river), is 325 miles long. It is proper to state here that all my estimates of distance are in geographical miles of sixty to the degree.

Chapter IX

❦

*Entrance into the Amazon—Upper and lower missions of
Mainas—Conversions of the Ucayali—Trade in Sarsaparilla—
Advantages of trade with this country*

THE RIVER UPON which we now entered is the main trunk of
the Amazon, which carries its Peruvian name of Marañón
as far as Tabatinga, at the Brazilian frontier; below which, and as
far as the junction of the Rio Negro, it takes the name of Solimoens;
and thence to the ocean is called Amazon. It is the same stream
throughout, and to avoid confusion I shall call it Amazon from this
point to the sea.

The march of the great river in its silent grandeur was sublime; but in the untamed might of its turbid waters, as they cut away
its banks, tore down the gigantic denizens of the forest, and built
up islands, it was awful. It rolled through the wilderness with a
stately and solemn air. Its waters looked angry, sullen, and relent-
less; and the whole scene awoke emotions of awe and dread—such
as are caused by the funeral solemnities, the minute gun, the howl
of the wind, and the angry tossing of the waves, when all hands
are called to bury the dead in a troubled sea.

I was reminded of our Mississippi at its topmost flood; the waters are quite as muddy and quite as turbid; but this stream lacked the charm and the fascination which the plantation upon the bank, the city upon the bluff, and the steamboat upon its waters, lends to its fellow of the North; nevertheless, I felt pleased at its sight. I had already travelled seven hundred miles by water, and fancied that this powerful stream would soon carry me to the ocean, but the water-travel was comparatively just begun; many a weary month was to elapse ere I should again look upon the familiar face of the sea; and many a time, when worn and wearied with the canoe life, did I exclaim, "This river seems interminable!"

Its capacities for trade and commerce are inconceivably great. Its industrial future is the most dazzling; and to the touch of steam, settlement, and cultivation, this rolling stream and its magnificent water-shed would start up into a display of industrial results that would indicate the Valley of the Amazon as one of the most enchanting regions on the face of the earth.

From its mountains you may dig silver, iron, coal, copper, quicksilver, zinc, and tin; from the sands of its tributaries you may wash gold, diamonds, and precious stones; from its forests you may gather drugs of virtues the most rare, spices of aroma the most exquisite, gums and resins of the most varied and useful properties, dyes of hues the most brilliant, with cabinet and building-woods of the finest polish and most enduring texture. Its climate is an everlasting summer, and its harvest perennial.

SEPTEMBER 4—The shores of the river are low, but abrupt. The lower strata next to the water's edge are of sand, hardening into rock from the superincumbent pressure of the soil with its great trees. There were a great many porpoises sporting in the river. At three P.M. we passed the narrow arm of the river that runs by

Urarinas, a small village situated on the left bank. The channel inside the island seemed nearly dry. Ijurra, however, passed through it in a small canoe, and bought some fowls and a small monkey at the *pueblo*. The channel of the river runs near the right bank. Population of Urarinas, eighty.

SEPTEMBER 5—The *patos reales,* a large and beautiful species of duck with which the river abounds, are now breeding. We saw numbers of pairs conducting their broods over the water. Though the young ones could not fly, they could dive so long and fast that we could not catch them. I brought home a pair of these ducks, and find that they answer exactly to the description of the Egyptian goose. They have small horns on their wings.

SEPTEMBER 6—We have had quite heavy squalls of wind and rain every day since entering the Amazon. The canoes are so low that they cannot ride the waves of mid-river, and are compelled to haul in for the land, and wait for the storm to pass. We saw alligators to-day for the first time.

SEPTEMBER 8—The Fiscales killed six howling monkeys with their *pucunas*. Passed the mouth of Tigre Yacu on the left. It is seventy yards broad, and looks deep and free from obstruction. Its waters are much clearer than those of the Amazon. It is navigable for canoes a long way up; and a considerable quantity of sarsaparilla is gathered on its banks, though inhabited by savages, who are said to be warlike and dangerous. We camped at night on an island near the middle of the river. A narrow island lay between us and San Regis, a small pueblo on the left bank, whence we could hear the sound of music and merry-making all night.

The Fiscales, cooking their big monkeys over a large fire on the beach, presented a savage and most picturesque night scene. They looked more like devils roasting human beings than like servants of the church.

SEPTEMBER 9—Passed a channel called Pucati, which is a small mouth of the Ucayali. It is now nearly dry. In the rainy season it is passable for canoes. Soon after leaving this, we passed another small channel, said to communicate with a large lake—a large one probably in the full, when this whole country between the Ucayali, Amazon, and channel of Pucati, is nearly overflowed. We arrived at Nauta at noon, having travelled two hundred and ten miles from the mouth of the Huallaga.

We called on the Governor General of the Missions of Mainas, Don José Maria Arebalo, who received us with some formality, and gave us lodgings in one of the houses of the village—I suspect, turning out the inhabitants for that purpose. My companion, Ijurra, was not sure of a cordial reception; for, when sub-prefect of the province, he had caused Arebalo to be arrested and carried prisoner from Balza Puerto to Moyobamba. But our friend was much too magnanimous to remember old feuds, and he and Ijurra soon became boon companions.

Nauta is a fishing village of one thousand inhabitants, mostly Indians of the Cocama tribe, which is distinct from that of the Cocamillas of Laguna. It has a few white residents engaged in trading with the Indians for salt fish, wax, and sarsaparilla, which are obtained from the Ucayali. Don Bernardino Cauper, an old Portuguese, does most of the business of the place. He sends parties of Indians to fish or gather sarsaparilla upon the Napo and Ucayali; and he has two or three boats (called in this part of the country *garreteas*) trading down the river as far as Egas. He supplies all the country above with foreign articles from Brazil, and receives consignments from the upper country, which he sends to Egas.

Don Bernardino lives in a sort of comfort. He has plenty of meat (calling turtle, salt fish, and fowls meat), with *farinha* from below, and beans and onions from his little garden. There is good tobacco from above to smoke, and wholesome, though fiery, Lisbon wine to drink. I have been frequently struck during my journey with the comparative value of things. The richest man of a village of one thousand inhabitants, in the United States, would think Bernardino's table poorly supplied, and would turn up his nose at a grass hammock slung between two hooks in the shop for a bed-place. Yet these things were regal luxuries to us; and, doubtless, being the best that are to be had, Don Bernardino is perfectly contented, and desires nothing better.

The old gentleman is very pious. The Cura of Pebas was at this time in Nauta, attending to the repairs of the church; and we celebrated a nine days' service (Novena) in honor of our Lady of Mercy, the patroness of the arms of Peru. The expenses of the service (being a fee for the padre and the lighting of the church with wax) were borne by individuals. The padre gave the first day; then Señor Cauper; then his wife, his wife's sister, his son, his pretty Brazilian niece, Doña Candida; then came Arebalo; then Ijurra and I; the priest winding up on Sunday. But my old friend was not contented with this; and when I shoved off on Monday for the Ucayali, I left him engaged in another church service, setting off rockets, and firing, from time to time, an old blunderbuss, loaded to the muzzle, in honor of a miracle that had happened in Rimini, in Italy, some year and a half ago, of which we had just received intelligence.

Arebalo gave me some statistics from which it appears that the province of Mainas is divided into the province proper (of which the capital is Moyobamba), the upper and lower Missions, and the Conversions of the Ucayali.

I know of no legal establishment in the Missions—the law proceeding out of the mouths of the governors. Indians are punished by flogging or confinement in the stocks; whites are sometimes imprisoned; but if their offence is of a grave nature, they are sent to be tried and judged by the courts of the capital.

Arebalo estimates the value of the commerce of the Missions with Brazil at $20,000 annually. The vegetable productions of the Missions do not equal the value of the imports. They send down tobacco, salt fish, straw hats, coarse cotton, wax, incense, balsam, and vanilla, and receive, in return, cattle, horses, goods of Europe, and a little money. The Brazilians bring up heavy articles and take back straw hats, hammocks, sarsaparilla, and money. The greatest profit is made on the fish, of which thirty thousand pieces are taken annually in the Ucayali and Amazon. It costs there about three cents the piece, and is worth in Tarapoto, Lamas, and other places of the province, about twelve and a half cents the piece. The profit is about 126 percent in thirty-six days.

The return-cargo also yields a profit, so that my friend Arebalo, who by virtue of his office can get as many men to take fish for him as he wants, will probably return to civilized parts in a few years with a snug little sum in his pocket. Old Cauper is rich, and the priest in comfortable circumstances.

The people engaged in this occupation make more profit by cheating the Indians in every possible mode. They also own the *garreteas,* and, by management, support their *peons* for less than three cents per day. This is an estimate made up from information given by Arebalo.

Sarsaparilla is to be found on the banks of almost every tributary of the great streams of the Montaña; but a great many of these are not worked, on account of the savages living on their banks, who frequently attack the parties that come to gather it. On the Pangoa are the Campas; on the Pachitea, the Aguaytia, and the Pisque are the Cashibos; and the whole southern border of the Amazon, from the mouth of the Ucayali to that of the Yavari, is inhabited by the Mayorunas; all savages, and averse to intercourse with the white man.

I have estimated the annual cost of running a small steamer between Loreto, the frontier port of Peru and Chasuta, a distance of eight hundred miles, entirely within the Peruvian territory, at $20,000, including the establishment of blacksmiths' and carpenters' shops at Nauta for her repairs. I estimate that the value of the imports and exports to and from Brazil is $20,000 annually. I have no doubt that the appearance of a steamer in these waters would at once double the value. A loaded canoe takes eighty days to ascend these eight hundred miles. A steamer will do it in twelve, giving ample time to take in wood, to land and receive cargo at the various villages on the river, and to lay by at night. When the river becomes better known she can run for a large part of the night, and thus shorten her time nearly one half. Men shrink at the eighty days in a canoe, when they will jump at the twelve in a steamer.

The steamer will also increase commerce and trade by creating artificial wants; men will travel who did not travel before; articles of luxury—such as Yankee clocks, cheap musical instruments, &c.—will be introduced, and the Indians will work to obtain them; and, in short, when the wonders that the steamboat and railroad have accomplished are taken into consideration, I shall not be thought rash in predicting that in one year from the time of the appearance of the steamer, the $20,000 will be made $40,000.

Thus we shall have $20,000 worth of goods going up from Loreto to Chasuta, paying at least 100 percent; and $20,000 going down, paying another 100 percent; giving to the steamboat company (who would monopolize the trade) $40,000 a year, against $20,000 of expenses.

There would be no difficulty in getting a supply of fuel. My Peruvian steamer would have to make her way slowly up, for the first time, by collecting and cutting up the abundant drift-wood on the islands; but she could readily contract with the governors of the thirty-six villages between Pará and Chasuta for a regular supply. The Indians of the Peruvian villages are entirely obedient to their governors; and a sufficient number of them may always be had, at wages of twelve and a half cents per day, with about three cents more for their maintenance.

The only difficulty that I have in my calculations is that I know there is not $40,000 in the whole province; its productions must find their way to the Pacific, on the one hand, and to the Atlantic, on the other, before they can be converted into money. My steamer, therefore, to be enabled to buy and sell, must communicate at Loreto with a larger steamer, plying between that place and Barra, at the mouth of the Rio Negro, a distance of 840 miles; and this with another still larger, between Barra and Pará, a distance of a thousand miles.

These three steamers could not fail to enrich their owners; for they would entirely monopolize the trade of the river, which is fairly measured by the imports and exports of Pará, which amounted in 1851 to two millions of dollars.

These two millions are now brought down to Pará, and carried away from Pará, by clumsy, inefficient river-craft, which would vanish from the main stream at the first triumphant whistle of the engine. These would, however, until the profits justified the putting on of more steamers, find ample employment in bringing down and depositing upon the banks of the main stream the productions of the great tributaries.

I can imagine the waking up of the people on the event of the establishment of steamboat navigation on the Amazon. I fancy I can hear the crash of the forest falling to make room for the cultivation of cotton, cocoa, rice, and sugar, and the sharp shriek of the saw, cutting into boards the beautiful and valuable woods of the country; that I can see the gatherers of India-rubber and *copaiba* redoubling their efforts, to be enabled to purchase the new and convenient things that shall be presented at the door of their huts in the wilderness; and even the wild Indian finding the way from his pathless forest to the steamboat depôt to exchange his collections of vanilla, spices, dyes, drugs, and gums, for the things that would take his fancy—ribbons, beads, bells, mirrors, and gay trinkets.

Brazil and Peru have entered into arrangements, and bound themselves by treaty, to appropriate money towards the establishment of steamboat navigation on the Amazon. This is well. It is doing something towards progress; but it is the progress of a denizen of their own forests—the sloth. Were they to follow the example lately set by the republics of the La Plata, and throw open their rivers to the commerce of the world, then the march of improvement would be commensurate with the importance of the act; and these countries would grow in riches and power with the rapidity of the vegetation of their own most fertile lands.

We, more than any other people, are interested in the opening of this navigation. As has been before stated, the trade of this region must pass by our doors, and mingle and exchange with the products of our Mississippi Valley. The greatest boon in the wide world of commerce is in the free navigation of the Amazon, its confluents and neighboring streams. The back-bone of South

America is in sight of the Pacific. The slopes of the continent look east; they are drained into the Atlantic, and their rich productions, in vast variety and profusion, may be emptied into the commercial lap of that ocean by the most majestic of water-courses.

The time will come when the free navigation of the Amazon and other South American rivers will be regarded by the people of this country as second only in importance to the acquisition of Louisiana.

Having traversed that water-shed from its highest ridge to its very caves and gutters, I find my thoughts and reflections overwhelmed with the immensity of this field for enterprise, commercial prosperity, and human happiness.

The Valley of the Amazon and the Valley of the Mississippi are commercial complements of each other—one supplying what the other lacks in the great commercial round. They are sisters which should not be separated. Had I the honor to be mustered among the statesmen of my country, I would risk political fame and life in the attempt to have the commerce of this noble river thrown open to the world.

Chapter X

❧

River Ucayali—Sarayacu—The missionaries—
The Indians of the Ucayali

SEÑOR CAUPER has four or five slaves in his house—blacks,
which he brought from Brazil. This is contrary to the law,
but it is winked at; and I heard the Governor say that he would
like much to have a pair. Mr. Cauper said they would be difficult
to get, and would cost him $500 in money. A slave that is a me-
chanic is worth $500 in Brazil.

The temperature of Nauta is agreeable. The lowest thermometer I observed was 71 degrees at six A.M., and the highest 89 degrees at three P.M. We have had a great deal of cloudy weather and
rain since we have been on the Amazon, and it is now near the commencement of the rainy season at this place. No one suffers from
heat, though this is probably the hottest season of the year; the air
is loaded with moisture, and heavy squalls of wind and rain sweep
over the country almost every day. In the dry months—from the
last of February to the first of September—a constant and heavy
breeze blows nearly all day against the stream of the river. The

river, which is three fourths of a mile wide opposite Nauta, and has an imposing appearance, has risen four feet between the sixteenth and twenty-fifth of September.

The town is situated on a hill, with the forest well cleared away from around it, and is a healthy place. I saw only two cases of sickness during my stay of two weeks. They were acute cases of disease, to which people are liable everywhere. Both patients died, probably for want of medical attention. I gave the man who had the dysentery some doses of calomel and opium (a prescription I had from Lima), but he died with the last dose. Though solicited, I would have nothing to do with the other case. It was a woman, and I had no confidence in my practice. I could only add my mite to a subscription raised by the whites for the benefit of her orphan children.

The Cocamas of Nauta are great fishermen and boatmen, and I think are bolder than most of the civilized tribes on the river. They make incursions, now and then, into the country of the Mayorunas—savages who inhabit the right banks of the Ucayali and Amazon—fight battles with them, and bring home prisoners, generally children. When travelling in small numbers, or engaged in their ordinary avocations on the river, they studiously avoid the country of their enemies, who retaliate whenever opportunity offers.

These Indians are jealous, and punish conjugal infidelity with severity, and also departure from the laws of chastity on the part of the unmarried female.

Arebalo thinks that the population of the Missions is increasing and found by the census, taken carefully last year by himself, that the number of women exceeded that of the men by more than one thousand.

A boat came in from above on the eighteenth, and reported the loss of another belonging to Enrique, one of the traders we had met at Laguna. She was loaded with salt and cotton cloth, and, in passing the mouth of Tigre Yacu in the night, struck upon a "saw-yer," capsized, and went down. A boy was drowned. Some would have envied the low, soft, sad tones and eloquent gestures, expressive of pity and horror, with which an Indian told us the disastrous story.

SEPTEMBER 30—We paid twelve rowers and a *popero,* and set them to work to fit up our boat with decks and coverings. I had purchased this boat from Mr. Cauper for $60, the price he paid for it when it was new. Most persons on the river held up their hands when I told them what I had paid for it; but I thought it was cheap, especially as I was obliged to have it on any terms. He had it repaired and calked for us.

The boat is thirty feet long, seven wide in its widest part, and three deep. The after-part is decked for about ten feet in length with the bark of a palm-tree, which is stripped from the trunk and flattened out by force. The deck is covered over by small poles, bent in hoop-fashion over it, and well thatched with palm-leaves, making quite a snug little cabin. The pilot stands or sits on this roof to direct and steer, and sleeps upon it at night, to the manifest danger of rolling off. About twelve feet of the middle of the boat is covered and decked in like manner, but the covering is lower and narrower, giving room for the rowers to sit on each side of it to paddle. Most of the cargo is stowed under the decks, thus leaving a cabin for both Ijurra and myself. There is a space between the two coverings which is not decked over that gives a chance for bailing the boat when she takes in water; and a sufficient space is left in the bow on which to place a large earthen vessel to make a fire in.

I bought from Señor Cauper some Portuguese axes, some small fish-hooks (called by the Indians *mishqui*), and some white beads, which are most coveted by the savages of the Ucayali.

SEPTEMBER 25—Having engaged a servant, a Tarapotino, named Lopez, and embarked our luggage and provisions, I hoisted a small American flag, given me from the frigate *Raritan,* and got under way for the Ucayali. We started with ten *peons,* but were joined by two others in a skiff next morning. In fifty-five minutes we arrived at the mouth of the Ucayali. It is a beautiful stream, with low, shelving green banks at its mouth. But I was disappointed in its size; it was not more than half as wide as the Amazon. It is the longest known tributary above Brazil, and is therefore called by some the main trunk of the Amazon. We poled and paddled slowly up the left bank for four and a half miles, and stopped at a bluff where there were one or two huts of Nauta people. Threatening rain, we attempted to sleep in the boat, but our *musquito* curtains not being properly prepared, we passed a wretched night.

SEPTEMBER 26—Taking advantage of the eddies and still water near the shore, we paddled and poled along at about the rate of a mile and a half per hour. Our men work well. They commence paddling with a strong, slow stroke, of about fifteen or twenty to the minute, and gradually quicken them till they get to be half-second strokes. They keep this up for about half an hour, when, at a shout from the bowman, they toss their paddles in the air, change sides, and commence the slow stroke again. They, however, prefer poling to padding, and will always make for a beach, when they can use their poles, which they do in a lazy, inefficient manner.

The shores of the river to-day, on the left bank, are abrupt, and about ten or fifteen feet high. They are of a light, loose earth, that is continually caving in by the action of the current, and carrying trees into the stream. On the other side the shores are low, green, and shelving. I think they are the shores of low, narrow islands. The trees are not very thick, and the country is more open than on the banks of the Huallaga. After breakfast we pulled nearly to the middle of the river, and, anchoring in thirty-three feet of water, we found the current to be a mile and three quarters the hour. We passed the mouth of a small stream called Chingana, up which there is a settlement of the Mayorunas. Our men are much afraid of this people, and always sleep on the left bank so long as they are in their country. All the *peons* on this river have their *musquito* curtains painted black, so that the Mayorunas may not see them in the night. The mode of attack of these savages is to wait till the travellers have fallen asleep, and then rush upon the *musquito* nets and plunge in their lances. None of the Indians that I have travelled with seem to have any idea of the propriety of posting a sentinel.

At noon the river, which has been from its mouth less than a quarter of a mile wide, spreads out, and is divided by islands. We anchored in twelve feet of water, sixty yards from the shore, and slept without *musquito* netting. It was windy, and these troublesome insects did not come off. Rain nearly all night.

SEPTEMBER 27—Two of our turtles died yesterday, and the Indians are eating them to-day. Ijurra suspects that they killed them by putting tobacco in their mouths, knowing that we would not eat them, and that they consequently would get them. But Ijurra is of a suspicious nature, especially where Indians are concerned, whom he thinks to be the vilest and most worthless of mankind. We found the current to-day to be two miles the hour. A fish about two feet long, and sharp-built, like a dolphin, jumped into the boat. It had two curved and very sharp teeth, like those of a squirrel, or the fangs of a serpent, in the lower jaw. It made us a very good mess. The river to-day is much divided by islands, the passages from one hundred to 150 yards wide. When running between the main shore, the river is about a quarter of a mile wide.

SEPTEMBER 30—Passed the mouth of an arm of the river, which is said to leave the main river many miles above, and make the large island of Paynaco. It is navigable for canoes in the wet season; but, on account of its windings, it takes nearly as long to pass it as it does to pass the main river, and it is seldom navigated. We see many cranes and *huananas* (the Egyptian goose before described), but no animals except flesh-colored porpoises, of which there are a great many. Occasionally we hear *cotomonos,* or howling monkeys, in the woods. Dull work ascending the river; anchored near low sand islands with abrupt banks, which were continually tumbling into the stream.

OCTOBER 1—After daylight we landed and shot at *cotomonos.* One is not aware of the great height of the trees until he attempts to shoot a monkey or a bird out of the topmost branches. He is then surprised to find that the object is entirely out of reach of his fowling piece, and that only a rifle will reach it. The trees throughout this country grow with great rapidity, and, being in a light, thin soil, with a sub-stratum of sand, the roots are superficial, and the trees are continually falling down. Nature seems to have made a provision for their support, for, instead of coming down round to the ground, the trunk, about ten feet above it, divides into thick, wide tablets, which, widening as they come down, stand out like buttresses for the support of the tree; but even with this provision no day passes that we do not hear the crashing fall of some giant of the forest. Re-stowed the boat, and repaired Ijurra's palace, making it narrower and higher.

OCTOBER 3—Many *huananas,* with their broods, upon the river. Shot a large brown bird called *chansu* (*cigana* in Brazil); it has a crest, erectile at pleasure, and looks like a pheasant. Large flocks frequent the cane on the banks of the river; they have a very game look, and are attractive to the sportsman, but the Indians call them a foul bird, and do not eat them; the crop of this was filled with green herbage.

OCTOBER 4—Clear all night, with heavy dew. The anchor, which is a sixty-four-pound weight, had sunk so deep in the thick dark sand of the bottom as to require the united exertions of all hands to get it. Met three canoes going down loaded with sarsaparilla; bought some *yuccas* and plantains at a settlement of five families of Conibos, on the left bank of the river. Got also specimens of the black wax of the country. The black wax is the production of a small bee very little larger than an ant, which builds its house in the ground. The white wax is deposited in the branches of a small tree, which are hollow, and divided into compartments like the joints of a cane. The wood is sufficiently soft to be perforated by the bee; the tree is called *cetica,* and looks, though larger, like our alder bush.

OCTOBER 7—River half a mile wide and rising fast. Trunks of trees begin to come down. Stopped at a settlement called Guanache. I saw only two houses, with four or five men and women; they said that the others were away gathering sarsaparilla. These people cannot count, and can never get from them any accurate idea of numbers. They are very little removed above the "beasts that perish." They are filthy, and covered with the sores and scars of *sarna*. The houses were very large, measuring between thirty and forty feet of length, and ten or fifteen in breadth. They consist of immense roofs of small poles and cane, thatched with palm, and supported by short stakes four feet high and three inches in diameter, planted in the ground three or four feet apart, and having the spaces, except between two in front, filled in with cane. Many persons "pig" together in one of these houses.

OCTOBER 9—Stopped at the village of Sta. Maria, a Pirros settlement, on the left bank, of 150 souls. The *curaca,* who seemed a more rational and respectable being than the rest, told me that there were thirty-three Matrimonios. These Indians ascend the Ucayali in their canoes to a point not very far from Cuzco, where they go to exchange rare birds and animals for beads, fish-hooks, and the little silver ornaments which they wear in their noses. They bury their dead in his canoe under the floor of his house. The *curaca* said that the Conibos buried the personal effects of the deceased with him, differing in this from his people, the Pirros. Their language is also different, but in all other things they are as like as peas. They have no idea of a future state, and worship nothing. In fact, I think they have no ideas at all, although they can make a bow or a canoe, and take a fish; and their women can weave a coarse cloth from cotton, and dye it. They asked us if we had not in our boxes some great and infectious disease, which we could take up and let loose among their enemies, the Cashibos of the Pichitea.

There were two Moyobambinos domiciliated in the village, purchasing salt fish from the Indians. One of them told me that an Indian would furnish eighty pieces of salt fish for eight yards of *tocuyo;* this man may have "let the cat out of the bag," and showed me how they cheat the Indians. A yard of *tocuyo* is the general price of three pieces. A fish called *payshi,* which is the fish ordinarily salted, was brought in and cut up whilst we were here. It is a powerful fish, about six feet long and one and one fourth in diameter. The head is fourteen inches long, with short jaws and rather small mouth. The tongue, when dried, is as hard as bone, and is commonally used as a rasp. The scales of the belly and tail are bordered with a bright red streak, which makes the fish appear to be nearly encircled with a number of scarlet rings, and gives it a very pretty appearance.

Two hours after leaving Sta. Maria we arrived at a beach where there was an establishment of Señor Cauper's for salting fish. These establishments are called *factorias*. Twenty-five Indians collect and salt four thousand pieces of fish in six weeks.

The Indians on this river have in their houses cotton, maize, ground peas (*mani*), sweet potatoes, *yuccas,* plantains, fowls and fish, bows and arrows, lances, clubs, paddles, and pretty baskets made of cane. The women weave their own clothes, and those of their husbands, and manage to paint figures and devices on the cotton after it is woven. The Pirros and Conibos seem taller than they really are, on account of their costume, which is a long cotton gown. I have seen a fellow in one of these gowns, slowly striding over a beach, look, at a distance, like a Roman patrician in his toga.

OCTOBER 10—Met a Conibo, with his wife and two children, on the beach. This man was evidently the dandy of his tribe. He was painted with a broad stripe of red under each eye; three narrow stripes of blue were carried from one ear, across the upper lip, to the other—the two lower stripes plain, and the upper one bordered with figures. The whole of the lower jaw and chin were painted with a blue chain-work of figures, something resembling Chinese figures. Around his neck was a broad tight necklace of black and white beads, with a breastplate of the same hanging from it, and partly concealed by the long gown, or *cushma*. His wrists were also adorned with wide bracelets of white beads, and above these a bracelet of lizard skins, set round with monkeys' teeth. He wore a little silver shield hanging from his nose, and a narrow, thin plate of silver, shaped like a paddle, two and a half inches long, thrust through a hole in the lower lip, and hanging on the chin. He had been to Cuzco, where he got his silver ornaments, and said it was a journey of four moons. We anchored in thirty-six feet water, and found a current of three miles the hour. Calm, clear night; much dew.

OCTOBER 11—Stopped to breakfast on a beach on the left bank, back of which, on the firm land, were two houses of Remos Indians. There were twenty-two of them—men, women, and children—with three men of the Shipebos tribe. There seemed to be no uniformity in their paint, each one consulting his own taste; though there was one man and a woman, whom I understood to be man and wife, painted exactly alike. The Remos were low and small; the Shipebos taller. They were dressed in the common costume of the Ucayali (the *cushma*), and had their hair cut straight across the forehead, just above the eyes, so as to show the face, set, as it were, in a frame of hair. They are all filthy, and some have *sarna*. As far as I have observed, more women have this disease than men. Passed more huts afterwards, and some Indians seeking the young of the turtle on a beach. These people eat anything. I have known them to eat the eggs of the turtle with the young in them, and also turtle that had died a natural death and had become offensive.

OCTOBER 13—Stopped at a little settlement of Shipebos on the right bank—twenty-five all told. Met three negroes, with a crew of Conibos, who had been up the river for sarsaparilla. They gathered the principal part of what they had (about sixty *arrobas*) in the Aguaytia, but had been five days up the Pachitea, and six up the Ucayali, above the Pachitea. They say that the Cashibos of that river would come to the beach in hostile attitude; but when they found that the strangers were not Indians of the Ucayali, but wore trousers and had guns, they fled.

Passed two houses of Conibos, about fifteen in number. One of them, taking us for padres, insisted that Ijurra should baptize his child, which was accordingly done. He gave it the name of the officiating priest, writing it on a bit of paper and giving it to the mother, who put it away carefully. I believe my companion was upbraided by the priest at Sarayacu for doing so. The head of the infant had been bound in boards, front and rear, and was flattened and increased in height. I do not observe that the heads of the adults bear any trace of this custom.

OCTOBER 15—Arrived at the village of Tierra Blanca, belonging to the Mission, having passed yesterday several settlements of the Indians, and seen for the first time the hills in the neighborhood of Sarayacu. It is a clean little town, of two hundred inhabitants, situated on an eminence on the left bank about twenty-five feet above the present level of the river. In the full the water approaches within a few feet of the lower houses.

A priest from Sarayacu has charge of the spiritual and pretty much of the temporal concerns of the village. He is here at this time celebrating some feast, and is the only white man present. The Indians, as usual at a feast time, were nearly all drunk, and made my men drunk also. When I wished to start, I sent Ijurra to a large house where they were drinking to bring our people to the boat; he soon came back, foaming with rage, and demanded a gun, that he might bring them to obedience; I soothed him, however, and went up to the house, where, by taking a drink with them, and practising the arts that I have often practised before in getting off to the ship refractory sailors who were drinking on shore, I succeeded in getting off a sufficient number of them to work the boat, and shoved off with as drunken a boat's crew as one could desire, leaving the small boat for the others to follow; this they are sure to

do when they find that their clothes and bedding have been taken away. The Padre said that if Ijurra had shot one, they would have murdered us all, but I doubt that, for we were well armed, and the Indians are afraid of guns.

OCTOBER 16—Started at six A.M.; stopped at half past five opposite the mouth of the Catalina. It seemed thirty yards wide, and had a small island in front.

The ascent of the river is very tedious; we barely creep along against the force of the current, and day after day "wearies by" in the most monotonous routine. I frequently land, and with gun on shoulder, and clad only in shirt and drawers, walk for miles along the beaches. My greatest pleasure is to watch the boat struggling up against the tide. This is always accompanied with emotions of pride, mingled with a curious and scarcely definable feeling of surprise. It was almost startling to see, at her mast-head, the beautiful and well-beloved flag of my country dancing merrily in the breeze on the waters of the strange river, and waving above the heads of the swarthy and grim figures below. I felt a proud affection for it; I had carried it where it had never been before; there was a bond between us, we were alone in a strange land, and it and I were brothers in the wilderness.

OCTOBER 18—At eleven A.M. we entered the Caño of Sarayacu; at this season this is not more than fifteen or eighteen feet wide, and nearly covered with a tall grass something like broom-corn, or a small species of cane. It soon contracts so as scarcely to allow room for my boat to pass, and becomes shallow and obstructed with the branches of small trees. We could not get our boat nearer than within a quarter of a mile of the town, so we took small canoes from the bank, and carried up our equipage in them. We were hospitably received by the padres, and lodgings were given us in the *convento,* a large house with several rooms in it.

We found Sarayacu a rather neat-looking Indian village, of about one thousand inhabitants, including Belen, a small town of 150 inhabitants, one and a half mile distant. The missionary station—including the towns of Sta. Catalina and Tierra Blanca—is governed by four Franciscan friars.

Father Calvo, meek and humble in personal concerns, yet full of zeal and spirit for his office, clad in his long serge gown, belted with a cord, with bare feet and accurate tonsure, habitual stoop, and generally bearing upon his shoulder a beautiful and saucy bird of the parrot kind, called *chiriclis,* was my beau ideal of a missionary monk. He is an Arragonese, and had served as a priest in the army of Don Carlos. Bregati is a young and handsome Italian, whom Father Calvo sometimes calls St. John. Lorente was a tall, grave, and cold-looking Catalan. A lay-brother named Maquin, who did the cooking, and who was unwearied in his attentions to us, made up the establishment. I was sick here, and think that I shall ever remember with gratitude the affectionate kindness of these pious and devoted friars of St. Francis.

The town is situated on a level plain elevated one hundred feet above the rivulet of the same name, which empties into the Ucayali at three miles distant.

The climate of Sarayacu is delightful; the average temperature of the day is 79; the nights are sufficiently cool to allow one to sleep with comfort under a *musquito* curtain made of gingham. These insects are less troublesome here than might be expected, which may be seen from the fact that the priests are able to live without wearing stockings; but it is a continual penance, quite equal, I should think, to self-flagellation once a week.

The fathers extract about three hundred *arrobas* of sarsaparilla, from the small streams above, and sell it to Señor Cauper in Nauta. This gives them a profit of about $500. The College at Ocopa allows them a dollar for every mass said or sung. The four padres are able to perform about seven hundred annually (those for Sundays and feast-days are not paid for). This income of $1,200 is appropriated to the repairs of the churches and *conventos,* church furniture, the vestments of the priests, their table and chamber furniture, and some little luxuries—such as sugar, flour, vinegar, &c., bought of the Portuguese below.

Each padre has two Mitayos, appointed monthly—one a hunter, the other a fisherman—to supply his table with the products of the forest and the river. The Fiscales cultivate him a small farm for his *yuccas* and plantains, and he himself raises poultry and eggs; they also make him rum from the sugar-cane, of which he needs a large supply to give to the constables, the Fiscales, and the Mitayos.

The government is paternal. The Indians recognise in the padre the power to appoint and remove *curacas,* captains, and other officers, to inflict stripes, and to confine in the stocks. They obey the priest's orders readily, and seem tractable and docile. They take advantage, however, of Father Calvo's good nature, and are sometimes a little insolent. On an occasion of this kind, my friend Ijurra, who is always an advocate of strong measures, and says that in the government of the Indians there is nothing like the *santo palo* (sacred cudgel), asked Father Calvo why he did not put the impudent rascal in the stocks. But the good Father replied that he did not like to do it—that it was cruel, and hurt the poor fellow's legs.

The Indians here, as elsewhere, are drunken and lazy. The women do most of the work, carry most of the burdens to and from the *chacras* and canoes, make the *masato,* and the earthen vessels out of which it is drunk, spin the cotton and weave the cloth, cook and take care of the children. And their reward is to be maltreated by their husbands, and, in their drunken frolics, to be cruelly beaten, and sometimes badly wounded.

The town is very healthy, there being no endemics, but only acute attacks from great exposure or imprudence in eating and drinking. From the parish register it appears that in the year 1850 there were ten marriages, sixty-two births, and twenty-four deaths. This appears, from an examination of the other years, to be a pretty fair average, yet the population is constantly decreasing. Father Calvo attributes this to desertion. He says that many go down the Amazon with passengers and cargoes, and, finding the return difficult, they either settle in the villages upon the river or join the Ticumas, or other Infidel tribes, and never come back.

The Spaniards, from the Huallaga, also frequently buy the young Indians from their parents, and carry them off for domestic services at home. Father Calvo spoke with great indignation of this custom and said if he could catch any person stealing his people he would hang him in the plaza. Our servant Lopez desired me to advance him nine hatchets, for the purpose of buying a young Indian which his father wished to sell. But I told Lopez of Father Calvo's sentiments on the subject, and refused him. Two boys, however, put off in a canoe the day before we did on our return, and joined us below Tierra Blanca. I did not clearly understand who they were, or I should have sent them back. I fear that many of those that came down with me did not get back for years, if at all, though I did all I could to send them back.

Thus Sarayacu is becoming depopulated in spite of the paternal kindness and mild government of Father Calvo. My own impression as to the reason of their desertion is not that it is on account of the difficulties of the return, or indifference, or a proclivity to fall back into savage life, but that the missionaries have civilized the Indians in some degree—have taught them the value of property, and awakened in their minds ambition and a desire to improve their condition. For this reason the Indian leaves Sarayacu and goes to Brazil. In Sarayacu there are comparatively none to employ him and pay for his services. In Brazil, the Portuguese *commerciante,* though he maltreats him, and does not give him enough to eat, pays him for his labor. Thus he accumulates, and becomes a man of property and in the course of time possibly returns to his family in possession of a wooden trunk painted blue, with a lock and key to it, and filled with hatchets, knives, beads, fish-hooks, mirrors, &c. He has seen the world, and is an object of envy to his kinsmen and neighbors.

The friars entertained us on Sunday evening with a dance of Indians. These were dressed in frocks and trousers, but had head-dresses made of a bandeau or circlet of short and rich-colored feathers, surmounted with the long tail-feathers of the scarlet macaw. They had strings of dried nut shells around their legs, which made an agreeable jingling in the dance. The half-bent knee, and graceful wave of the plumed hat towards the priest before the dance commenced, with the regularity of the figure, gave unmistakable evidence of the teaching of the Jesuits, who appear to have neglected nothing, however trivial, that might bind the affections of the proselytes, and gain themselves influence.

The inhabitants of Sarayacu are divided into three distinct tribes, called Panos, Omaguas, and Yameos. They dwell in different parts of the town. Each tribe has its peculiar dialect, but they generally communicate in the Pano language. These last are the whitest and best-looking Indians I have seen.

I was unable to gather much authentic information concerning the Infidels of the Ucayali. The padres had only been in Sarayacu a few years, and had never left their post to travel among the Indians.

The Campas are the most numerous and warlike tribe, and are resolute in forbidding strangers to enter their territory. They inhabit all the upper waters of the Ucayali, and I think it probable that they are the same who, under the name of Chunchos, are so hostile to the whites about Chanchamayo, and on the *haciendas* to the eastward of Cuzco. These are the people who, in 1742, swept away all the Missions of the Cerro de la Sal; and I have very little doubt that they are descendants of the Inca race. From the extent of their territory, one might judge them to be the most numerous body of savages in America, but no estimate can be formed of their numbers, as no one capable of making one ever ventures among them.

The Cashibos, or Callisecas, are found principally on the Pachitea. They also make war upon the invaders or visitors of their territory, but they only venture to attack the Indians who visit their river and who often come to make war upon them and carry off their children. They rarely trust themselves within gun-shot of the white man; they are bearded, and are said to be cannibals.

The Sencis occupy the country above Sarayacu, and on the opposite side of the river. They are said by the previous missionary governor to be a numerous, bold, and warlike tribe. He said that some whom he saw at Sarayacu exhibited much interest in his astronomical observations. They had names for some of the fixed stars and planets, two of which struck me as peculiarly appropriate. They called the brilliant Canopus *Noteste,* or thing of the day, and the fiery Mars *Tapa* (forward). I saw some of these people at Sarayacu. They frequently come to the mission to get their children baptized, to which ceremony most of the Indians seem to attach some virtue (as they probably would to any other ceremony), and to purchase the iron implements.

The missionary governor also states that the Sencis are a very industrious people, who cultivate the land in common, and that they kill those who are idle and are indisposed to do their fair share of the work. If this be true, they are very different from the savages of the Ucayali whom I have met with, who are all drones, and who would be rather disposed to kill the industrious than the lazy, if they were disposed to kill at all, which I think they are not.

The Conibos, Shipebos, Setebos, Pirros, Remos, and Amajuacas are the vagabonds of the Ucayali, wandering about from place to place, and settling where they take a fancy. They are great boatmen and fishermen, and are the people employed by the traders to gather sarsaparilla and salt fish, and make oil or lard from the fat of the *vaca marina,* and turtle's eggs. They have settlements on the banks of the river, but many of them live in their canoes, making huts of reeds and palms upon the beaches in bad weather. I could never ascertain that they worshipped anything or had any ideas of a future state. Many have two or three wives; they marry young and have many children, but do not raise more than half of them. They seem docile and tractable, though lazy and faithless. They will not trust the white man, for which they have probably good cause, and the white man would not trust them if he could help it, but the Indian will do nothing unless he is paid in advance.

Finally, the Mayorunas occupy the right bank of the Ucayali, near its mouth, and extend along the southern borders of the Amazon as far as the Yavari. Very little is known of this tribe. They are said to be whiter than the other tribes, to wear their beards, and to go naked. They attack any person who comes into their territory, and our Nauta boatmen were careful not to camp on their side of the river.

When I left Nauta I intended to ascend the Ucayali, if possible, as far as Chanchamayo, and also to examine the Pachitea. On arriving at Sarayacu I consulted Father Calvo on the subject. He at first spoke discouragingly, said that the larger part of the population of his village were away fishing, and that I would have great difficulty in recruiting a sufficient number of men for the expedition; for that Padre Cimini, year before last, with a complement of 150 men, had been beaten back by the Campas when within one day of Jesus Maria, at the confluence of the Pangoa and Perené, and had declared it was folly to attempt it with a less number, and these well armed. Father Calvo also said that, could he raise the men by contributions from Tierra Blanca and Sta. Catalina, he could not possibly furnish provisions for half that number. I told him I was ready to start with twenty-five men: fifteen for my own boat, and ten for a lighter canoe, to act as an advanced guard, and to depend upon the river itself for support; that I had no idea of invading the Infidel country, or forcing a passage, and that the moment I met with resistance, or want of provisions, I would return.

Upon this reasoning the Padre said he would do his best, and sent off expresses to Fathers Bregati and Lorente with instructions to recruit men in Tierra Blanca and Sta. Catalina, and send them, with what provisions could be mustered, to Sarayacu. In the mean time we commenced beating up recruits, and gave orders to make *farinha,* gather *barbasco* for fishing on the route, and distill *aguadiente.*

We found, however, although I offered double pay, that we could not get more than eight men in Sarayacu who were willing to go at this season. Many of the Sarayacu people had been with Father Cimini on his expedition. They said that the current was so strong then, when the river was low, that they were forced to drag the canoes by ropes along the beaches; that now the current was stronger, and the river so full that there were no beaches, and consequently no places for sleeping, or on which to make fires for cooking. In short, they made a thousand excuses for not going, but I think the principal reason was fear of the Campas.

Fathers Bregati and Lorente reported that they could not raise a man, so I saw myself obliged to abandon the expedition upon which I had rather set my heart; for I thought it possible that I might gather great reputation with my Chanchamayo friends by joining them again from below, and showing them that their darling wish (a communication with the Atlantic by the Perené and Ucayali) might be accomplished.

I felt, in turning my boat's head down stream, that the pleasure and excitement of the expedition were passed, that I was done, and had done nothing. I became ill and dispirited, and never fairly recovered the gaiety of temper and elasticity of spirit which had animated me at the start, until I received the congratulations of my friends at home.

Chapter XI

❧

*Upper Ucayali—M. Castelnau—Length of navigation—Loss of
the priest—Departure from Sarayacu—Iquitos—Mouth of the
Napo—San José de los Yaguas—State of Indians of Peru*

I COULD GET ANY number of men for the voyage down, and on
October 28, at ten A.M., we left Sarayacu and dropped down to the
mouth of the *caño,* where we stopped to re-stow and shake things
together. We found the Ucayali a very different-looking stream
from what it was when we left it; it was much higher, with a stronger current, and covered with floating trees. At three P.M. we took
leave of good Father Calvo with much regret and started in company with Father Bregati and with a large canoe that we were
carrying down for the return of our *peons* from Pebas.

I was much pleased with our new men, particularly with our
pilot, old Andres Urquia, a long, hard-weather, Tom Coffin—
looking fellow, whom travel and exposure for many years seemed
to have hardened into a being insensible to fatigue and impervi-
ous to disease. He has navigated the rivers of the country a great
deal and was with Father Cimini when driven back by the
Campas.

We passed the distance from Sarayacu to Nauta in eight days, which had cost us twenty-three in the ascent. The distance from Sarayacu to the mouth by the channel is 270 miles—in a straight line 150. We travelled all one night when near the mouth, but this is dangerous on the Ucayali and Huallaga. The channels on these rivers are frequently obstructed by grounded trees, striking one of which the boat would almost inevitably perish. It is safer on the broader Amazon.

The Ucayali, as far as Sarayacu, averages half a mile of width, twenty feet of depth at its lowest stage, and three miles the hour of current.

The difference between high- and low-water mark is about thirty-five feet. I planted a pole at a settlement called Guanache as I went up on the ninth of October; when I passed it going down on the first of November, I found the river had risen nine feet seven inches. It did not, however, commence its regular and steady rise till the fifteenth of October. A mile inside of the mouth, in the middle of the river, I found seventy-two feet of depth, and two and three-quarter miles current per hour. The bottom of the river is full of sunken trees. I lost two sounding-leads and three axe-heads in the descent. My sounding-line, however, had become very rotten from the dampness of the atmosphere, and did not even stand the strain of the current upon the log-chip, which I also lost.

I had intended to stay at Nauta some days, for I found that so much canoe life was beginning to affect my health, and that I was getting weaker day by day; but Nauta seemed a different place than when I left it. Arebalo, Father Valdivia, and Antonio the Paraguá were gone, and Señor Cauper seemed out of humor, and not glad to see us.

I wished to get a few more *peons,* but there were no authorities, and the Indians were engaged in drinking and dancing. Two of my men, whom I had picked up at a settlement called Santos Guagua, on the Ucayali, deserted, though paid as far as Pebas. I feared to lose more. Collecting the few birds and animals I had left there, I started at half past five P.M. on the fifth of November, having slept in my boat on the night of the fourth for the want of a house, and been nearly devoured by the *musquitoes.*

I left Lopez, the servant, who had only engaged for the Ucayali trip, and two of my Sarayacu people, who were reported to have gone into the woods to gather *chambira,* but who I suspected were drinking with the Cocamas, and did not wish to be found.

We drifted with the current all night. The soundings at the mouth of the Ucayali were forty-two feet. The Amazon looked grand in the moonlight, below the island of Omaguas, where I judged it to be a mile and a half wide.

NOVEMBER 6—Omaguas is situated on a height on the left bank. The number of inhabitants is 232, of the tribes of Omaguas and Panos. They are *peons* and fishermen, cultivate *chacras,* and live in the usual filthy and wretched condition of all these people. I gave some calomel, salts, and spermaceti ointment to the Governor's wife, who was a pitiable object—a mere skeleton, and covered with inveterate-looking sores. I was reminded of Lazarus, or old Job in his misery. I doubt if my remedies were of the proper sort, but her husband and she were anxious to have them, and she will probably die soon at any rate and cannot well be worsted.

Left Omaguas at a quarter past nine. At noon, moderate breeze from the northward and eastward. Thermometer 86 degrees. Most of the men and animals fast asleep. Even the monkeys, except a restless friar (who seems as sleepless as I am), are dozing. The friar gapes and closes his eyes now and then, but at the next instant appears to have discovered something strange or new, and is as wide awake and alert as if he never slept.

There was a great disturbance among the animals this morning. The *Pumagarza,* or tiger crane (from being speckled and colored like the tiger of the country), with a bill as long and sharp as an Infidel's spear, has picked to pieces the head of a delicate sort of turkey-hen. The *diputado* (as we call a white monkey, because Ijurra says he is the image of the worthy deputy in Congress from Chachapoyas) has eaten off the ear of the *maquisapa* (a stupid-looking black monkey) and the tail of another. Some savage unknown, though I strongly suspect my beautiful *chiriclis,* has bitten off the bill of the prettiest paroquet. There was a desperate battle between the friar and the *chiriclis,* in which one lost fur and the other feathers, and symptoms of warfare between a wild pig and a Mexican mongoose. The latter, however, fierce as he generally is, could not stand the gnash of the wild boar's teeth, and prudently "fled the fight." The life of the fowls is a state of continued strife, and nothing has kept the peace except an affectionate and delicate Pinshi monkey (Humboldt's *Midas Leonina*), that sleeps upon my beard, and hunts game in my moustachios.

We encountered two canoes that had come from near Quito by the Napo, and were bound to Tarapoto. They told me that I could reach the mouth of the river Coca, which empties into the Napo, in two and a half months from the mouth but could go no further in my boat for want of water. There are very few christianized towns upon the Napo, and the rowers of these boats were a more savage-looking set than I had seen.

Fearful of going to the right of Iquitos Island, and thus passing the town, I passed to the left of some islands, and in running between the one just above Iquitos Island and the left bank of the river, the boat grounded near the middle of the passage, which was 150 yards broad, and came near rolling over from the velocity of the current. We hauled over to the left bank and passed close along it in forty-two feet of water. At half past nine P.M. we arrived at Iquitos.

NOVEMBER 7—Iquitos is a fishing village of 227 inhabitants, a considerable part of them, to the number of ninety-eight, being whites and Mestizos of San Borja and other settlements of the upper Mission, who were driven from their homes a few years ago by the Huambisas of the Pastaza and Santiago. This occurred in 1841. In 1843, these same Indians murdered all the inhabitants of a village called Sta. Teresa, situated on the upper Marañón, between the mouths of the rivers Santiago and Morona. My companion Ijurra was there soon after the occurrence. He gave the dead bodies burial, and published in his *Travels in Mainas* a detailed account of the affair:

In October 1843, Ijurra, with seventeen other young men of Moyobamba, formed a company for the purpose of washing for gold the sands of the Santiago. They were furnished with arms by the prefecture, and recruited sixty-six Cocamillas of Laguna, armed with bows and arrows, as a light protecting force. They also engaged eighty-five of the Indians of Jeveros as laborers at the washings, and, after they started, were joined by 450 of the people who had been expelled in 1841 from Santiago and Borja, desirous of recovering their homes and taking vengeance of the savages.

The party went by land from Moyobamba to Balza Puerto, thence north to Jeveros, and thence to the port of Barranca, at the mouth of the river Cahuapanas, when they embarked to ascend the Amazon to the mouth of the Santiago. At Barranca they received intelligence of the massacre at Sta. Teresa with the details.

A Moyobambino, fearing that the company would get all the gold, and that he should not be able to collect a little that was due him by the people about Sta. Teresa, hastened on before. He met at Sta. Teresa with a large party of Huambisas, who had come down the Santiago for the ostensible purpose of trade. Conversing with the *curaca* of the tribe, the Moyobambino told him that a multitude of Christians were coming with arms in their hands to conquer and enslave his people. The *curaca* asked the Moyobambino what he had in his packages. The reply was more foolish and wicked than the other speech, for, desirous to play upon the credulity of the Indian, or to overawe him, he said that he had in his packages a great many epidemic diseases, with which he could kill the whole tribe of the Huambisas. It was his death warrant. The *curaca* plunged his spear into his body, and giving a shrill whistle, his people, who were scattered about among the houses, commenced the massacre. They killed forty-seven men, and carried off sixty women; some few persons escaped into the woods. The Indians spared two boys—one of seven and one of nine years—and set them adrift upon the Amazon on a raft, with a message to the gold-hunting company that they knew of their approach, and were ready, with the assistance of their friends, the Paturos and Chinganos, to meet and dispute with them the possession of the country. The raft was seen floating past Barranca and brought in.

The gold-seekers found no gold upon the borders of the Marañón, quarrelled, became afraid of the savages, broke up and abandoned their purpose before they reached the mouth of the Santiago.

Ijurra and a few others then turned their attention to the collection of Peruvian bark. They spent two or three years in the woods, about the mouth of the Huallaga, gathered an enormous quantity, and floated it down to Pará on immense rafts that Ijurra describes as floating-houses, with all the comforts and conveniences of the house on shore. When they arrived at Pará the cargo was examined by chymists, said by them to be good, and a mercantile house offered $80,000 for it. They refused the offer, chartered a vessel, and took the cargo to Liverpool, where the chymist pronounced the fruit of years of labor to be utterly worthless.

We left Iquitos at half past nine A.M. The shores of the river just below are bold, and of white clay. At a quarter to eleven we passed the mouth of the Nanay, about 150 yards broad. The depth of the Amazon at the junction of the two rivers is fifty feet. At half past five we arrived at Pucallpa, where we passed the night.

NOVEMBER 8—Pucallpa, or New Oran, is a small settlement, of twenty houses, and 111 inhabitants, who formerly belonged to Oran, but who, finding their situation uncomfortable, removed and settled here. It is one of the most pleasantly situated places I have seen—on a moderate eminence, with green banks shelving to the river. The water is bold (twenty-five to thirty feet deep) close to the shore. Two islands—one above and one below the town, with a narrow opening in front—gave the place the appearance of a snug little harbor. We bought at this place two of the great cranes of the river, called Tuyuyú. These were gray.

NOVEMBER 9—We started at five, and arrived at Pebas at ten A.M. We found that the people of Pebas, under the direction of Father Valdivia (my Nauta friend), were establishing a new town about a quarter of a mile up a stream called Ambiyacu, which enters into the Amazon two miles above Pebas. We pulled up this stream, and found the good priest and the Governor General Arebalo busy in directing the felling of trees and building of houses. I determined to stay here for some time, for I was now getting so weak that I could scarcely climb the banks upon which the towns are situated. Father Valdivia received us with great cordiality, and gave us quarters in a new house he was building for himself.

The new settlement had not yet a name; Ijurra wished it called Echenique, after the new president, while I insisted on Ambiyacu, as being Indian and sonorous. The population already numbered 328—almost all the people of Pebas having come over. The inhabitants are principally *Oregones,* or Big Ears, from the custom of introducing a bit of wood into a slit in the ear and gradually increasing the size of it until the lobe hangs upon the shoulder. They have, however, now discontinued the custom, and I saw only a few old people thus deformed.

They are fishermen, and serve as *peons,* but their condition seems better than that of the inhabitants of the other towns on the river, which is doubtless owing to the presence and exertions of the good priest, who is very active and intelligent.

Visited Pebas in the afternoon. We found it nearly abandoned and overgrown with grass and weeds. We saw some cattle roving about, which were fat, and otherwise in good condition. The town is situated immediately on the banks of the river, which is here unbroken by islands, three quarters of a mile broad, and apparently deep and rapid. We carried over to the new town specimens of black clay slate that crops out in narrow veins on the banks and made a fire of it, which burned all night with a strong bituminous smell.

NOVEMBER 10—I gave Arebalo the message sent him by Padre Calvo, which was a request that the Sarayacu men be sent back in the larger canoe that we had brought down for that purpose. However, two of them went up the river with a trader and one down.

The others started back in the canoe, but much to my surprise, and even regret, I found in the evening that they had returned, turned over their canoe, sold their pots and other utensils, and expressed their determination to go down the stream. They said that if I would not take them they would go with anybody that would. I of course was glad to have them, and I quieted my conscience in thus robbing Father Calvo by the reflection that if they went with me to the end of my voyage, I could give them my boat and fit them out for the return; whereas, if they separated, they might never go back. I think that Arebalo winked at their conduct in returning, because he and the padre were busy with their new town, and did not wish to furnish me with men of their own. But I think we are all culpable. The *peons* were culpable for not going back; I was culpable for taking them further, and Arebalo was culpable for permitting it; and thus it is that the population of Sarayacu diminishes, and the friars are cheated out of the hard earned fruits of their labor.

NOVEMBER 15—Ijurra and I went with the Padre to visit his mission of San José of the Yaguas. This is a settlement of Yaguas Indians, of 260 inhabitants, about ten miles in a northeast direction from Ambiyacu, or Echenique.

San José is reached by a path through the woods over a rather broken country. There were two or three rivulets to pass on the road, which have pebbly beds, with black slate rock cropping out of the sides of the ravine—the first stones I have seen since leaving the Pongo of Chasuta. The soil is dark clay and deeper than I have seen it elsewhere on the river. Birds of a brilliant plumage occasionally flitted across our path, and the woods were fragrant with aromatic odors.

The Yaguas received their priest in procession, with ringing of the church bell and music of drums. They conducted him, under little arches of palm branches stuck in the path, to the *convento,* and politely left us to rest after the fatigue of the walk. These are the most thorough-looking savages in their general appearance and costume, though without anything savage in the expression of their countenances, which is vacant and stupid. Their ordinary dress consists of a girdle of bark around the loins, with a bunch of fibres of another kind of bark, looking like a swab or mop, about a foot in length, hanging down from the girdle in front and rear. Similar, but smaller bunches, are hung around the neck and arms by a collar and bracelets of small beads. This is the every-day costume. On festivals they stain all their bodies a light brown, and on this ground they execute fantastic devices in red and blue. Long tail-feathers of the macaw are stuck in the armlets, reaching above the shoulders, and a chaplet, made of white feathers from the wings of a smaller bird, is worn around the head. This generally completes the costume, though I did see one dandy who had stuck short white feathers all over his face, leaving only the eyes, nose, and mouth exposed.

The *curaca,* and some one or two of the Varayos, wore frocks and trousers, but I was told they had the national costume underneath these. The dress of the women is a yard or two of cotton cloth rolled around the hips. They are strong people for drinking and dancing, and hate work.

Their houses are peculiar. Very long, slender poles are stuck in the ground opposite each other, and about thirty feet apart; their ends are brought together at the top, forming a Gothic arch about twenty feet high. Similar poles, of different lengths, are planted in front of the openings of the arch, and their ends are brought down and lashed to the top and sides of the openings. They are secured by cross-poles, inside and out, and the whole is thickly thatched to the ground, leaving two or three apertures for entrance. The house looks, on the outside, like a gigantic bee-hive. On the inside, small cabins of cane are built at intervals around the walls, each one of which is the sleeping-room of a family. Four or five families generally occupy one house, and the middle space is used in common. This is never cleaned, nor even levelled, and is littered with all manner of abominations. There is a puddle of water before each door, for, from the construction of the house, the rain, both from the heavens and the roof, pours directly into it.

After evening service, the Indians went off to their houses to commence the festival. They kept the drums going all night, and until ten o'clock next morning, when they came in a body to conduct us to mass. Most of them were the worse for their night's debauch, and sat upon the ground in a listless and stupid manner, occasionally talking and laughing with each other, and little edified, I fear, by the sacred ceremony.

I was annoyed at the poverty of the church, and determined, if I ever went back, that I would appeal to the Roman Catholics of the United States for donations. The priestly vestments were in rags. The lavatory was a gourd, a little earthern pitcher, and a jack towel of cotton; and it grieved me to see the host taken from a shaving box, and the sanctified wine poured from a vinegar cruet.

After mass, and a procession, the Indians went back with us to the *convento,* and entertained us with music whilst we breakfasted. It was well that the drums were small, or we should have been fairly deafened. There were six of them, and they were beaten without intermission. One fellow dropt to sleep, but we gained nothing by this, for his neighbor beat his drum for him. Nearly the whole male population were crowded into the *convento.* The breakfast was furnished by the Indians, each family contributing a dish. The old women were proud of their dishes, and seemed gratified when we partook of and commended them. They continued their frolic all day and night.

On Monday we visited the houses of the Indians to see what curiosities we could get. We found the men stretched in their hammocks, sleeping off the effects of the *masato,* and the patient, much-enduring women at work twisting *chambira* for hammocks, or preparing *yuccas* or plantains to make drink for their lords. We could get nothing except a hammock or two, and some twisted *chambira* to make me a lead line. The Indians had hidden their hammocks, and we had to go poking about with our sticks, and searching in corners for them. The reason of this was that most of them owe the Padre, and this paying of debts seems as distasteful to the savage man as to the civilized.

The only article of manufacture is a coarse hammock made of the fibres of the budding top of a species of palm, called *chambira.* The tree is very hard, and is defended with long sharp thorns, so that it is a labor of a day to cut a *cogollo,* or top, split the leaves into strips of convenient breadth, and strip off the fibres, which are the outer covering of the leaves, and which is done very dexterously with the finger and thumb. A top, of ordinary size, yields about half a pound of fibres, and when it is reflected that these fibres have to be twisted, a portion of them dyed, and then woven into hammocks of three or four pounds' weight, it will be seen that the Indian is very poorly paid for his labor when he receives for a hammock twelve and a half cents in silver, or twenty-five cents in *efectos.*

The women twist the thread with great dexterity. They sit on the ground, and, taking two threads, which consist of a number of minute fibres, between the finger and thumb of the left hand, they lay them, separated a little, on the right thigh. A roll of them down the thigh, under the right hand, twists each thread, when, with a scarcely perceptible motion of the hand, she brings the two together, and a roll up the thigh makes the cord. A woman will twist fifty fathoms about the size of a common twine in a day.

The Indians brought me some few birds, but they were too drunken and lazy to go out into the forest to hunt rare birds, and only brought me those that they could shoot about their houses.

The climate of San José is very agreeable. It seems drier and more salubrious than that of Pebas and there are fewer *musquitoes*. The atmosphere was very clear for the two nights I spent there, and I thought I could see the smaller stars with more distinctness than I had seen them for a long time.

The history of the settlement of this place is remarkable, showing the attachment of the Indians to their pastor and their church. Some years ago, Padre Jose de la Rosa Alva had established a mission at a settlement of the Yaguas, about two days' journey to the northward and eastward of the present station, which he called Sta. Maria, and where he generally resided. Business took him to Pebas, and unexpectedly detained him there for fifteen days. The Indians, finding he did not return, reasoned with themselves and said, "Our father has left us; let us go to him." Whereupon they gathered together the personal property the priest had left; shouldered the church utensils and furniture, even to the doors; set fire to their houses, and joined the Padre in Pebas. He directed them to the present station, where they built houses and established themselves.

Our little Padre has also considerable influence over them; though, when he will not accede to all their demands, they contrast his conduct with that of Father Rosa, call him mean, get sulky, and won't go to mass.

It is sad to see the condition of the Peruvian Indians. (That of the Indians of Brazil is worse.) They make no progress in civilization, and they are taught nothing. The generally good, hard-working, and well-meaning padres, who alone attempt anything like improvement, seem contented to teach them obedience to the church, observance of its ceremonies, and to repeat the *doctrina* like a parrot, without having the least idea of what is meant to be conveyed. The priests, however, say that the fault is in the Indian—that he cannot understand. Padre Lorente, of Tierra Blanca, thought he had his flock a little advanced, and that now he might make some slight appeal to their understanding. He accordingly gathered them together, and exhibiting a little plaster image of the Virgin that they had not yet seen, he endeavored to explain to them that this figure represented the Mother of God, whom he had taught them to worship and pray to, that She was the most exalted of human beings, and that through Her intercession with Her Son, the sins and crimes of men might be forgiven, &c. The Indians paid great attention, passing the image from hand to hand, and the good Father thought that he was making an impression, but an unlucky expression of one of them showed that their attention was entirely occupied with the image, and that the lesson was lost upon them. He stopped the priest in his discourse, to know if the image were a man or a woman. The friar gave it up in despair, and fell back upon the sense-striking ceremonial of the church, which I think (humanly speaking) is far better calculated to win them to respect and obedience, and thus advance them in civilization, than any other system of religious teaching.

The mind of the Indian is exactly like that of the infant, and it must grow rather by example than by precept. I think that good example, with a wholesome degree of discipline, might do much with this docile people; though there are not wanting intelligent men, well acquainted with their character, who scruple not to say that the best use to which an Indian can be put is to hang him, that he makes a bad citizen and a worse slave, and (to use a homely phrase) "that his room is more worth than his company." I myself believe—and I think the case of the Indians in my own country bears me out in the belief—that any attempt to communicate with them ends in their destruction. They cannot bear the restraints of law or the burden of sustained toil, and they retreat from before the face of the white man, with his improvements, till they disappear. This seems to be destiny. Civilization must advance, though it tread on the neck of the savage, or even trample him out of existence.

I think that in this case the government of Peru should take the matter in hand—that it should draw up a simple code of laws for the government of the Missions, appoint intelligent governors to the districts with salaries paid from the treasury of the country suppress the smaller villages and gather the Indians into fewer, appoint a governor-general of high character with dictatorial powers and large salary, tax the inhabitants for the support of a military force of two thousand men to be placed at his disposal, and throw open the country to colonization, inducing people to come by privileges and grants of land. I am satisfied that in this way, if the Indian be not improved, he will at least be cast out, and that this glorious country may be made to do what it is not now doing—that is, contribute its fair proportion to the maintenance of the human race.

NOVEMBER 18—Returned to Echenique; the walk occupied three hours without stopping. Although the Orejones have left off some of their savage customs and are becoming more civilized, they are still sufficiently barbarous to permit their women to do most of the work. I saw to-day twenty of the lazy rascals loitering about, whilst the same number of women were fetching earth and water, trampling it into mud, and plastering the walls of the *convento* with it. I also saw the women cleaning up and carrying away the weeds and bushes of the town, most of them, too, with infants hanging to their backs. These marry very young. I saw some, whom I took to be children, with babies that I was told were their own. They suffer very little in parturition, and, in a few hours after the birth of a child, they bathe, go to the *chacra,* and fetch home a load of *yuccas.*

The *musquitoes* are very troublesome here. I write my journal under a *musquito* curtain, and whilst I am engaged in skinning birds, it is necessary to have an Indian with a fan to keep them off; even this does not succeed, and my face and hands are frequently quite bloody, where he has to kill them with his fingers. The Indians bring me a number of very beautiful birds every evening, and I have my hands full, even with the occasional assistance of Arebalo and the Padre's servant. I do not know if it arises from the constant tugging at the birds' skins, or the slovenly use of arsenical soap, but the blood gathered under nearly all the nails of my left hand, and they were quite painful.

We have increased our stock of animals largely at this place. They now number thirteen monkeys, a mongoose, and a wild pig (the Mexican peccary), with thirty-one birds, and one hundred skins. I bought a young monkey off an Indian woman to-day. It had coarse gray and white hair, and that on the top of its head was stiff, like the quills of the porcupine, and smoothed down in front as if it had been combed. I offered the little fellow some plantain, but finding he would not eat, the woman took him and put him to her breast, when he sucked away manfully and with great "gusto." She weaned him in a week so that he would eat plantain mashed up and put into his mouth in small bits, but the little beast died of mortification, because I would not let him sleep with his arms around my neck.

I had two little monkeys not so large as rats; the peccary ate one, and the other died of grief. My howling monkey refused food and grunted himself to death. The friars ate their own tails off and died of the rot. The mongoose, being tied up on account of eating the small birds, literally cut out his entrails with the string before it was noticed. The peccary jumped overboard and swam ashore; the *tuyuyús* grabbed and swallowed every paroquet that ventured within reach of their bills; and they themselves, being tied on the beach at Eyas, were devoured by the crocodiles. My last monkey died as I went up New York bay. I only succeeded in getting home about a dozen *mutuns,* or curassows, a pair of Egyptian geese, a pair of birds, called *pucacunga,* a pair of macaws, a pair of parrots, and a pair of large white cranes, called *jaburú*, which are the same, I believe, as the birds called *adjutants* in India.

NOVEMBER 24—Preparing for departure. Our boat, which had been very badly calked in Nauta, required re-calking. The tow, or fill-ing, used is the inner bark of a tree called *machinapuro,* beaten and mashed into fibres. It answers very well, and there is great abun-dance in the forest. Its cost is twelve and a half cents the *mantada,* or as much as an Indian can carry in his blanket. An Indian can gather and grind two *mantadas* in a day. Ten or twelve *mantadas* are required to calk such a boat as mine. The pitch of the country is said to be the deposit of an ant in the trees. I never saw it in its original state. It is gathered by the Indians, heated till soft, made into the shape of wide, thin bricks, and is worth sixty-two and a half cents the *arroba.* It is very indifferent. A better kind is made by mixing black wax with gum copal.

Father Valdivia entertained us most kindly. His *aguadiente* gave out, and he occasionally regaled us with a glass of wine, bought for the church in Loreto. It is a weak white wine. I suppose I could not drink it at home, but here it seems very good. I find that this is the case with a great many things. The green plantains, roasted, which were at first an abomination to me, have now become a very good substitute for bread, and a roasted *yucca* is quite a treat. We have some small red-headed pan fish that are very fine, and, at my suggestion, the Padre had two or three fried, added to his usual evening cup of chocolate. I look forward to this meal with considerable pleasure. I do not know if it arises from the fact of our seeing so few things that are good to eat, or from the freshness of the cocoa, but chocolate, which I could not touch before this, is now very palatable and refreshing. The bean is simply toasted and pulverized, and the chocolate is made nearly as we make coffee.

After supper, we—that is, the Padre, the Governor General, Ijurra, and I, provided with fans to keep off the *musquitoes*—light our cigars, stretch ourselves at full length in a hammock, and pass an hour before bed-time in agreeable conversation. The priest, in this country, has more power, though it is by force of opinion, than the governor of the districts, or even than the governor general. I saw an instance in Nauta, where a man withstood Arebalo to his face, but yielded without a struggle, though growlingly, to the mandate of the Padre. Father Valdivia, though half Indian, and exceedingly simple-minded, is a very resolute and energetic person. On one occasion the Governor of Pebas succeeded in carrying off the Indians of that village to the Napo to gather *sarza,* against the wish of the Padre, who wanted them to clear the forest and build the new town. When the Governor returned, the priest told him that they two could not live together, that one or the other must resign his office and go away; and the man, knowing the power and influence of the priest, retired from the contest and his post. The Padre had great opposition and trouble in forming his new settlement. Even the women (wives of the white men) of Pebas came over to laugh at and ridicule his work; but the good Father called his Varayos, had the ladies conducted to their canoes, and, with much ceremonious politeness, directed them to be shoved off.

We obtained from the Indians more of the poisonous milk of the *catao,* and also the milk of the cow-tree. This they drink when fresh; and, when brought to me in a calabash, it had a foamy appearance, as if just drawn from the cow, and looked very rich and tempting. It, however, coagulates very soon, and becomes as hard and tenacious as glue. The Indians make use of this property of it to eradicate their eyebrows. This is not so painful an operation as it would seem, for the Indians have never suffered the eyebrows to grow and become strong, and the hair is only down, which is easily plucked up. When the milk coagulates, it expands, so that it forced the glass stopper out of the bottle I put it in, though sealed with pitch. We also got some of the almonds of the country, which I have not seen elsewhere. They are about the size, and have something the appearance, of our common black walnut, with a single oblong kernel, similar in taste to the Brazil nut.

NOVEMBER 26—We had much heavy rain for the last day or two. A number of persons were affected with catarrh and headache. The Padre told me that half of the population were ill of it, and that this always happens at the commencement of the rains. The disease is called *romadizo,* and is like our influenza. Ijurra and I were both indisposed with rheumatic pains in the back of the neck and shoulders. I don't wonder at this, for we have slept all the time in a room just plastered with mud, and so damp that, where my bed-clothes came in contact with the wall, they were quite wet, and the rain beat in upon my head and shoulders through an open window nearly over head. My boots are covered with mould every morning, and the guns get half-full of water.

I gave the Padre's servant, who was suffering very much from *romadizo,* fifteen grains of Dover's powder (Heaven knows if it were proper or not), and also to the Padre's sister, who had been suffering for some days with painful diarrhœa, forty drops of laudanum. The old lady was cured at once, and said she had never met with so great a *remedio.* I left her a phial of it with directions for its use, telling her (at which she looked aghast) that it was a deadly poison. It is curious to see how entirely ignorant the best-informed people out here are concerning the properties of medicines. Most of them do not know the names, much less the effects, of even such common drugs as calomel and opium. I suspect this is the case among most Spanish people, and think that Spanish physicians have always made a great mystery of their science.

We sailed from Echenique at half past one P.M. Father Valdivia, who is musical, but chanted the mass in a falsetto that would be very difficult to distinguish, at a little distance, from the rattling of a tin pan, commissioned me to bring him out (should I ever return) a small piano and a French horn, which he would pay for in salt fish and sarsaparilla. I cannot refrain from expressing my grateful thanks, for much attention and much information, to my friends—the well-informed and gentlemanlike Arebalo, and the pious, simple-minded, single-hearted little Indian priest of Pebas. We arrived at Cochiquinas (twenty-five miles distant) at half past eight P.M.

Chapter XII

❧❧

Caballococha—Alligators—Indian incantations—
Tabatinga—River Yavari—San Paulo—Making manteiga—
River Juruá—River Japurá

COCHIQUINAS, or New Cochiquinas, is a miserable fishing village of 240 inhabitants, though at this time there did not appear to be forty in the village, most of them being absent fishing and seeking a livelihood. Old Cochiquinas is four miles further down the river, and seems a far better situation; but the people there were afraid of the attacks of the savages of the Yavari, and removed up to this place.

The old town, to which place we dropped down to breakfast, has 120 inhabitants, of which twenty-five are white, and the rest Indians of the Yavari, called Marubos. These are dressed with even more simplicity than the Yaguas, dispensing with the mop behind. They have small, curly moustaches and beards, are darker than the other Indians, and do nothing but hunt for their living.

The Governor treated us very civilly, and gave us a good breakfast of soup, chickens, rice, and eggs, with milk just taken from the cow. What a luxury! I saw before his door a large canoe filled with unshelled rice of very good quality. The Governor told us that rice grew very well and gave about forty-fold in five months. He seemed a very gay and good-tempered young person, with a fine family of a wife and eleven remarkably handsome children—some born in lawful wedlock, others natural—but all cared for alike, and brought up together. I had the impertinence to ask him how he supported so many people. He said that the forest and the river yielded abundantly, and that he occasionally made an expedition to the Napo, and collected sarsaparilla enough to buy clothes and luxuries for his family in Loreto. The Napo, he says, is very full of sand-banks, and that twenty days from its mouth the men have to get overboard and drag the canoes.

We sailed at noon, and arrived at Peruaté at five P.M. (twenty miles).

NOVEMBER 28—From Peruaté to Camucheros is thirty miles. Just below Camucheros we had apparently all the width of the river in view—about a mile broad. We arrived at Moromoroté at a quarter past six P.M. (distance fifteen miles). This consists of one house of Christianized Indians. There is a house of Ticunas a mile further inland. We could hear the sound of their music and sent them word that we wanted to buy animals and food from them. They came to see us after night, but were drunk and had nothing to sell.

NOVEMBER 29—At nine A.M., after a journey of twenty miles, we entered the *caño* of *Caballococha* (Horse Lake). It is about eighty yards wide, and has eighteen feet of depth in the middle. The water is clear and makes an agreeable contrast with the muddy waters of the Amazon, but, there being no current in the *caño*, the water is supposed to be not so good to drink as that of the main river, which is very good when it is allowed to settle.

The village is situated on the *caño* about a mile and a half from the entrance and at the same distance from the lake. It contains 275 inhabitants, mostly Ticunas Indians. These are darker than the generality of Indians of the Marañón, though not so dark as the Marubos; and they are beardless, which frees them from the negro-look that these last have. Their houses are generally plastered with mud inside and are far neater-looking and more comfortable than the other Indian residences that I have seen. This is, however, entirely owing to the activity and energy of the priest, Father Flores, who seems to have them in excellent order. They are now building a church for him, which, when finished, will be the finest in the Montaña.

The men are all decently clad in frocks and trousers, and the women, besides the usual roll of cotton cloth around the loins, wear a short tunic covering the breast. I think that Father Flores, though he wants the honest simplicity and kindness of heart of Valdivia, and the noble patience, magnanimity, and gentleness of dear Father Calvo, is a better man for the Indians, and more successful in their management, than either of the others. He does not seem to care about their coming to church, for there was not an Indian at mass Sunday morning (though the padre did give us a little homily on the importance of attending worship); but he has them afraid of him, keeps them at work, sees that they keep themselves and their houses clean and the streets of the village in order; I saw none of the abominable drinking and dancing with which the other Indians invariably wind up the Sunday.

It is very dangerous to bathe in the *caño,* on account of the alligators. Not long before my arrival, a woman, bathing after nightfall in company with her husband, was seized and carried off by one of those monsters. She was not even in the *caño,* but was sitting on the bank, pouring water over her head with a gourd, when the reptile crawled from behind a log, where it had been lying, and carried her off in its mouth, though struck several heavy blows with a stick by the unfortunate husband. The padre next morning declared war upon the alligators and had the Indians out with their harpoons and lances to destroy them. They killed a number, and they thought it remarkable that the first they killed should have parts of the woman yet undigested in its stomach. I think it probable that a good many alligators had a bite.

The lake is a pretty and nearly circular sheet of water of two and a half miles in diameter, and is twenty feet deep in the centre. There were a great many water-fowl in it, but principally cranes and cormorants.

Padre Flores, as usual, gave us a room in his house and seats at his table. I admired a very old-looking silver spoon that he had on the table, and which Ijurra judged to be of the date of Ferdinand and Isabella from the armed figures and lion's head upon the handle; whereupon the padre, with the courtesy that belongs to his race, insisted upon my accepting it. I was glad to have it in my power to acknowledge the civility by pressing upon the padre a set of tumblers neatly put up in a morocco case, which had been given me by the first lieutenant of the Vandalia.

After dark he proposed that we should go out and see some of the incantations of the Indians for the care of the sick. We heard music at a distance and approached a large house whence it proceeded, in which the Padre said there was almost always someone sick. We listened at the door, which was closed. There seemed to be a number of persons singing inside. I was almost enchanted myself. I never heard such tones and think that even instrumental music could not be made to equal them. I have frequently been astonished at the power of the Indians to mock animals, but I had heard nothing like this before. The tones were so low, so faint, so guttural, and at the same time so sweet and clear that I could scarcely believe they came from human throats; and they seemed fitting sounds in which to address spirits of another world.

Someone appearing to approach the door, the priest and I fled, for, though we were mean enough to listen at a man's door, we were ashamed to be caught at it; but hearing nothing further we returned, and Ijurra, with his usual audacity, pushed open the door and proposed to enter. The noise we made in opening the door caused a hasty retreat of some persons, which we could hear and partly see; and when we entered, we found but two Indians—an old man and a young one—sitting on the floor by a little heap of flaming copal, engaged in chewing tobacco and spitting in an earthern pot before them. The young man turned his face to the wall with a sullen look, and although the old man smiled when he was patted on the head and desired to proceed with his music, yet it was with a smile that had no mirth or satisfaction in it, and that showed plainly that he was annoyed, and would have expressed his annoyance had he dared.

The hut was a large one, and appeared larger in the gloom. There was a light burning in the farther end of it, which looked to be a mile off; Ijurra strode the distance and found it to be just twenty-four paces. There were a number of hammocks slung one above the other between the posts that supported the roof, and all seemed occupied. In one corner of the house was built a small partition of cane, in which I understood was confined a young girl, who was probably looking at us with curious eyes, but whom we could not see. I had been told before that it was the custom among most of the Indians of the Montaña to shut up a girl when she entered into the period of womanhood, until the family could raise the means for a feast, when everybody is invited, all hands get drunk, and the maiden is produced with much ceremony, and declared a woman of the tribe, whose hand may be sought in marriage. The confinements sometimes last several months, for the Indians do not hurry themselves in making their preparations, but are ready when the *yuccas* are gathered, the *masato* made, and there is a sufficient quantity of dried monkey in the house; so that it sometimes happens, when the poor girl is brought out, that she is nearly white. It is said that she frequently conceals her situation from her family, preferring a sound beating, when the time betrays her, to the dreary imprisonment.

DECEMBER 1—I lost my beautiful and valued *chiriclis,* which died of the cold. It was put to bed as usual under the wash-basin, but the basin was not put under the *armayari,* its usual place, and it rained heavily all night. I was surprised at the delicacy of feeling shown by my Indian boatmen on the occasion; they knew how much I was attached to the bird, and, instead of tossing the carcass overboard, as they would have done with that of any other animal that I had, one of them brought it into my room before I was awake and laid it decently, and with care, on a table at my bed-side. I felt the loss very sensibly—first, because it was a present from good Father Calvo, upon whose head and shoulder I had so often seen it perched; and, secondly, on account of the bird itself. It was beautiful, gentle, and affectionate; and so gallant that I called it my Mohawk chief. I have seen it take the food, unresisted, out of the mouths of the parrots and macaws many times its size, by the mere reputation of its valor; and it waged many a desperate battle with the monkeys. Its triumphant song when it had vanquished an adversary was most amusing. It was very pleasant, as the cool of night came on, to find it with beak and claws climbing up the leg of my trousers until it arrived at the opening of my shirt, and to hear its low note of satisfaction as it entered and stowed itself snugly away

in my armpit. It was as sensible of caresses, and as jealous, as a favorite; and I could never notice my little Pinshi monkey in its sight
that it did not fly at it and drive it off.

This bird is the *psit melanocephalus* of Linnaeus. It is about the
size of a robin, has black legs, yellow thighs, a spotted white breast,
orange neck and head, and a brilliant green back and wings. There
is another species of the same bird in Brazil. It is there called
periquito, and differs from this in having the feathers on the top of
the head black, so as to have the appearance of wearing a cowl. An
Italian resident at Barra gave me one of this species, which was even
more docile and affectionate than the present of Father Calvo; but,
to my infinite regret, he flew away from me at Pará.

I noticed growing about the houses of the village a couple of
shrubs, six or eight feet high, called, respectively, *yanapanga* and
pacapanga. From the leaves of the first is made a black dye, and
from those of the second a very rich scarlet. I surmised that a dye,
like the indigo of commerce, though of course of different color,
might be made of these leaves; and when I arrived in Brazil, I found
that the Indians there were in the habit of making a scarlet powder of the *pacapanga,* called *carajurú,* quite equal, in brilliancy of
color, to the dye of the cochineal. I believe that efforts have been
made to introduce this dye into commerce, and I do not know why
they have failed. I brought home a specimen.

Two brothers of Father Flores were quite sick with a *tertiana,*
taken in gathering sarsaparilla up on the Napo. This is an inter-
mittent fever of a malignant type. The patient becomes emaci-
ated and yellow, and the spleen swells. I saw several cases as I
came down the Marañón, but all were contracted on the tributaries. I saw or heard of no cases that originated upon the main
trunk.

DECEMBER 2—Much rain during the night. Sailed from Caballococha at half past two P.M. Ijurra liked the appearance of things so much at this place that he determined, when he should leave me, to return to it and clear land for a plantation, which he has since done.

I lost my sound-lead soon after starting, and had no soundings to Loreto, where we arrived at half past seven P. M. (twenty miles). Loreto is situated on an eminence on the left bank, having the large island of Cacao in front. There are a number of cattle and hogs running about the village and trampling the clay into mire.

There are three mercantile houses in Loreto, all owned by Portuguese. About $10,000 a year passes through their hands. They tell me that they sell the goods from below at about 20 percent on Pará prices, which of course I did not believe. I saw a schooner-rigged boat lying along-side the bank. She was about forty feet long and seven broad, was built in Coari, and sold here for $200, silver. The houses at Loreto are better built, and better furnished, than those of the towns on the river above. We are approaching civilization.

The population of Loreto is 250, made up of Brazilians, mulattoes, negroes, and a few Ticunas Indians. It is the frontier post of Peru. There are a few miles of neutral territory between it and Tabatinga, the frontier of Brazil.

DECEMBER 4—We left Loreto at half past six A.M., with a cold wind from the northward and eastward, and rain. Thermometer, 76 degrees. It seems strange to call the weather cold with the thermometer at 76 degrees, but I really was very uncomfortable with it, and the monkeys seemed nearly frozen. I estimate the length of the neutral territory, by the windings of the river, at twenty miles.

Since I purchased a boat at Nauta I had worn an American flag over it. I had been told that I probably would not be allowed to wear it in the waters of Brazil. But when the boat was descried at Tabatinga, the Brazilian flag was hoisted at that place; and when I landed, which I did dressed in uniform, I was received by the Commandant, also in uniform, to whom I immediately presented my Brazilian passport.

As soon as my rank was ascertained (which appeared to be that of a captain in the Brazilian army), I was saluted with seven guns. The Commandant used much stately ceremony towards me, but never left me a moment to myself until he saw me safely in bed on board my boat. I did not know, at first, whether this was polite attention or a watch upon me, but I think it was the latter, for, upon my giving him the slip, and walking over towards the old fort, he joined me within five minutes, and when we returned to his house he brought a dictionary, and, pointing with a cunning expression to the verb *traçar* (to draw), asked me to read it. I did so, and handed the book back to him, when he pointed out to me the verb *delinhar*. I was a little fretted, for I thought he might as well ask me at once, and told him that I had no intention of making any drawings whatever, and had merely intended to take a walk. He treated me with great civility, and entertained me at his table, giving me roast beef, which was a great treat.

It was quite pleasant, after coming from the Peruvian villages, which are all nearly hidden in the woods, to see that Tabatinga had the forest cleared away from about it for a space of forty or fifty acres, was covered with green grass, and had a grove of orange-trees in its midst, though they were now old and past bearing. There are few houses to be seen, for those of the Ticunas are still in the woods. Those that are visible are the soldiers' quarters and the residences of a few whites that live here—white, however, in contradistinction to the Indian; for I think the only pure white man in the place was a Frenchman, who has resided a long time in Brazil, and has a large Brazilian family. The post is garrisoned by twenty soldiers, commanded by O Illustrissimo Señor Tenente José Virisimo dos Santos Lima, a cadet, a sergeant, and a corporal. The population of Tabatinga is about two hundred, mostly Indians of the Ticuna tribe. It is well situated for a frontier post, having all the river in front, only about half a mile wide, and commanded from the fort by the longest range of cannon-shot. The fort is at present in ruins and the artillery consists of two long brass twelve-pounder field-guns.

I did not hoist my flag again, and the Commandant seemed pleased. He said that it might give offence down the river, and told me that Count Castelnau, who had passed here some years before, borrowed a Brazilian flag from him and wore that. He also earnestly insisted that I should take his boat in lieu of my own, which he said was not large enough for the navigation of the lower part of the Amazon. I declined for a long time, but finding that he was very earnest about it, and embarrassed between his desire to comply with the request of the Brazilian minister at Washington, contained in my passport—"that Brazilian authorities should facilitate me in my voyage, and put no obstacle in my way"—and the requirements of the law of the empire forbidding foreign vessels to navigate its interior waters, I accepted his proposition, and exchanged boats, thus enabling him to say, in a frontier passport which he issued to me, that I was descending the river in Brazilian vessels.

He desired me to leave his boat at Barra, telling me he had no doubt but that the government authorities there would furnish me with a better one. I told him very plainly that I had doubts of that, and that I might have to take his boat on to Pará, which I finally did, and placed it in the hands of his correspondent at that place. I was correct in my doubts, for, so far from the government authorities at Barra having a boat to place at my disposal, they borrowed mine and sent it up the river for a load of wood for building purposes. The Commandant at Tabatinga, I was told, compelled the circus company that preceded me to abandon their Peruvian-built raft and construct another of the wood of the Brazilian forests.

DECEMBER 5—We were employed in fitting up the new boat, to which the commandant gave his personal attention. I asked him to give me some more *peons*. He said, "Certainly," sent out a guard of soldiers, pressed five Tucunas, and put them in the guard house till I was ready to start, when they were marched down to the boat, and a negro soldier sent along to take charge of them. He gave me all the beasts and birds he had, a demijohn of red wine, salt fish, and *farinha* for my men, and in short loaded me with kindness and civility. I had already parted with all the personal "traps" that I thought would be valuable and acceptable to my friends on the route, and could only make a show of acknowledgment by giving him, in return, a dozen masses of tobacco—an article which happened at this time to be scarce and valuable.

DECEMBER 6—We embarked at half past one P.M., accompanied by the Commandant, the cadet, and the Frenchman, Jeronymo Fort, who had been kind enough to place his house at Egas at my disposal. Ijurra had privately got all the guns and pistols ready, and we received the Commandant with a salute of, I should think, at least one hundred guns, for Ijurra did not leave off shooting for half an hour.

DECEMBER 7—The river now has lost its name of Marañón, and is called Solimoens. It is here a mile and a half wide, sixty-six feet deep in the middle, and has a current of two miles and three quarters per hour. The small boat in which we carry our animals did not stop with us last night, but passed on without being noticed. She had all our fowls and turtles; so that our breakfast this morning consisted of boiled rice. We drifted with the tide all night, stopping for an hour in consequence of a severe squall of wind and rain from the eastward.

DECEMBER 8—Rainy morning. We arrived at San Paulo at ten A.M. This village is on a hill two or three hundred feet above the present level of the river—the highest situation I have yet seen. The ascent to the town is very difficult and tedious, particularly after a rain, the soil being of white clay. On the top of this hill is a moist, grassy plain, which does not extend far back. The site is said not to be healthy, on account of swamps back of it. The population is 350, made up of thirty whites, and the rest Tucunas and Juries Indians. We left San Paulo at half past three P.M. and drifted with the current all night. Distance from Tabatinga to San Paulo, ninety-five miles.

DECEMBER 9—At half past eight A.M. we arrived at Maturá, a settlement of four or five huts (with only one occupied), on a muddy bank. Its distance from San Paulo is fifty miles. The shores of the river are generally low, though there are reaches where its banks are forty or fifty feet high, commonly of white or red clay. There is much colored earth on the banks of the river—red, yellow, and white—which those people who have taste make use of to plaster the inside of their houses. The banks are continually falling into the stream, sometimes in very large masses, carrying trees along with them and forming one of the dangers and impediments to upward navigation where the boats have to keep close in shore to avoid the current.

At half past four we entered the mouth of the Iça, or Putumayo, fifteen miles from Maturá. This is a fine-looking river, half a mile broad at the mouth, and opening into an estuary (formed by the left bank of the Amazon and islands on the right hand) of a mile in width. The water is clearer than that of the Amazon. Many slaves of the Brazilians escape by way of this river into New Granada.

San Antonio is a village about two miles below the mouth of the Iça. It is a collection of four or five houses of Brazilians, and a few Indian huts. The people seemed mad for tobacco, and begged me earnestly to sell them some. I told them I would not sell for money, but I was willing to exchange for things to eat or for rare birds and beasts. They ransacked the town, but could only raise five fowls, half a dozen eggs, two small turtles, and three bunches of plantains. They had no animals but such as I already had, and I only bought a macaw and a *pavoncito,* or little peacock. The little tobacco I gave for these things, however, was not enough to give everybody a smoke, and they implored me to sell them some for money. They came to the canoe after night, and showed so strong a desire to have it that I feared they would rob me. Finding me inexorable, they went off abusing me, which excited the wrath of Ijurra to a high pitch.

Our stock of tobacco, which we had bought in Nauta, was now very much reduced. We had used it, during our voyage on the Ucayali, to purchase food and curiosities and to give to the *peons,* who were not satisfied or contented unless they had an occasional smoke. We also had been liberal with it to governors and curates, who had been civil to us, and now we had barely enough for our own use to last us to Barra. I gave twenty-five cents the mass for it in Nauta, though the Paraguá cheated me and should only have charged me twelve and a half. We could have sold it all the way to Barra for thirty-seven and a half, and fifty cents.

DECEMBER 10—Between San Antonio and Tunantins we met the governor of San Antonio, a military-looking white man, returning with his wife and children from a visit to Tunantins. I showed him my passport, which he asked for, and we interchanged civilities and presents, he giving me a *chiriclis,* like the one I lost at Caballococha, and water-melons, and I making him a present of tobacco and a tinder-box. The species of bird he gave me is called, in Brazil, *marianita.* This one took a singular disease by which it lost the use of its legs—hopped about for some days on the knee-joints, with the leg and foot turned upwards in front, and then died.

At twenty miles from San Antonio we entered the mouth of the Tunantins River. The town is prettily situated on a slight green eminence on the left bank. It is composed of the tribes of Cayshanas and Juries and about twenty-five whites. One sees very few Indians in the Portuguese villages. They seem to live apart and in the woods and are, I think, gradually disappearing before the advance of civilization. They are used as beasts of burden, and are thought no further of.

DECEMBER 11—We stopped at a *factoria* on the left bank, sixty-five miles from Tunantins, where people were making *manteiga.* The effect of "mirage" was here very remarkable. When within a mile or two of the *factoria,* I thought I saw quite a large town, with houses of two or three stories built of stone and brick with large heaps of white stone lying about in several places. There was a vessel lying off the town that I was satisfied was a large brig-of-war. But upon drawing near, my three-story houses dwindled to the smallest palm *ranchos,* my heaps of building stones to piles of egg-shells, and my man-of-war to a schooner of thirty tons.

The season for making *manteiga* on the Amazon generally ends by the first of November; but the rise of the river this year has been unusually late and small. The people are still collecting the eggs, though they all have young turtles in them.

A commandant, with soldiers, is appointed every year by some provincial or municipal authority to take care of the beaches, prevent disorder, and administer justice.

Sentinels are placed at the beginning of August, when the turtles commence depositing their eggs, and are withdrawn when the beach is exhausted. They see that no one wantonly interferes with the turtles or destroys the eggs. Those engaged in the making of *manteiga* pay a capitation tax of twelve and a half cents' duty to the government.

The process of making it is very disgusting. The eggs, though they be rotten and offensive, are collected, thrown into a canoe, and trodden in a mass with the feet. The shells and young turtles are thrown out. Water is poured on, and the residue is left to stand in the sun for several days. The oil rises to the top and is skimmed off and boiled in large copper boilers. It is then put in earthen pots of about forty-five pounds' weight. Each pot of oil is worth on the beach one dollar and thirty cents, and in Pará usually sells at from two and a half to three dollars.

A turtle averages eighty eggs; forty turtles will give a pot. Twenty-five men will make two hundred pots in twelve days. The beaches of the Amazon and tributaries yield from five to six thousand pots annually. Prolific as they are, I think the turtle is even now diminishing in number on the Amazon. Vast numbers of the young are eaten by the Indians, who take them by the time they are able to crawl and when they do not measure more than an inch in diameter; boil them, and eat them as a delicacy. One Indian will devour two dozen of these three or four times a day. The birds also pick up a great number of them as they crawl from their nest to the water, and I imagine the fish, too, make them pay toll as they pass. I heard complaints of the growing scarcity, both of fish and *manteiga,* as I came down the river.

This *factoria* is a small one and will give but two or three hundred pots. One requires a good stomach to be able to eat his breakfast at one of these places. The stench is almost intolerable, the beach is covered with greedy and disgusting-looking buzzards, and the surface of the water dotted with the humps of the deadly alligator.

The Ticunas whom I brought with me from Tabatinga are even more lazy and careless than the Sarayaquinos. I fancied that it was because they were forced into the service, and did not think that they would be paid, so I gave each one, as a gratuity, a knife, a pair of scissors, and a small mirror; but they were no better afterwards than before. Poor fellows! they have been abused and maltreated so long that they are now insensible even to kindness. The negro soldier who was sent along, either as a pilot or to govern the Ticunas, or as a watch upon me, is drunken and worthless. He knows nothing of the river, and I believe steals my liquor.

DECEMBER 12—There are evidently many newly formed islands in the river. We ran, all the morning, through narrow island passages, the channels, in some places, not over forty yards wide, but of twenty and thirty feet of depth.

DECEMBER 13—At eight A.M. we entered a narrow arm of the river, sixty miles from the mouth of the Jutay, that leads by Fonteboa.

The population of Fonteboa is 250. There are eighty whites. We met several traders at this place bound up and down the river. One had a variety of articles. I bought some red wine and rum for stores, and Ijurra bought very good shoes and cotton stockings.

DECEMBER 14—Started at half past four A.M. Misty morning. At ten entered the mouth of the Juruá, thirty-six miles from Fonteboa. The Indians of the Juruá, I was afterwards told by Señor Batalha, are Arauas and Catauxis, who are met with at eight days' journey up. Some of these are baptized Indians; but the Arauas are described as a treacherous people, who frequently rob and murder the traders on the river. Two months further up are the Culinos and Nawas Infidels. Between these two was a nation called the Canamaris, but they have been nearly entirely destroyed by the Arauas. This year all the expeditions to the Juruá were failures, on account of the hostility of the Arauas.

M. Castelnau, in summing up the accounts of this river, collected some very curious stories concerning the Indians who dwell upon the banks of the Juruá. He says (vol. 5, p. 105),

I cannot pass over in silence a very curious passage of Padre Noronha, which one is astonished to find in a work of so grave a character in other respects. The Indians, Cauamas and Uginas (says the Padre), live near the sources of the river. The first are of very short stature, scarcely exceeding five palms (about three and a half feet), and the last (of this there is no doubt) have tails, and are produced by a mixture of Indians and Coata monkeys. Whatever may be the cause of this fact, I am led to give it credit for three reasons: first, because there is no physical reason why men should not have tails; secondly, because many Indians, whom I have interrogated regarding this thing, have assured me of the fact, telling me that the tail was a palm and a half long; and, thirdly, because the Reverend Father Friar José de Santa Theresa Ribeiro, a Carmelite, and Curate of Castro de Avelaeñs, assured me that he saw the same thing in an Indian who came from Japurá, and who sent me the following attestation:

I, José de Santa Theresa Ribeiro, of the Order of our Lady of Mount Carmel, Ancient Observance, &c., certify and swear, in my quality of Priest, and on the Holy Evangelists, that, when I was a missionary in the ancient village of Parauaù, where was afterwards built the village of Noguera, I saw, in 1755, a man called Manuel da Silva, native of Pernambuco, or Bahia, who came from the river Japurá with some Indians, amongst whom was one—an Infidel brute—who the said Manuel declared to me had a tail; and as I was unwilling to believe such an extraordinary fact, he brought the Indian and caused him to strip, on pretence of removing some turtles from a "pen" near which I stood to assure myself of the truth. There I saw, without possibility of error, that the man had a tail, of the thickness of a finger, and half a palm long, and covered with a smooth and naked skin. The same Manuel assured me that the Indian had told him that every month he cut his tail, because he did not like to have it too long, and it grew very fast. I do not know to what nation this man belonged, nor if all his tribe had a similar tail; but I understood afterwards that there was a tailed nation upon the banks of the Juruá; and I sign this act and seal it in affirmation of the truth of all that it contains.

ESTABLISHMENT OF CASTRO DE AVELAEÑS, October 14, 1768.

FR. JOSÉ DE STA. THERESA RIBEIRO.

M. Castelnau says, after giving these relations, "I will add but a word. Descending the Amazon, I saw one day, near Fonteboa, a black Coata of enormous dimensions. He belonged to an Indian woman, to whom I offered a large price, for the country, for the curious beast, but she refused me with a burst of laughter. 'Your efforts are useless,' said an Indian who was in the cabin. 'That is her husband.'"

These Coatas, of which I had several, are a large, black, pot-bellied monkey. They average about two and a half feet of height, have a few thin hairs on the top of their head, and look very like an old negro.

We breakfasted at the mouth of the river. After breakfast one of the Ticunas from Tabatinga was directed by the soldier to take up one of the macaws that was walking on the beach and put it in the boat preparatory to a start. The man, in an angry and rude manner, took the bird up and tossed it into the boat to the manifest danger of injuring it. I was standing in the larger boat close by, and saw his insolent manner. I took up a paddle and beckoned him to come to me, but he walked sulkily up the beach. I thought it a good time to see whether, in the event of these surly fellows becoming mutinous, I could count upon my Sarayacu people, so I directed two of them to bring the Ticuna to me. They turned to obey, but slowly, and evidently unwillingly, when my quick and passionate friend Ijurra sprang upon the Indian, and, taking him by the collar, jerked him to where I was. I made great demonstrations with my paddle, though without the slightest idea of striking him (for I always shunned, with the utmost care, the rendering myself amenable to any of the tribunals or authorities of Brazil), and abused him in English, which I imagine answered quite as well as any other language but his own would have done. I think this little "fracas" had a happy effect upon all the Indians, and they improved in cheerfulness and willingness to work afterwards. The Ticunas that I had with me, however, were far the laziest and most worthless people that I had hitherto had anything to do with. I believe that this is not characteristic of the tribe, for they seemed well enough under Father Flores at Caballococha, and they have generally rather a good reputation among the whites on the river. I imagine that the proximity of the garrison at Tabatinga has not a good effect upon their manners and morals, but, however that may be, these men were too lazy to help to cook the provisions, and when we stopped to breakfast they generally seated themselves on the thwarts of the boat, or on the sand of the beach, whilst the Sarayaquinos fetched the wood and made the fire. They were ready enough to eat when the breakfast was cooked. I couldn't stand this, when I observed that it was a customary thing and accordingly caused the provisions issued to be divided between the two parties, and told my Ticuna friends, "No cook, no eat." It would take many years of sagacious treatment on the part of their rulers to civilize this people, if it be possible to do so at all.

DECEMBER 15—We travelled till eleven P.M., for want of a beach to camp on; the men disliking to sleep in the woods on account of snakes.

DECEMBER 16—Finding that I was on the southern bank, and having an opening between two islands abreast of me, I struck off to the eastward for the mouth of the Japurá. We ran through island passages till we reached it at three P.M., distant 105 miles from the mouth of the Juruá.

The Indians of the Japurá are called Mirauas (a large tribe), Curitus, and Macus. The traveller reaches them in sixteen days from the mouth. The Macus have no houses, but wander in the woods, infest the river banks, and rob and kill when they can. (These are the fruits of the old Brazilian system of hunting Indians to make slaves of them.)

I judge the width of the Amazon, opposite the mouth of the Japurá, to be four or five miles.

DECEMBER 17—At half past eight we entered a narrow channel between a small island and the right bank, which conducted us into the river of Teffé, about a mile inside of its mouth. The river at this point is 180 yards broad, water clear and apparently deep. Just below Egas, where we arrived at half past ten, a lake contracts into the river. The town is situated on a low point that stretches out into the lake, and has a harbor on each side of it.

On landing we showed our passports to the *sub-delegado,* an officer of the general government who has charge of the police of the district and to the military commandant, and forthwith inducted ourselves into the house of M. Fort, our French friend of Tabatinga, who had placed it at our disposal.

Chapter XIII

❧❧

Egas—Trade—Lake Coari—Mouth of the Rio Negro—
Barra—Trade—Productions

EGAS HAS a population of about eight hundred inhabitants, and is the largest and most thriving place above Barra. It occupies an important position with regard to the trade of the river, being nearly midway between Barra and Loreto (the Peruvian frontier), and near the mouths of the great rivers Juruá, Japurá, and Teffé.

There are now eight or ten commercial houses at Egas that drive a tolerably brisk trade between Peru and Pará, besides employing agents to go into the neighboring rivers and collect from the Indians the productions of the land and the water.

Trade is carried on in schooners of between thirty and forty tons burden, which commonly average five months in the round trip between Egas and Pará, a distance of 1,450 miles.

Major Batalha (for my friend commands a battalion of the Guarda Policial of the province divided between San Paulo, San Antonio, Egas, and Coari) complains, as all do, of the want of energy of the people. He says that as long as a man can get a bit of turtle or salt fish to eat, a glass of *caçacha,* and a cotton shirt and trousers, he will not work. The men who fish and make *manteiga,* although they are employed but a small portion of the year in this occupation, will do nothing else. There is wanting an industrious and active population who know what the comforts of life are and who have artificial wants to draw out the great resources of the country.

Although the merchants sell their foreign goods at an advance of 25 percent, this is on credit, and they say they could do much better if they could sell at 15 percent for cash. Moreover, in this matter of credit they have no security. When a trader has made sufficient money to enable him to leave off work with his own hands, the custom is for him to supply some young dependent with a boat-load of goods and a crew, and send him away to trade with the Indians, depending upon his success and honesty for the payment of the 25 percent. The young trader has no temptation to desert or abandon his patron, but much is lost from the dangers incident to the navigation, and the want of judgment and discretion in the intercourse of the employer with the Indians, and in the hostile disposition of the Indians themselves.

There is much in this life of the *habilitado,* or person employed by the traders, to attract the attention of the active, energetic young men of our country. It is true that he will encounter much hardship and some danger. These, however, are but stimulants to youth. It is also true that he will meet with a feeling of jealousy in the native towards the foreigner, but this feeling is principally directed towards the Portuguese, who are hard-working, keen, and clever, and who, as a general rule, go to that country to make money, and return home with it. This is their leading idea, and it makes them frugal, even penurious, in their habits, and indisposes them to make common cause with the natives of this country. Not so with the Italians, the French, the English, and the Americans, whom I have met with in this country. I do not know more popular people than my friends Enrique Antonii, the Italian, and his associate, Marcus Williams, the Yankee, who are established at Barra. Everywhere on the river I heard sounded the praises of my countryman. At Sarayacu, at Nauta, at Pebas, and at Egas, men said they wished to see him again and to trade with him. He himself told me that, though the trade on the river was attended with hardships, exposure, and privation, there was a certain charm attending the wild life, and its freedom from restraint, that would always prevent any desire on his part to return to his native country. I heard that he carried this feeling so far as to complain bitterly, when he visited Norris, the consul at Pará, of the restraints of society that compelled him to wear trousers at dinner.

Any number of *peons,* or as they are called in Brazil, *tapuios,* may be had for an almost nominal rate of pay for this traffic with the Indians. All the christianized Indians of the province of Pará are registered and compelled to serve the State, either as soldiers of the Guarda Policial, or as a member of "Bodies of Laborers," distributed among the different territorial divisions of the province. There are nine of these bodies, numbering in the aggregate 7,444. It is from these bodies that the trader, the traveller, or the collector of the fruits of the country is furnished with laborers, but little care is taken by the government officials in their registry or proper government, and a majority of them are either entire drones, or have become, in fact, the slaves of individuals. It is now difficult for the passing traveller to get a boat's crew, though I have no doubt that judicious and honest dealing with them would restore to civilization and to labor many who have retired from the towns and gone back to a nomadic and nearly savage life.

Most of the leading men at Egas own negro slaves, but these are generally employed in household and domestic work. A young negro man is worth $250—if a mechanic, $500. Major Batalha tells me that he will purchase no more slaves; he has had ill luck both with them and with his *tapuios*. The slaves desert to Spain (as Peru, Ecuador, and New Granada are called here), and he has lost six *tapuios,* by a sort of bloody flux, within the last two months. I asked him if the disease was confined to his household, but he told me that it was general, and supposed that it was caused by drinking the water of the lake, which was thought to be, in some small degree, impregnated with the poisonous milk of the *assacu* trees, many of which grow on its borders. I have no idea that this is the cause, but suppose the disease originates from exposure, bad food, and an imprudent use of fruit, though I see no fruit except a few oranges and limes. It is even difficult to purchase a bunch of bananas. There are no other diseases in Egas except *tertiana*, caught in gathering sarsaparilla on the tributaries.

DECEMBER 25—We are very gay at Egas with Christmas times. The people keep it up with spirit, and with a good deal of spirits, too, for I see a number of drunken people in the streets. I attended midnight mass last night. The church was filled with well-dressed people, and with some very pretty, though dark-complexioned ladies. The congregation was devout, but I could not very well be so, on account of the music, which was made by a hand-organ that wouldn't play. It gave a squeak and a grunt now and them, but there were parts of the music when nothing could be heard but the turning of the handle. There was also a procession on the lake. A large, very well-illuminated boat, with rockets and music moving about, and a long line of lights on logs or canoes anchored in the lake, had a very pretty effect. Processions of negroes, men and

women, with songs and music of tambourines and drums, were parading the streets all night.

The higher classes are taking a little champagne, Teneriffe wine, or English ale. Ginger beer is a favorite and wholesome drink in this climate. I was surprised to see no cider. I wonder some Yankee from below has not thought to send it up.

DECEMBER 26—I had requested the Commandante-militar to furnish me with a few more Tapuios, and he had promised to send out an expedition to catch me some. He now says there are none to be had, but I suspect he gave himself no trouble about it. Many persons go down the river with only two rowers and a steersman, and I having six, I have no doubt he thought that I had a sufficient number.

My Ticunas, and the negro soldier sent with them, gave me a great deal of trouble—the soldier with his drunkenness and dishonesty, and the Indians by their laziness and carelessness, suffering the boat to be injured for the want of care and permitting the escape and destruction of my animals and birds. It is as much as my patience and forbearance towards a suffering and ill-treated people can stand to refrain from reporting them to the Commandant, who would probably punish them with severity. Last night they broke the leg of one of my *tuyuyús,* and an alligator carried off the other. I am told that these animals have killed three persons at this same place. I had bathed there twice a day until I heard this, but after that, although I knew that they only seize their prey at night, it was going too close to danger, and I chose another place.

I saw a very peculiar monkey at Egas. It is called *acaris,* and has a face of a very pretty rose color. The one I saw here was nearly as large as a common baboon. He had long hair, of a dirty-white color, and was evidently very old. Two that I saw at a *factoria,* on a beach of the Amazon, had hair of a reddish-yellow color; the tail is very short. Castelnau says that the vermilion color of the face disappears after death, and during life it varies in intensity, according to the state of the passions of the animal. The owners would not sell me those at the *factoria,* and I would not buy the one at Egas, because his face was blotched with some cutaneous affection, and he was evidently so old that he would soon die.

During our stay at Egas we had our meals cooked by an old negro woman who has charge of M. Fort's house, furnishing her with money to buy what she could. It is very difficult to get anything but turtle even here. I counted thirty-nine cattle grazing on the green slope before our door, yet neither for love nor money could we get any beef, and with difficulty a little milk for our coffee. We sent to Nogueyra for fowls and eggs, but without success. These are festival times, and people want their little luxuries themselves, or are too busily engaged in frolicking to care about selling.

Major Batalha treated us with great kindness, sending us delicacies from his own table—the greatest of which was some well-made bread. We had not tasted any since leaving Huanuco—now five months, and of course it was very welcome. On Christmas day he sent us a pair of fine, large sponge-cakes. A piece of these, with a glass of tolerable ale, was a princely luncheon to us wayfarers, who had lived so long on salt fish and *farinha.* It fairly made Ijurra grin with delight. We could always get a cup of very good chocolate by walking round to the Major's house, and the only thing I had to find fault with was that I was always received in the shop. The Brazilians, as a general rule, do not like to introduce foreigners to their families, and their wives lead a monotonous and somewhat secluded life.

An intelligent and spirited lady friend told me that the customs of her country confined and restrained her more than was agreeable, and said, with a smile, that she would not like to say how much she had been influenced in the choice of a husband by the hope that she would remove to another country, where she might see something, learn something, and be somebody.

DECEMBER 28—We left Egas at half past two P.M., in the rain. We seemed to have travelled just ahead of the rainy season, and whenever we have stopped at any place for some days, the rains have caught up with us.

I now parted with my Sarayacu boatmen, and very sorry I was to lose them. They were lazy enough, but were active and diligent compared with the stupid and listless Ticunas. They were always (though somewhat careless) faithful and obedient. I believe that the regret at parting was mutual. Their earnest tone of voice and affectionate manner proclaimed their feeling, and a courtier, addressing his sovereign, would have envied the style in which old Andres bent his knee and kissed my hand, and the tremulous tones, indicating deep feeling, with which he uttered the words *"A dios, mi patrón."* They are all going back to Sarayacu but one, who has engaged himself to Señor Batalha. It is a curious thing that so many Peruvian Indians should be working in Brazil, but it shows that they are removed above the condition of savages, for, though worse treated in Brazil, and deprived of the entire freedom of action they have in Peru, yet they are paid something, they acquire property, though it be nothing more than a painted wooden box with hinges and a lock to it (the thing they most covet), with a colored shirt and trousers to lock up in it and guard for feast-days. With such a box and contents, a hatchet, a short sabre, and red woollen cap, the Peruvian Indian returns home a rich and envied man, and others are induced to go below in hopes of similar fortune. They are frequently gone from their homes for years. Father Calvo complained that they abandoned their families, but in my judgment this was a benefit to them, rather than an injury, for the man at home is, in a great measure, supported by the woman.

We entered the Amazon at four P.M. The mouth of the Teffé is three hundred yards wide, and has thirty feet of depth and one mile per hour of current. This is an inconsiderable stream, and may be ascended by canoes to near its sources in twenty days. In ten or twelve days' ascent, a branch called the Rio Gancho is reached, which communicates by a portage with the Juruá. Indians of the Purus, also, sometimes descend the Teffé to Egas.

I shall give the height of Egas above the level of the sea, from the temperature of boiling water (208.2 degrees) at 2,052 feet. Egas is about eighteen hundred miles from the sea; this would give the river a descent of a little more than a foot per mile, which would about give it its current of two and a half miles per hour.

DECEMBER 29—We drifted with the current, and a little paddling on the part of the crew, until ten P.M., when we made fast to a tree on the right bank.

DECEMBER 30—We started at five A.M. At three P.M., where the river was quite a mile wide, I found but thirty feet in mid-channel. At six P.M., I judged from the appearance of the shores on each side (bold, red cliffs) that we had all the width of the river. It was only about a mile wide, and I thought it would be very deep, but I found only sixty feet. I could not try the current for the violence of the wind. At seven we arrived at the mouth of the Lake Coari, 115 miles from Egas, and made fast to a schooner at anchor near the right bank.

This schooner seemed to have no particular owner or captain, but to be manned by a company of adventurers, for all appeared on an equality. They were from Obidos, upwards of two months; and twenty-eight days from Barra, which place we reached from here in five. They were travelling at their leisure, but complained much of the strength of the current and the want of strength of the easterly winds. I heard the same complaints at Egas, but I have found the winds quite fresh from the eastward, and the current, compared with that above, slight.

The fault of the vessels navigating the Amazon is the breadth of beam and want of sail. I am confident that a clipper-built vessel, sloop, or rather ketch-rigged, with a large mainsail, topsail, topgallant-sail, and studding sails—the last three fitted to set going up before the wind, and to strike, masts and all, so as to beat down with the current under mainsail, jib, and jigger—would make good passages between Pará and Egas. The vessels used now on the river are built broad and flat-bottomed, to warp along shore when the wind is light or contrary. Their sails are much too small, and are generally made of thin, bad material.

DECEMBER 31—We pulled into the Lake of Coari; but being told that it would take nearly all day to reach the village of Coari, and that it was an insignificant place, where I would get neither supplies nor information, I decided not to go.

It may seem strange that just out of Egas I should need supplies, but all I could purchase there were half a dozen fould, four turtles, and some farinha; and upon opening the baskets of farinha, it was found to be so old and sour that, though the Indians could eat it, I could not; and thus we had no bread, nor even the substitute for it—plaintains and farinha; and had to eat our meat with some dried peas that we fortunately found at Egas.

We pulled up the right bank of the lake about a mile, and stopped at a little settlement of ten or twelve houses, but could get nothing. The people seemed afraid of us and shut their doors in our faces. The Lieutenant, or principal man of the place, said that if we would give him money, he would send out and get us some fowls and plantains, but as he was a little drunk at this hour (seven in the morning), I would not trust him. We breakfasted, and sailed at eleven.

JANUARY 1, 1852—At nine A.M. we had the easterly breeze so strong that we were compelled to keep close in shore to avoid the sea raised by it. Our heavy, flat-bottomed boat rolls nearly gunwales under. Some of the Indians look alarmed, and Tomas, a servant whom we brought from Caballococha, is frightened from all propriety. He shouts to the men to make for the land, and, seizing a paddle, makes one or two vigorous strokes, but fear takes away his strength, and he stretches himself on his face, and yields to what appears his inevitable destiny. Ijurra is much scandalized at his cowardice, and asks him what he would do if he got upon the sea.

At half past four we passed the mouth of the Codajash. The mouth appeared a quarter of a mile wide, but I was afterwards told that this was not the largest mouth, and that the true mouth lay opposite to the island of Coro. The Amazon, at a small sand island just below this mouth, commenced falling day before yesterday. A boat which arrived at Egas from Tabatinga the day before we left there reported that the river had commenced falling at Tabatinga on the twentieth of December. This is probably the fall due to the *Verano del Niño* of the Cordillera, and will only last a week or ten days, when the river will again commence to swell.

JANUARY 2—The usual fresh easterly wind commenced at nine. The only time to make progress is at night; during the day the breeze is so fresh, and the sea so high, that very little is made. The wind usually subsides about four or five P.M., and concludes with a squall of wind and rain, leaving heavy-looking thunder-clouds in the southward and westward. The easterly wind often rises again, and blows for a few hours at night.

JANUARY 3—We stopped to breakfast at nine, in company with a schooner bound up. She was three months from Pará and expected to be another month to Egas. Two others also passed us at a distance this morning. We arrived at the mouth of the Purus, 145 miles from Lake Coari. It is a fine-looking river, with moderately bold shores, masked by a great quantity of bushes growing in the water. These bushes bore a great number of berries, which, when ripe, are purple, and about the size of a fox-grape. They were, at this time, green and red. The pulp is sweet, and is eaten.

The water of the river is of the same color, and scarcely clearer, than that of the Amazon. We pulled in about a mile, and found 108 feet of water, rather nearer the left than the right bank, with a bottom of soft blue mud. Temperature of the Purus, 84½ degrees; that of the Amazon, 83 degrees; and the air, 82 degrees. Drifted with the current all night; beautifully calm and clear.

JANUARY 4—We travelled slowly all day, on account of the fresh wind and sea. At seven P.M. we stopped at the village of Pesquera, at the mouth of the Lake Manacapuru, forty-five miles from the mouth of the Purus. All this country seems cut up with channels from river to river, but I believe they are canoe channels, and only passable for them at high water. In many instances these channels, in the rainy season, widen out into lakes.

The banks of the river are now losing the character of savage and desolate solitude that characterizes them above, and begin to show signs of habitation and cultivation. We passed today several farms, with neatly framed and plastered houses, and a schooner-rigged vessel lying off several of them.

JANUARY 5—At three A.M. we passed a rock in the stream called *Calderon,* or Big Pot, from the bubbling and boiling of the water over it when the river is full. At this time the rock is said to be six or eight feet above the surface of the water. We could hear the rush of the water against it, but could not see it on account of the darkness of the night.

We stopped two hours to breakfast, and then drifted with the current broadside to the wind (our six men being unable to keep the boat "head to it") until four, when the wind went down. At five we entered the Rio Negro. We were made aware of our approach to it before getting into the mouth. The right bank at the mouth is broken into islands, and the black water of the Negro runs through the channels between these islands and alternates, in patches (refusing to mingle), with the muddy waters of the Amazon. The entrance is broad and superb. It is far the largest tributary of the Amazon I have yet seen, and I estimate its width at the mouth at two miles. There has been no exaggeration in the description of travellers regarding the blackness of its water. Lieut. Maw describes it perfectly when he says it looks like black marble. It well deserves the name of "Rio Negro." When taken up in a tumbler, the water is a light-red color, like a pale juniper water, and I should think it colored by some such berry. A body immersed in it has the color, though wanting the brilliancy, of red Bohemian glass.

It may have been fancy, but I thought the light cumuli that hung over the river were darker here than elsewhere. These dark, though peaceful-looking clouds, the setting sun, the glitter of the rising moon upon the sparkling ripples of the black water, with its noble expanse, gave us one of the fairest scenes upon our entrance into this river that I ever recollect to have looked upon.

JANUARY 6—Started at one A.M. Moderate breeze from the eastward, blowing in squalls, with light rain. The left bank of the river is bold and occasionally rocky. At five A.M. we arrived at Barra. My countryman, Mr. Marcus Williams, and Señor Enrique Antonii, an Italian (merchants of the place), came on board to see me. Williams was fitting out for an expedition of six months up the river, but Antonii took me at once to his house, and established me there snugly and comfortably. The greatest treat I met here, however, was a file of New York papers. They were not very late, it is true, but still six months later than anything I had seen from home, and I conned them with great interest and no small anxiety.

The Comarca of the Rio Negro, one of the territorial divisions of the great province of Pará, has, within the last year, been erected into a province, with the title of Amazonas.

I have not seen yet any laws regulating its trade, but presume that a custom-house will be established at Barra. The income of the province would be much increased by making Barra a port of entry for the trade with Peru, Bolivia, Ecuador, Venezuela, and New Granada; and I have no doubt that industry and enterprise will, in the course of time, bring goods of European manufacture.

The province has six hundred thousand square miles of territory, and but thirty thousand inhabitants—whites and civilized Indians. (No estimate can be made of the number of *Gentios,* or savages, but I think this is small.) It is nobly situated. By the Amazon, Ucayali, and Huallaga, it communicates with Peru and Bolivia, with Ecuador, New Granada, Venezuela and the Guayanas, and with the rich interior provinces of Brazil. I presume that the

Brazilian government would impose no obstacles to the settlement of this country by any of the citizens of the United States who would choose to go there and carry their slaves; and I know that the thinking people on the Amazon would be glad to see them. The President, who is laboring for the good of the province, and sending for the chiefs of the Indian tribes for the purpose of engaging them in settlement and systematic labor, said to me, at parting, "How much I wish you could bring me a thousand of your active, industrious, and intelligent population, to set an example of labor to these people"; and others told me that they had no doubt that Brazil would give titles to vacant lands to as many as came.

Foreigners have some advantage over natives in being exempt from military and civil services, which are badly paid, and a nuisance. There is still some jealousy on the part of the less educated among the natives against the foreigners, who, by superior knowledge and industry, monopolize trade, and thus prosper. This produced the terrible revolution of the *Cabanos* (serfs, people who live in cabins) in the years from 1836 to 1840, when many Portuguese were killed and expelled. These are the most numerous and active foreigners in the province. I have been told that property and life in the province are always in danger from this cause, and it was probably for this reason that the President, in his speech to the provincial assembly, reminded that body, in such grave terms, that laws must be made for the control and government of the sixty thousand *tapuios*, who so far outnumbered the property-holders, and who are always open to the influence of the designing, the ambitious, and the wicked.

Chapter XIV

❧

Town of Barra—Foreign residents—Population—Rio Negro—
Connexion with the Oronoco—River Purus—Rio Branco—
Vegetable productions of the Amazon country

THE TOWN OF BARRA, capital of the province of Amazonas, is built on elevated and broken ground, on the left bank of the river, and about seven miles from its mouth. Its height above the level of the sea is, by boiling point, 1,475 feet. It is intersected by two or three ravines, containing more or less water, according to the state of the river, which are passed on tolerably constructed wooden bridges. The houses are generally of one story, though there are three or four of two, built of wood and *adobe,* and roofed with tiles. The floors are also of tiles, and the walls are plastered with the colored earth which abounds on the banks of the Amazon.

Every room has several hooks driven into the walls, for the purpose of hanging hammocks. People find it more comfortable, on account of the heat, to sleep in hammocks, though I always suffered from cold, and was obliged every night to wrap myself in a blanket. There are few *musquitoes,* these insects always avoiding black water.

I was surprised to find, before I left Barra, that provisions were getting very scarce. The supply of flour gave out, so that for some time there was no bread in the city, and beef was killed but once a fortnight. Even the staples of the country were difficult to procure, and I heard the President say that he was desirous of recruiting some fifty or sixty *tapuios* to work on the new government buildings, but that he really did not know where he should get a sufficient quantity of salt fish and *farinha* to feed them on. Just before I sailed, a boat-load of turtles came up from the Amazon for Enrique, and his house was besieged by the poorer part of the population, begging him to sell to them.

Soon after my arrival the President did me the honor to ask me to dine with him, to meet the officers of the new government. There seemed then a great abundance of provisions. We had fish, beef, mutton, pig, turtle, and turkey. There are very fine fish taken about Barra; they come, however, from the Amazon, and, unless cooked immediately on their arrival, invariably spoil. The best fish is called *pescado;* it is very delicate, and quite equal, if not superior, to our striped bass, or rock-fish, as it is called in the Southern States. Cut into pieces, fried, and potted with vinegar and spices, it makes capital provisions for a voyage of a week or two.

Williams is the only American resident in Barra. He was in partnership with an Irishman named Bradley, who died a few months ago of yellow fever in Pará. There had been another American in Barra a year ago. This was a deaf mute named Baker, who was travelling in this country for his amusement. He carried with him tablets and a raised alphabet, for the purpose of educating the deaf, dumb, and blind. He died on the twenty-ninth of April, 1850, at San Joachim, the frontier port of Brazil, on the Rio Branco.

I heard some muttered suspicions that the poor man had possibly met with foul play, if not in relation to his death, at least in relation to his property; and understanding that the soldier in whose house he died was then in prison in Barra, I directed a communication to the President, requesting an interview with this soldier. His Excellency did not think it proper to grant that, but sent for the soldier and himself examined him. He then replied to my communication that he could find nothing suspicious in the matter of Mr. Baker's death, but enough in regard to his property to induce him to send for the commandant of the port of San Joachim, and bring the whole matter before a proper tribunal, which he should do at the earliest opportunity, and communicate the result to the American Minister at Rio.

Enrique had told me that he saw in Mr. Baker's possession a rouleau of doubloons, which he judged amounted to $2,000, besides a large bag of silver. A military gentleman whom I was in the habit of meeting at Enrique's house told me that he himself had heard the soldier say that he should be a rich man when he got back to San Joachim, all of which I communicated to the President. The soldier's imprisonment at Barra was on account of some military offence and had nothing to do with this case.

The President also sent me a list of the personal effects of Mr. Baker, which had been sent down by the commandant of San Joachim to Col. Albino, the Commandante General of the Comarca. Amongst them were some things that I thought might be valuable to his family—such as daguerreotypes, maps, and manuscripts, and I requested his Excellency to place them at my disposal for transportation to the United States, but he replied that by a law of the empire the effects of all foreigners belonging to nations who have no special treaty upon the subject, who die in Brazil, are subject to the jurisdiction of the Juiz de Orfaos y Difuntos, and that it was therefore out of his power to comply with my request. I am told (though this may be scandal) that if property once gets into this court, the heir, if he ever succeeds in getting a settlement, finds but a Flemish account of his inheritance.

Our intelligent and efficient consul at Pará, Henry L. Norris, has represented this matter to the government in strong terms, showing the effect that such a law has upon the credit and standing of large mercantile houses in Brazil. I am not aware of any other nation than the French being exempted from its operation. It is clear that the credit of a house whose property may be seized by such a court as this on the death of its resident principal will not be so good, *coeteris paribus,* as that of a house exempted from the operation of such a law. The Brazilian authorities are very rigid in its execution, and I was told that a file of soldiers was sent to surround the house of a dying foreigner to see that no abstraction of property was made, and that the whole might be taken possession of, according to law, on the decease of the moribund.

There were two English residents at Barra—Yates, a collector of shells and plants, and Hauxwell, a collector of bird-skins, which he prepares most beautifully. He used the finest kind of shot, and always carried in his pocket a white powder, to stop the bleeding of the birds when shot. In the preparation of the skins he employed dry arsenic in powder, which is much superior, in this humid climate, to arsenical soap. He admired some of my birds very much and went with Williams up to Pebas, in Peru, where I procured most of them.

The chief engineer of the steamer was a hard-headed, hot-tempered old Scotchman, who abused the steamer in particular, and the service generally, in no measured terms. He desired to know if ever I saw such beef as was furnished to them, and if we would give such beef to the dogs in my country. I told him that I thought he was fortunate to get beef at all, for that I had not seen any for a fortnight, and that if he had made such a voyage as I had recently, he would find turtle and salt fish no such bad things. The steamer, though preserving a fair outside, is, I believe, very inefficient— the machinery wanting in power, and being much out of order; indeed, so much so that on her downward passage she fairly broke down and had to be towed into Pará. She, however, made the trip up in eighteen days, which, considering that the distance is full a thousand miles, that this was the first trip ever made up by steam, that the wood prepared for her had not had time to dry, and that there is nearly three-miles-an-hour current against her for about one third of the distance, I do not consider a very bad run. The officers did not call to see me or invite me on board their vessel, though I met some of them at the dinner and evening parties of the President.

Mr. Potter, a daguerreotypist, and watch-maker, who came up in the steamer, and my good friend Enrique Antonii, the Italian, with his father-in-law, Señor Brandâo, a Portuguese, make up the list of the foreigners of Barra, as far as I know them. Señor Brandâo, however, has lived many years in the country, has identified himself with it, and all his interests are Brazilian. He is a very intelligent man; and I observe that he is consulted by the President and other officials in relation to the affairs of the new government.

Whilst speaking of persons, I should be derelict in the matter of gratitude if I failed to mention Doña Leocadia, the pretty, clever, and amiable wife of Enrique. She exhibited great interest in my mission and was always personally kind to myself. When our sunrise meal of coffee and buttered toast gave out, she would always manage to send me a tapioca custard, a bowl of *caldo,* or something nice and comfortable for a tired invalid. Unlike most Brazilian ladies, whenever her household duties would permit, she always sat with the gentlemen, and bore an intelligent part in the conversation, expressing her desire to speak foreign languages, and to visit foreign countries, that she might see and know what was in the world. A son was born to her whilst I was in the house, and we had become such friends that the young stranger was to be called Luis, and I was to be *compadre* (godfather). But the church, very properly, would not give its sanction to the assumption of the duties belonging to such a position by a heretic.

Ijurra left me here, and returned up stream with Williams. He laid out nearly all the money received for his services in such things as would best enable him to employ the Indians in the clearance of the forest and the establishment of a plantation, which he proposed to "locate" at Caballococha, saying to me that he would have a grand crop of cotton and coffee ready against the arrival of my steamer.

Ijurra has all the qualities necessary for a successful struggle with the world, save two—patience and judgment. He is brave, hardy, intelligent, and indefatigable. The river beach and a blanket are all that are necessary to him for a bed, and I believe that he could live on coffee and cigars. But his want of temper and discretion mars every scheme for prosperity. He spent a noble fortune, dug by his father from the Mina del Rey, at Cerro Pasco, in the political troubles of his country. He was appointed governor of the large and important province of Mainas, but, interfering with the elections, he was driven out. He then joined a party for the purpose of washing the sands of the Santiago for gold, but quarrels with his companions broke that up. With infinite labor he then collected an immense cargo of Peruvian bark, but, refusing $80,000 for it in Pará, he carried it to England, where it was pronounced worthless; and he lost the fruits of his enterprise and industry.

He gave me infinite concern and some apprehension in the management of the Indians, but I shall never forget the untiring energy, the buoyancy of spirits, and the faithful loyalty, that cheered my lonely journey, and made the little Peruvian as dear to me as a brother.

The official returns for the year 1848 gave the population of the town of Barra at 3,614 free persons, and 234 slaves; the number of marriages, 115; births, 250; and deaths 25; the number of inhabited houses, 470; and the number of foreigners, twenty-four.

The Indians of the neighborhood are called Muras; they lead an idle, vagabond life, and live by hunting and fishing. A few of them come in and take service with the whites, and nearly all bring their children in to be baptized. Their reason for this is not that they care about the ceremony, but they can generally persuade some good-natured white man to stand as godfather, which secures the payment of the church fee, a bottle of spirits to the father, and a yard or two of cotton cloth to the mother. Antonii tells me that he is *compadre* with half the tribe.

They are thorough savages and kill a number of their children from indisposition to take care of them. My good hostess told me that her father, returning from a walk to his house in the country, heard a noise in the woods, and, going towards the spot, found a young Indian woman, a *tapuia* of his, digging a hole in the ground for the purpose of burying her infant just born. He interfered to prevent it, when she flew at him like a tiger. The old gentleman, however, cudgelled her into submission and obedience, and compelled her to take the child home, where he put it under the care of another woman.

The women suffer very little in parturition, and are able to perform all the offices of a midwife for themselves. I am told that sometimes, when a man and his wife are travelling together in a canoe, the woman will signify to her husband her desire to land, will retreat into the woods, and in a very short time return with a newly born infant, which she will wash in the river, sling to her back, and resume her paddle again. Even the ladies of this country are confined a very short time. The mother of my little namesake was about her household avocations in seven days after his birth. This probably arises from three causes: the climate, the habit of wearing loose dresses, and the absence of dissipation.

The Rio Negro, opposite the town, is about a mile and a half wide, and very beautiful. The opposite shore is masked by low islands, and, where glimpses of it can be had, it appears to be five or six miles distant. The river is navigable for almost any draught to the Rio Maraya, a distance of twenty-five days, or, according to the rate of travelling on these streams, about four hundred miles; there the rapids commence, and the further ascent must be made in boats. Though large vessels may not ascend these rapids, they descend without difficulty.

A few hours above Barcellos is the mouth of the river Quiuni, which is known to run up to within a very short distance of the Japurá; nearly opposite to San Isabel is the mouth of a river called Jurubashea, which also runs up nearly to the Japurá. Between these rivers is the great Puxiri country; it is covered with water when the rivers are full. There is a vagabond tribe of Indians living in this country called Magu. They use no canoes, and when they cannot travel on the land, for the depth of water, they are said to make astonishing progress from tree to tree, like monkeys, the men laden with their arms and the women with their children.

I have estimated that the distance between Barra and San Carlos at the mouth of the Cassiquiari is about 660 miles. A flat-bottomed iron steamer calculated to pass the rapids of the Rio Negro will make seventy-five miles a day against the current. This will take her to San Carlos in nine days. She will ascend the Cassiquiari 180 miles in two and a half days. From the junction of the Cassiquiari and the Oronoco to Angostura is 780 miles. The steamer has the current with her, and, instead of seventy-five, will run 125 miles a day. This will bring her to Angostura in six days;

thence to the ocean, 250 miles, in two days. This allows the steamer abundance of time to take in fuel, and to discharge and take in cargo, at the many villages she finds on her route; with a canal cut over the portage of six hours at Pimichim, she will make the voyage in five days less.

The mind is confused with the great images presented to it by the contemplation of these things. We have here a continent divided into many islands (for most of its great streams inosculate), whose shores produce, or may be made to produce, all that the earth gives for the maintenance of more people than the earth now holds. We have also here a fluvial navigation for large vessels, by the Amazon and its great tributaries, of (in round numbers) about six thousand miles, which does not include the innumerable small streams that empty into the Amazon, and which would probably swell the amount to ten thousand; neither does it include the Oronoco, with its tributaries, on the one hand, nor the La Plata, with its tributaries, upon the other.

Let us now suppose the banks of these streams settled by an active and industrious population, desirous to exchange the rich products of their lands for the commodities and luxuries of foreign countries; let us suppose introduced into such a country the railroad and the steamboat, the plough, the axe, and the hoe; let us suppose the land divided into large estates, and cultivated by slave labor, so as to produce all that they are capable of producing: And with these considerations, we shall have no difficulty in coming to the conclusion that no territory on the face of the globe is so favorably situated, and that, if trade there is once awakened, the power, the wealth, and grandeur of ancient Babylon and modern London must yield to that of the depots of this trade that shall be established at the mouths of the Oronoco, the Amazon, and the La Plata.

A glance at the map, and a reflection upon the course of the trade-winds, will show conclusively that no ships can sail from the mouths of the Amazon and Oronoco without passing close by our southern ports. Here, then, is the natural depot for the rich and varied productions of that vast region. Here, too, can be found all that the inhabitants of that region require for their support and comfort; and I have not the slightest doubt, if Brazil should pursue a manly policy, and throw open her great river to the trade of the world, that the United States would reap for the largest share of the benefits to be derived from it.

There is scarcely any attempt at the regular cultivation of the earth in all the province of Amazonas, but the natural productions of its soil are most varied and valuable. In the forest are twenty-three well-known varieties of palm, all more or less useful. From the *piassaba* bark is obtained cordage which I think quite equal in quality to the *coir* of India. From the leaves of the *tucum* are obtained the fibres of which all the hammocks of the country are made. Roofs of houses thatched with the gigantic leaves of the *bussu* will last more than ten years. The seed of the *urucurí* and *inaja,* are found to make the best fires for smoking India-rubber; and most of the palms give fruit, which is edible in some shape or other.

Of trees fitted for nautical constructions, there are twenty-two kinds; for the construction of houses and boats, thirty-three; for cabinet-work, twelve (some of which—such as the *jacarandá,* the *muirapinima,* or tortoise-shell wood, and the *macacauba*—are very beautiful); and for making charcoal, seven.

There are twelve kinds of trees that exude milk from their bark; the milk of some of these—such as the *arvoeiro* and *assacú*—is poisonous. One is the *seringa,* or India-rubber tree, and one the *mururé,* the milk of which is reported to possess extraordinary vir-

286   *William Lewis Herndon*

tue in the cure of mercurialized patients, or those afflicted with syphilitic sores. Mr. Norris told me that a young American, dreadfully afflicted with the effects of mercury, and despairing of cure, had come to Pará to linger out what was left of life in the enjoyment of a tropical clime. A few doses of the *mururé* sent him home a well man, though it is proper to say that he died suddenly a few years afterwards. Captain Littlefield, the master of the barque *Peerless,* told me that he had a seaman on board his vessel covered with sores from head to foot, who was radically cured with a few teaspoonfuls of *mururé*. Its operation is said to be very powerful, making the patient cold and rigid, and depriving him of sense for a short time. Mr. Norris has made several attempts to get it home, but without success.

It is idle to give a list of the medicinal plants, for their name is legion. The Indians use nearly everything as a *remedio*. One, however, is peculiar—it is called *manacá*. Its virtue in rheumatic affections was much extolled, and, as I was suffering from pains in the teeth and shoulder, I determined to try its efficacy; but, understanding that its effects were powerful, and made a man feel as if a bucket of cold water were suddenly poured down his back, I begged my kind hostess, Doña Leocadia, to make the decoction weak. Finding no effects from the first teacupful, I took another, but either I was a peculiar patient, or we had not got hold of the proper root. I felt nothing but a very sensible coldness of the teeth and tip of the tongue. Next morning I took a stronger decoction, but with no other effect. I think it operated upon the liver, causing an increased secretion of bile. I brought home the leaves and root.

The root of the *murapuama,* a bush destitute of leaves, is used as an analeptic remedy, giving force and tone to the nerves.

A little plant called *douradinha,* with a yellow flower, something like our dandelion, that grows in the streets at Barra, is a powerful emetic.

A clear and good-burning oil is made from the Brazil nut. Another very pretty oil or resin is called *tamacuaré;* its virtues are much celebrated for the cure of cutaneous affections.

The banks of the rivers and inland lakes abound with wild rice, which feeds a vast number of water-fowl; it is said to be edible.

The Huimba of Peru—a sort of wild cotton, with a delicate and glossy fibre, like silk—abounds in the province. It grows in balls on a very large tree, which is nearly leafless; it is so light and delicate that it would be necessary to strip a number of these large trees to get an *arroba* of it. It is used in Guayaquil to stuff mattresses. I brought home several large baskets of it. Some silk manufacturers in France thought that, mixed with silk, it would make a cheap and pretty fabric, but they had not a sufficient quantity to test it. The tree will give good cotton for three years.

The tree that gives the Brazil nut is not more than two or three feet in diameter, but very tall; the nuts, in number about twenty, are enclosed in a very hard, round shell, of about six inches in diameter. The crop is gathered in May and June. It is quite a dangerous operation to collect it; the nut, fully as large and nearly as heavy as a nine-pounder shot, falls from the top of the tree without warning, and would infallibly knock a man's brains out if it struck him on the head.

There is a variety of this tree, called *sapucaia,* that grows on low lands subject to overflow. Ten or fifteen of the nuts, which are long, corrugated, and very irregular in shape, are contained in a large outer shell; the shell, unlike that of the *castanha,* does not fall entire from the tree, but when the nuts are ripe the bottom falls out, leaving the larger part of the shell, like the cup of an acorn, hanging to the tree. The nuts are scattered upon the water that at this season surrounds the trees and are picked up in boats or by wading. The bark of the nut is fragile, easily broken by the teeth, and its substance is far superior in delicacy of flavor to that of the Brazil nut. This nut as yet must be scarce, or it would have been known to commerce. The tree is a very large one, the flowers yellow and pretty, but destitute of smell. The wood is one of those employed in nautical construction.

Rains at Barra commence in September; the force of the rain is in February and March, but there is scarcely ever a continuous rain of twenty-four hours—one day rainy and one day clear.

Chapter XV

❦

Departure from Barra—River Madeira—Villa Nova—
Cocoa plantations—Obidos

HAVING HAD MY BOAT thoroughly repaired, calked, and well fitted
with palm coverings, with a sort of Wandering Jew feeling that I
was destined to leave everybody behind and never to stop, I sailed
from Barra on the eighteenth of February. The President had
caused me to be furnished with six *tapuios,* but unwilling to dis-
possess himself at this time of a single working hand, he could not
let them carry me below Santarem. The President is laboring in
earnest for the good of the province, and if anything is to be done
for its improvement he will do it. He paid me every attention and
kindness during my stay at Barra.

But to my host (Antonii, the Italian) I am most indebted for
attention and information. From his having been mentioned the
head of trade at Barra sixteen years ago, I had fancied that I should
find him an elderly man, but he is a handsome, gay, active fellow,
in the prime of life. His black hair is somewhat sprinkled with gray,
but he tells me that this arises not from age, but from the worry

and vexation he has had in business on account of the credit system. He is as agreeable as good sense, much information about the country, and open-hearted hospitality can make a man. I asked him to look out for Gibbon and make him comfortable and was charmed with the frank and hearty manner in which he bade me to "have no care of that."

I fear that I behaved a little churlishly about the mails. There are post offices established in the villages on the Amazon, but no public conveyances are provided to carry the mails. The owner or captain of every vessel is required to report to the postmaster before sailing, in order to receive the mails, and he is required to give a receipt for them. I did not like to be treated as an ordinary voyager upon the river, and, therefore, object to receipt for the mails, though I offered to carry all letters that should be intrusted to my care. My principal reason for declining, however, was that my movements were uncertain, and I did not wish to be trammelled. The postmaster would not give me the mail without a receipt, but I believe I brought away all the letters. I am now sorry, as I came direct, that I did not give the required receipt in return for the kindness that had been shown me.

Mr. Potter, the daguerreotypist and watch-maker, sailed in company with me. We found the current of the Negro so slight that, with our heavy boat and few men, we could make no way against a smart breeze blowing up the river. We, therefore, a mile or two below Barra, pulled into the shore and made fast till the wind should fall, which it did about three P.M., when we got under way and entered the Amazon.

Entering this river from the Negro, it appears but a tributary of the latter, and it is generally so designated in Barra. It is very curious to see the black water of the Negro appearing in large circular patches, amid the muddy waters of the Amazon and entirely distinct. I did not observe that the water of the Amazon was at all clearer after the junction of the Negro; indeed, I thought it appeared more filthy.

About sixty miles below the mouth of the Rio Negro we stopped at the establishment of a Scotchman named McCulloch situated on the left bank of the river. There is a very large island opposite, which reduces the river in front to about one hundred yards in width, so that the establishment seems to be situated on a creek.

McCulloch, in partnership with Antonii, at Barra, is establishing here a sugar plantation, and a mill to grind the cane. He dams, at great cost of time and labor, a creek that connects a small lake with the river. He will only be able to grind about six months in the year, when the river is falling and the water runs from the lake into the river; but he proposes to grind with oxen when the river is rising. The difference between high- and low-water mark in the Amazon at this point is, by actual measurement, forty-two feet.

McCulloch has already planted more than thirty acres of sugarcane on a hill eighty or one hundred feet above the present level of the river. It seems of tolerable quality, but much overrun with weeds, on account of want of hands. I gave him a leaf from my experience, and advised him to set fire to his field after every cutting. The soil is black and rich-looking, though light, and McCulloch supposes that in such soil his cane will not require replanting for twenty years.

This is the man who, in partnership with the Brazilian, built the sawmill at Barra, which was afterwards burned down. He sawed 130,000 feet the first year, but not more than half that quantity the second. In the third, by making a contract with Antonii, who was to furnish the wood and receive half the profits, he sawed eighty thousand. This plank is sold in Para at $40 the thousand, but the expenses of getting it there, and other charges, reduce it to about $28. The only wood sawed is the *cedro;* not that it is so valuable as other kinds, but because it is the only wood of any value that floats and thus can be brought to the mills. There are no roads or means of hauling timber through the forests. McCulloch told me that a young American in Pará offered to join him in the erection of a sawmill and to advance $10,000 towards the enterprise. He said that he now thought he was unwise to refuse it, for with that sum he could have purchased a small steamer with which to cruise on the river, picking up the *cedros* and taking them to the mill.

These are not our cedars, but a tall, branching tree, with leaves more like our oak. There are two kinds—red and white, the former of which is most appreciated. Some of them grow to be of great size; between Serpa and Villa Nova we made our boat fast to one that was floating on the river, which measured in length from the swell of the root to that of the first branches (that is a clear, nearly cylindrical trunk) ninety-three feet, and was nineteen feet in circumference just above the swell of the roots, which would probably have been eight feet from the ground when the tree was standing.

The distance hence to the mouth of the Madeira is about thirty miles. After passing the end of the long island, called Tamitari, that lies opposite McCulloch's, we had to cross the river, which there is about two miles wide. I always felt some anxiety in crossing so large an expanse of water in such a boat as ours, where violent storms of wind are of frequent occurrence. Our men, with their light paddles, could not keep such a haystack as our clumsy, heavy boat either head to wind or before it, and she would, therefore, lie broadside to in the trough of the sea, rolling fearfully, and threatening to swamp. I should have had sails fitted to her in Barra.

After crossing the river, we passed the mouth of two considerable streams. At half past eight P.M. we made fast for the night to some bushes on the low, western bank of the Madeira.

A large island occupies the middle of the Amazon, opposite the mouth of the Madeira. This mouth is also divided by a small island. The western mouth is three quarters of a mile wide. The eastern mouth is a mile and a quarter. The island which divides the mouth is low and grassy at its outer extremity, but high and wooded at its upper. I looked long and earnestly for the broad L that Gibbon was to cut on a tree at the mouth of whatever tributary he should come down, in hope that he had already come down the Madeira, and, not being able to go up stream to Barra, had gone on down; but it was nowhere to be seen.

The Madeira is by far the largest tributary of the Amazon. Once past its cascades, which are about 450 miles from its mouth, and occupy a space of 350 miles in length, it is navigable for large vessels by its great tributaries— the Beni and Mamoré—into the heart of Bolivia.

The village of Serpa, where we arrived in the afternoon, is situated on the left bank of the Amazon, thirty miles below the mouth of the Madeira. It is a collection of mud-hovels of about two hundred souls, built upon a considerable eminence, broken and green with grass, that juts out into the river.

We left Serpa at six P.M., and drifted all night. We are compelled to travel at night, for there is so much wind and sea during the day that we make no headway. We are frequently compelled to lay by, and are sometimes in danger of being swamped, even in the little nooks and bays where we stop. The most comfortable way of travelling is to make the boat fast to a floating tree, for this keeps the boat head on to the wind and sea, and drags her along against these with the velocity of the current.

About fifteen miles above Villa Nova, a boat manned by soldiers pulled out from a hut on the shore, and told us we must stop there until examined and despatched by the officer in charge, called inspector. I could not well pull back against the stream, for we had already passed the hut; so I sent word to the inspector that I had letters from the President, and pulled in shore abreast of where I was. The inspector had the civility to come down to me and inspect my papers. This is a *resisto,* or coast-guard, stationed above the port of entry of Villa Nova, to stop vessels from passing, and to notify them that they must go into that port. There is another below Villa Nova to stop vessels coming up, and to examine the clearances from the custom-house of those coming down.

The inspector told me I was within four hours of Villa Nova, but I kept in shore, for fear of squalls, and thus, in the darkness of night, pulled around the shore of a deep bay, where there was little current, and did not arrive for eight hours, passing the mouth of the small river Limao, about a mile and a half above Villa Nova, where we arrived at two A.M.

Villa Nova de Rainha is a long straggling village of single story mud-huts, situated in a little bend on the right bank of the Amazon. The temperature of boiling water gives its elevation above the level of the sea at 959 feet. This being the frontier town of the province of Amazonas, there is a custom-house established here. I heard that it had collected $1,000 since the steamer passed up in December. This gives an indication of the trade of the country; foreign articles, which are the cargoes of vessels bound up, paying 1½ percent on their value; and articles of domestic produce, which the vessels bound down carry, paying a half percent. The collection of $1,000 was made in two months.

The people valued their fowls at fifty cents apiece. We thought them extortionate and would not buy, but we happened to arrive on fresh-beef day and got a soup-piece. These fresh-meat days are a week apart, though this is a cattle producing country. It is an indication of the listless indifference of the people.

About a league below Villa Nova we passed the mouth of the river Ramos on the right. It is two hundred yards wide, and is a *paranimiri,* which leaves the Amazon nearly opposite Silves. It is the general route to Maués—a considerable village in the interior, four days from the mouth of the Ramos.

The country about Maués is described as a great grazing plain, intersected and cut up with streams and canals, all navigable for the largest class of vessels that now navigate the Amazon. The soil is very rich, and adapted to the cultivation of cotton, coffee, and cocoa. The rivers give abundance of fish, any number of cattle may be pastured upon the plains, and the neighboring woods yield cloves, cocoa, *castanhas,* India-rubber, *guaraná,* sarsaparilla, and *copaiba.* If this country be not sickly (and the *sub-delegado* at Villa Nova, who gave me a little sketch of it, told me that it was not) it is probably the most desirable place of residence on the Amazon.

Just below the mouth of the Ramos, quite a neatly rigged boat, carrying the Brazilian flag, put off from a house on shore, and seemed desirous to communicate with us, but she was so badly managed that, although there was a fine breeze, she could not catch us, though we were but drifting with the current. Had I known her character I would have paddled up against the stream to allow her to join company, but my companion, Mr. Potter, said that she was a boat belonging to the church, and begging for Jerusalem.

Finding that she could not come up with us, she put back, and a light canoe with a soldier in it soon overtook us. The soldier told me that this was another custom-house station, and that I must pull back and show my clearance from the collector at Villa Nova. I was a good deal annoyed at this, for I thought the said collector, to

whom I carried letters from the President, might have had the fore-
thought to tell me about this station, so that I might have stopped
there and saved the time and labor of pulling back. The soldier,
seeing my vexation, told me that if I would merely pull in shore
and wait, the inspector, who was then a few miles down the river,
would soon be by on his way up, and I could communicate with
him there.

To do this even carried me some distance out of my way, but
I had previously resolved to conform scrupulously to the laws and
usages of the country, so I smothered my annoyance, pulled in, and
had the good luck to meet the inspector before reaching the land.
This was a mere boy, who looked at my papers coldly and without comment, except (prompted by an old fellow who was steering his boat) he asked me if I had no paper from the collector at
Villa Nova. I told him no, that I was no *commerciante,* had nothing to sell, and that he had read my passports from his government.
After a little hesitation he suffered me to pass.

The pull into the right bank had brought me to the head of an
island. The inspector told me that the passage was as short on that
side, but that it was narrow and full of *carapana,* as *musquitoes* are
called on the Amazon. Although I have a *musquito* curtain which
protects me completely, yet the *tapuios* had none, and, whenever I
stopped at night, they had a wretched time, and could not sleep a
moment. This was one of the reasons why I travelled at night. All
persons are so accustomed to travel from Barra downwards at
night, and to keep out far from the shore, that they do not carry
musquito curtains, which the travellers on the upper Amazon and
its tributaries would perish without.

We pulled back into the main stream and drifted all night,
passing the small village of Parentins, situated on some high

lands that form the boundary between the provinces of Pará and Amazonas.

We now enter the country where the cocoa is regularly cultivated, and the banks of the river present a much less desolate and savage appearance than they do above. The cocoa-trees have a yellow-colored leaf, and this, together with their regularity of size, distinguishes them from the surrounding forest. At eight P.M., February 25, we arrived at Obidos, 105 miles below Villa Nova. Several gentlemen offered to furnish me a vacant house, but I was surly and slept in my boat.

Whilst at Obidos, I took a canoe to visit the *cacoaes,* or cocoa plantations, in the neighborhood; the fruit is called *cacao.* We started at six A.M., accompanied by a gentleman named Miguel Figuero, and stopped at the mouth of the Trombetas, which empties into the Amazon four or five miles above Obidos. It enters the Amazon at a very sharp angle; its waters are clear, and the dividing-line between them and those of the Amazon is preserved distinct for more than a mile.

The Trombetas is said to be a very large river, in some places as wide as the Amazon is here—about two miles. It is very productive in fish, *castanhas,* and sarsaparilla, and runs through a country well adapted to raising cattle. I have heard several people call it a world; they may call it so on account of its productions, or it may be a "world of waters," for the whole country, according to the description of it, is entirely cut up with lakes and water-communications.

Near the mouth of this river we stopped at an establishment for making pots and earthenware, belonging to a gentleman named Bentez, who received us with cordiality. This country house was neat, clean, and comfortable. I caught glimpses of some ladies neatly

dressed and with very pretty faces and was charmed with the sight
of a handsome pair of polished French leather boots sitting against
the wall. This was the strongest sign of civilization that I had met
with and showed me that I was beginning to get into communication with the great world without. Señor Bentez gave me some eggs
of the *enambu,* a bird of the pheasant or partridge species, some of
which are as large as a turkey.

In crossing the Amazon we were swept by the current below
the plantation we intended to visit, and thus had a walk of a mile
through the cocoa plantations, with which the whole right bank
of the river between Obidos and Alemquer is lined. I do not know
a prettier place than one of these plantations. The trees interlock
their branches, and, with their large leaves, make a shade impen-
etrable to any ray of the sun. The earth is perfectly level, and covered with a carpeting of dead leaves, and the large golden-colored
fruit, hanging from branch and trunk, shine through the green
with a most beautiful effect. The only drawback to the pleasure of
a walk through them arises from the quantity of *musquitoes,* which
in some places, and at certain times, are unendurable to one not
seasoned to their attacks. I could scarcely keep still long enough to
shoot some of the beautiful birds that were flitting among the trees.

This is the time of the harvest, and we found the people of every
plantation engaged, in the open space before the house, in break-
ing open the shells of the fruit, and spreading the seed to dry in
the sun on boards. They make a pleasant drink for a hot day by
pressing out the juice of the gelatinous pulp that envelops the seeds.
It is called *cacao* wine, is a white, rather viscid liquor, has an agreeable, acid taste, and is very refreshing; fermented and distilled, it
will make a powerful spirit.

The ashes of the burnt hull of the *cacao* contains a strong al-
kali, and it is used in all the *cacoaes* for making soap.

We were kindly received by the gentleman whom we went to visit, Señor José da Silva, whom we found busily engaged in gathering the crop. When he discovered that we had eaten nothing since daylight, he called out in true hospitable country fashion, "Wife, cook something for these men; they are hungry," and we accordingly got some dinner of turtle and fowl.

In addition to the gathering of his cocoa, Señor da Silva was engaged in expressing a clean, pretty-looking oil from the *castanha*. The nut was first toasted in the oven, then pulverized in a wooden mortar, and the oil was pressed out in the same sort of wicker-bag that is used for straining the *mandioc*. He said that the oil burned well and was soft and pleasant to put on the skin or make unguents of, though it had not a pleasant smell. This oil has not yet found its way into foreign commerce.

Obidos is situated upon a high, bold point, and has all the river (about a mile and a half in width) in front of it. The shores are bold, and the current very rapid. The land may be called mountainous, in comparison to the general low land of the Amazon; and far back in the direction of the course of the Trombetas were seen some very respectable mountains.

The town of Obidos proper contains only about five hundred inhabitants, but the district is populous, and is said to number about fourteen thousand. There is quite a large church in the town, built of stone and mud, with some pretensions to architecture; but, though only built in 1826, it seems already falling into ruins and requires extensive repairs.

There are several shops, apparently well stocked with English and American clothes and French fripperies. I heard a complaint that the trade was monopolized by a few who charged their own prices, but I judged, from the number of shops, that there was quite competition enough to keep the prices down to small profits.

I have my information from Señor Antonio Monteiro Tapajos, who was very kind to me during my stay in Obidos. He gave me some specimens of Indian pottery, and his wife, a thin, delicate-looking lady, apparently much oppressed with sore eyes and children (there being nine of the latter, the oldest only thirteen years of age), gave me a very pretty hammock.

Señor Joao Valentin de Couto, whose acquaintance I made by accident, gave me a live young *peixe-boi,* which unfortunately died after it had been in my possession but a day. He also made me a present of some statistical tables of the affairs of the province, and not being able to find, at the time, the report of the President that accompanied these tables, he had the courtesy to send it to me in a canoe, after I had left the place and was engaged in sounding the river.

It will be seen that here, as elsewhere, during my travels, I met with personal attention, kindness, and liberality. Everyone whom I conversed with on the subject of the Amazon advocates with earnestness the free navigation of the river and says that they will never thrive until the river is thrown open to all and foreigners are invited to settle on its banks. I think that they are sincere, for they have quite intelligence enough to see that they will be benefitted by calling out the resources of the country.

Obidos has a college, lately established, which has some assistance from the government. It has yet but twenty-four scholars, and one professor—a young ecclesiastic, modest and intelligent, and enthusiastic and hopeful about the affairs of his college.

Antonio, a Portuguese, with whom I generally got my breakfast, told me that there were many poisonous serpents in the neighborhood of Obidos, and showed me a black swelling on the arm of his little son, the result of the bite of a scorpion. In five minutes after the boy was bitten, he became cold and senseless, and foamed at the mouth, so that for some hours his life was despaired of. The remedies used were homœopathic, and, what is a new thing to me, were put in the corners of the eye, as the boy could not swallow. I found homœpathy a favorite mode of practice from Barra downwards. It was introduced by a Frenchman, a few years ago, and there are now several amateur practitioners of it.

We left Obidos, in the rain, at one P.M., on the twenty-ninth of February. Our long stay at Barra had brought the rains upon us, and we now had rain every day.

We travelled all night, and at half past nine A.M., on the first of March, we entered a *furo* of the Tapajos, which, in one hour and three quarters, conducted us into that river opposite the town of Santarem. We presented our passports and letters to the Delegado and obtained lodgings in the hired house of a French Jew of Pará, who was engaged in peddling watches and jewelry in Santarem.

Chapter XVI

❧

Santarem—Population—Trade—River Tapajos—
Diamond region

SANTAREM, 460 miles from the mouth of the Rio Negro and 650 miles from the sea, is the largest town of the province, after Pará. By official returns it numbers 4,977 free, and 1,591 slave inhabitants.

I would estimate the population of the town of Santarem at about two thousand souls. In the official returns all the settlers on the cocoa plantations for miles around, and all the *tapuios* engaged in the navigation of the river, are reckoned in the estimate. This, I believe, is the case with all the towns, and thus the traveller is continually surprised to find population rated so high in places where he encounters but few people. There is said to be a good deal of elephantiasis and leprosy among the poorer class of its inhabitants. I did not visit their residences, which are generally on the beach above the town and therefore saw nothing of them; nor did I see much poverty or misery.

There are tokens of an increased civilization in a marble monument in the cemetery, and a billiard table. The houses are com-

fortably furnished, though I believe everyone still sleeps in a hammock. The rides in the environs are agreeable, the views picturesque, and the horses good. A tolerably good and well-bitted horse
may be had for $75; they graze in the streets and outskirts of the
town and are fed with Indian corn.

There is a church (one of the towers has lately tumbled down)
and two or three primary schools. The gentlemen all wear gold
watches and take an immoderate quantity of snuff.

The voyage to the head of navigation on the Rio Preto, a
confluent of the Tapajos, occupies about two months. At this place
mules are found to carry the cargo fifteen miles to the village of
Diamantino, situated on the high lands that divide the headwaters of the streams flowing south from those of the streams flowing north, which approach each other at this point very closely.
These high lands are rich in diamonds and minerals. I saw some
in possession of a captain. The gold dust is apparently equal in
quality to that I had seen from California.

One will readily perceive, from certain estimates, that dia-
mond-hunting as a business is unprofitable. But this, like all mining operations, is a lottery. A man in the diamond region may
stumble upon a fortune at an instant of time and without a dollar
of outlay, but the chances are fearfully against him.

Chapter XVII

◠◠

Departure from Santarem—Monte Alegre—Prainha—River
Xingu—Great estuary of the Amazon—India-rubber country—
Method of collecting and preparing the India-rubber—
Bay of Limoeiro—Arrival at Pará

M. ALFONSE WAS MORE generous than the Tuchao, for I could do
nothing for him; yet he gave me his *paricá,* his Mundrucus gloves,
and a very valuable collection of dried leaves and plants that he had
gathered during his tour.

I spent a very agreeable day with him at the country house of
M. Gouzennes, situated on the Igarapé-assu, about three miles from
Santarem. The house is a neat little cottage, built of *pisé,* which is
nearly the same thing as the large sun-dried bricks, called by the
Spaniards *adobe,* though more carefully prepared. I supposed that
this house, situated in the midst of a cocoa plantation, on low land,
near the junction of two great rivers, under a tropical sun, and with
a tropical vegetation, would be an unhealthy residence; but I was
assured there was no sickness here. We put up in earth, for transportation to the United States, plants of arrow-root, ginger, *manacá,*
and some flowers. I believe that some of these reached home alive,
and are now in the public garden.

Other gentlemen were also kind and civil to me. Mr. Bates, a young English entomologist, gave me a box of very beautiful butterflies; and the Vicario Gêral, the foetus of a *peixe-boi,* preserved in spirits. Señor Pinto, the Delegado, furnished me with horses to ride; and I took most of my meals with Capt. Hislop.

An attempt was made to murder the old gentleman a few weeks before I arrived. Whilst sleeping in his hammock, two men rushed upon him, and one of them gave him a violent blow in the breast with a knife—the point of the knife, striking the breast-bone, broke or bent. The robbers then seized his trunk and made off, but were so hotly pursued by the captain's domestics, whom he had called up, that they dropped their booty and fled.

A young Englishman named Golden, who had married a Brazilian lady, and was engaged in traffic on the river, was also kind to me, giving me specimens of India-rubber and cotton.

We had a great deal of heavy rain during our stay at Santarem (generally at night), with sharp lightning and strong squalls of wind from the eastward. The river rose with great rapidity for the last three or four days of my stay. The beach on which I was accustomed to bathe, and which was one hundred yards wide when I arrived, was entirely covered when I left. There were no symptoms of tide at that season, though I am told it is very perceptible in the summer time. Water boiled at Santarem at 210.5, indicating a height of 846 feet above the level of the sea.

I left Santarem at seven P.M., March 28. The Delegado could only muster me three *tapuios* and a pilot, and I shipped a volunteer. I believe he could have given me as many as I desired (eleven), but that he had many employed in the building of his new house, and, moreover, he had no conception that I would sail on the day that I appointed; people in this country never do, I believe, by any chance. If they get off on a journey within a week of the time appointed, they think they are doing well, and I have known several instances where they were a month after the time.

When the Delegado found that I would go with what men I had, he begged me to wait till morning, saying that the military commandant, who had charge of the Trabalhadores, had sent into the country for two, and was expecting them every hour. But I too well knew that it was idle to rely on expectations of this sort, and I sailed at once, thanking him for his courtesy.

I had several applications to ship for the voyage from Indians at Santarem, but I was very careful not to take any who were engaged in the service of others, for I knew that custom, if not law, gave the *patrón* the service of the *tapuio,* provided this latter were in debt to the former, which I believe the *patrón* always takes good care shall be the case.

I paid these men—the pilot forty, and the crew thirty cents per day. The Ticunas, who formed my crew from Tabatinga to Barra, I paid partly in money and partly in clothes, at the rate of four dollars per month. I paid the Muras, from Barra to Santarem, at the same rate. The Peruvian Indians were generally paid in cotton cloth, at the rate of about twelve and a half cents per day.

We gave passage to the French Jew who had given us lodgings in his house at Santarem. I had great difficulty in keeping the peace between him and Potter, who had as much antipathy towards each other as an uneducated Frenchman and Englishman might be supposed to have.

We drifted with the current all night, and stopped in the morning at a small cocoa plantation belonging to someone in Santarem. The water of the river was, at this time, nearly up to the door of the house, and the country seemed to be all marsh behind. I never saw a more desolate, sickly-looking place; but a man who was living there with his wife and six children (all strong and healthy-looking) told me they were never sick there. This man told me that he could readily support himself and his family but for the military service he was compelled to surrender at Santarem, which took him away from his work and his family for several months in every year.

We stopped at nine P.M. under some high land close to the mouth of a small river called Curuá, on account of heavy squall of wind and rain.

MARCH 30—We passed this morning the high lands on the left bank of the river, among which is situated the little town of Monte Alegre. This is a village of fifteen hundred inhabitants, who are principally engaged in the cultivation of cocoa, the raising of cattle, and the manufacture of earthern-ware and drinking cups made from gourds, which they varnish and ornament with goldleaf and colors in a neat and pretty style.

In the afternoon we crossed the river, here about four miles wide, and stopped at the village of Prainha, a collection of mud huts on a slight green eminence on the left bank of the river, ninety miles below Santarem. The inhabitants, numbering five hundred, employ themselves in gathering India-rubber and making *manteiga*. The island opposite the town has a lake in the centre abounding with turtle.

We saw several persons at this place who were suffering from *sezoens,* or *tertianas,* but all said they took them whilst up the neighboring rivers. If general accounts are to be relied on, there seems to be really no sickness on the main trunk of the Amazon, but only on the tributaries, though I saw none on the Huallaga and Ucayali.

I have no doubt of the fact that sickness is more often taken on the tributaries than on the main trunk, but I do not think it is because there is any peculiar malaria on the tributaries from which the main trunk is exempt. The reason, I think, is this: When persons leave their homes to ascend the tributaries, they break up their usual habits of life, live in canoes exposed to the weather, with bad and insufficient food, and are engaged in an occupation (the collection of India-rubber or sarsaparilla) which compels them to be nearly all the time wet. It is not to be wondered at that, after months of such a life, the voyager should contract chills and fever in its most malignant form.

The mere traveller passes these places without danger. It is the enthusiast in science, who spends weeks and months in collecting curious objects of natural history, or the trader, careless of consequences in the pursuit of dollars, who suffers from the *sezoens.*

Although there were a number of cattle grazing in the streets of Prainha, we could get no fresh meat, and indeed, but for the opportune arrival of a canoe with a single fish, our *tuyuyús,* or great cranes, would have gone supperless. These birds frequently passed several days without food—and this on a river abounding with fish, which shows the listless indifference of the people.

The banks of the river between Monte Alegre and Gurupá are bordered with hills that deserve the name of mountains. In this part of our descent we had a great deal of rain and bad weather; for wherever the land elevates itself in this country, clouds and rain settle upon the hills. But it was very pleasant, even with these accompaniments, to look upon a country broken into hill and valley, and so entirely distinct from the low flat country above, that had wearied us so long with its changeless monotony.

It is very difficult to get any information from the Indian pilots on the river. When questioned regarding any stream, the common reply is, "It runs a long way up, it has rapids, savages live upon its banks, everything grows there." (*Vai longe, tem caxoieras, tem gentios, tem tudo*.) I was always reminded of the Peruvian Indian with his *"Hay platanos, hay yuccas, hay todo."*

Our pilot, however, told me that the river was navigable for large vessels twenty days to the first rapids; that the current was very strong; that there was much *sezoens* on it; and that much sarsaparilla and cloves could be collected there.

The immediate banks of the river at its mouth are low, but close to the left bank commences a short but quite high range of hills that runs parallel to the Amazon. Six miles below this we passed the village of Almeirim on the left bank but did not stop. Fifty miles below Almeirim we steered across the river for Gurupá, running under sail from island to island. The river here is about ten miles wide. Large islands divide it into the Macapá and Gurupá channels, the latter conducting to Pará, the former running out to sea by the shores of Guyana.

After crossing, we fell into the dark waters of the Xingu, whose mouth we could see some six or eight miles above. Fifteen miles further brought us to Gurupá, where we arrived at a quarter past nine P.M.

Gurupá is a village of one street, situated on a high grassy point on the right bank, with large islands in front, diminishing the width of the river to about a mile and a half. It contains about three hundred inhabitants, though the *sub-delegado* said it had two or three thousand, and the official report states the number at over one thousand.

The principal trade of the place is in India-rubber, obtained on the Xingu and the neighboring smaller streams. We found at this place, as at every other place below Barra, a great demand for salt fish. Everybody asked us if we had any to sell, and we could readily have obtained three dollars the *arroba,* for which we had paid but seventy-five cents in Barra. The scarcity of the fish is attributable to the fact that the river has fallen very little this year, but I incline to believe that the fish are not so plentiful, and that the people are not so active in taking them as before. It was amusing at Santarem to see the gathering of the population around a canoe, recently arrived with fish, as if this were a thing of rare occurrence. The people seemed so lazy that they would prefer eating *farinha* alone, rather than take the trouble to go down to the Amazon and catch fish.

I met, at the house of the Commandante-militar, with an old gentleman who was on his way to Porto de Moz, near the mouth of the Xingu, to take the office of municipal judge of the district. He seemed to be a man well informed with regard to all the river below Barra. He told me that the Xingu was obstructed by rapids for navigation in large vessels within four days' travel from its mouth, and that boats could not go far up on account of the savages. These rapids, however, cannot be a serious impediment for boats, for I was told at Santarem that the caravans from Cuiabá to Rio Janeiro passed the Xingu in boats, and found at that place porpoises of the Amazon, from which they inferred that there were no falls or serious obstacles in the river below them.

The judge asked me for accounts from Barra, and when he received the usual answer, that the town was not in a flourishing condition, and was short of the necessaries of life, he shrugged his shoulders (as all in the lower province do when speaking of the new province), as if to say, "I knew it."

He said that it might come to something in forty years, but that nothing could be expected of a place that furnished nothing to commerce but a few oils, and a little *piassaba,* and where the population was composed of Muras and Araras. He spoke bitterly of the Mura tribe of Indians, and said that they were lazy and deceitful.

According to his account, the white man furnishes the Mura with a boat, pays him, beforehand, a jacket, a shirt, a pair of trousers, and a hat; furnishes him with fish and *farinha* to eat, and tobacco to smoke, and sends him out to take Pirarucu; but when the Indian gets off, it is "Good-bye Mura," or, if he does come back, he has spent so much time in his fishing that the fish are not worth the outlay and the time lost.

It was true, he said, there were cattle on the Rio Branco, but they could only be sent for and traded in when the river was full, and he concluded by making a great cross in the air and lifting up his eyes to give vent to the expression, "Heaven deliver me from Barra!"

I conversed with the old gentleman on some projects of reform as regarded the Indian population. He thought that a military force should be employed to reduce them to a more perfect system of subjection, and that they should, by all means, be compelled to work. I told him that a Portuguese had said that the best reform that could be made would be to hang all the Indians. My friend seemed a little shocked at this, and said that there was no necessity for such root-and-branch work. He said he would grant that the old ones might be killed to advantage, but he thought they might be shot and not hung. This, I believe, was said *bona fide*. I was amused at the old gentleman's philanthropy, and thought that, as a judge, he might have preferred the hanging process.

The tide is very apparent at Gurupá. The river fell several feet during the morning whilst we were there. This point is about five hundred miles from the sea.

After we had sailed, the Commandante-militar, to whom I had applied for more men, and who had told me there were none to be had, sent a man in a canoe after us. I suspected so much courtesy, and found, accordingly, that the man (a negro) was a cripple, and utterly worthless. He had evidently been palmed off upon us to get rid of him. I made him feed the birds and cook for the men. These men made the best and hardest-working crew I had during my voyage.

About thirty-five miles below Gurupá commences the great estuary of the Amazon. The river suddenly flares out into an immense bay, which is probably 150 miles across in its widest part. This might appropriately be called the "Bay of the Thousand Islands," for it is cut up into innumerable channels. The great island of Marajo, which contains about ten thousand square miles, occupies nearly the centre of it, and divides the river into two great channels: one, the main channel of the Amazon, which runs out by Cayenne; and the other, and smaller one, the river of Pará. I imagine that no chart we have gives anything like a correct idea of this bay. I think it would cost a steamer a year of uninterrupted labor to make a tolerably correct chart of this estuary.

At this point we turned into a small creek that penetrated the right bank, and ran for days through channels varying from fifty to five hundred yards in width, between innumerable islands. This is the India-rubber country. The shores of the islands were all low; and, indeed, we seldom saw the land at all, the trees on the banks generally standing in the water.

We stopped (April 3) at one of the establishments on the river for making, or rather for buying, India-rubber. The house was built of light poles, and on piles to keep it out of the water, which, at this time, flowed under and around it. The owner had a shop containing all the necessaries of life, and such articles of luxury as were likely to attract the fancy of the Indian gatherers of the rubber. It was strange, and very agreeable, to see flour-barrels marked Richmond, and plain and striped cottons from Lowell and Saco, with English prints, pewter ear and finger rings, combs, small guitars, cheese, gin, and *aguadiente,* in this wild and secluded-looking spot.

This house was a palace to the rude shanty which the *seringero,* or gatherer of the rubber, erects for a temporary shelter near the scene of his labors.

The owner of the house told me that the season for gathering the rubber, or *seringa,* as it is here called, was from July to January. The tree gives equally well at all times, but the work cannot be prosecuted when the river is full, as the whole country is then under water. Some, however, is made at this time, for I saw a quantity of it in this man's house, which was evidently freshly made.

The process of making it is as follows: A longitudinal gash is made in the bark of the tree with a very narrow hatchet or tomahawk; a wedge of wood is inserted to keep the gash open, and a small clay cup is stuck to the tree beneath the gash. The cups may be stuck as close together as possible around the tree. In four or five hours the milk has ceased to run, and each wound has given from three to five tablespoonfuls. The gatherer then collects it from the cups, takes it to his *rancho,* pours it into an earthen vessel, and commences the operation of forming it into shapes and smoking it. This must be done at once, as the milk soon coagulates.

A fire is made on the ground of the seed of nuts of a palm-tree. An earthen pot with the bottom knocked out is placed, mouth down, over the fire, and a strong pungent smoke from the burning seeds comes up through the aperture in the bottom of the inverted pot.

The maker of the rubber now takes his last, if he is making shoes, or his mould, which is fastened to the end of a stick, pours the milk over it with a cup, and passes it slowly several times through the smoke until it is dry. He then pours on the other coats until he has the required thickness, smoking each coating until it is dry. From twenty to forty coats make a pair of shoes. The soles and heels are, of course, given more coats than the body of the shoe. The figures on the shoes are made by tracing them on the rubber whilst soft with a coarse needle or bit of wire. This is done in two days after the coating. In a week the shoes are taken from the last. The coating occupies about twenty-five minutes.

Moulds are made either of clay or wood; if of wood, it is smeared with clay, to prevent the adhesion of the milk. When the rubber has the required thickness, the moulds are either cut out or washed out.

Smoking changes the color of the rubber very little. After it is prepared, it is nearly as white as milk and gets its color from age.

An industrious man is able to make sixteen pounds of rubber a day, but the collectors are not industrious. I heard a gentleman in Pará say that they rarely average more than three or four pounds.

The tree is tall, straight, and has a smooth bark. It sometimes reaches a diameter of eighteen inches or more. Each incision makes a rough wound on the tree, which, although it does not kill it, renders it useless, because a smooth place is required to which to attach the cups. The milk is white and tasteless, and may be taken into the stomach with impunity.

We navigated all day, after leaving this place, through a labyrinth of island channels, generally one or two hundred yards wide, and forty-eight feet deep. No land is seen in threading these channels, it being all covered; and the trees and bushes seem growing out of the water. Occasionally the bushes are cleared away, and one sees a shanty mounted on piles in the water, the temporary residence of a *seringero*. At a place in one of these channels, I was surprised to find 192 feet of water, with a rocky bottom. The lead hung in the rocks, so that we had difficulty in getting it again.

APRIL 4—The channels and shores are as before; though we occasionally see a patch of ground with a house on it. This is generally surrounded with cocoa-nut trees and other palms, among which the *miriti* is conspicuous for its beauty. This is a very tall, straight, umbrella-like tree, that bears large clusters of a small nut, which is eaten.

We employed the fifth, sixth, and seventh of April in running through inland passages, and occasionally touching on the main stream, anchoring during the flood-tide.

I could keep no account of the tide in these passages. We would encounter two or three different tides in three or four hours. I imagine the reason of this was that some of the passages were channels proper of the Amazon; some of them small, independent rivers; and some, again, *furos,* or other outlets of these same rivers. On the morning of the seventh, we were running down on the main river, here about three miles wide, and with a powerful ebb-tide. Suddenly we turned to the right, or southward, into a creek about forty yards wide, and with twelve feet of water, and found a small tide against us. After pulling up this creek an hour, we found a powerful tide in our favor, without having observed that we had entered another stream; so that from five A.M. to three P.M., we had had but a small tide of one hour against us.

I could get no information from our pilot. He seems to me to say directly contrary things about it. The old man is very timid, and will never trust himself in the stormy waters of the main river if he can find a creek, though it go a long distance about.

The channels are so intricate that we find, at the bifurcations, bits of sail cloth hung on the bushes, to guide the navigators on the route to Pará. Those channels which lead to Cametá, on the Tocantins, and other places, are not marked.

At eight P.M. on the seventh, we arrived at the mouth of the creek, which debouches upon the bay of Limoeiro, a deep indentation of the right bank of the Amazon, at the bottom of which is the mouth of the river Tocantins. We had a stormy night, with a fresh wind from the eastward, and much rain, thunder, and lightning.

APRIL 8—The pilot objected to attempt the passage of the bay; but another pilot, who was waiting to take a vessel across the next day, encouraged him, telling him that he would have *feliz viagem.*

We pulled a mile to windward, and made sail across, steering east-southeast. The wind from the northward and eastward, encountering the ebb-tide which runs from the southward, soon made a sharp sea, which gave us a rough passage. The canoe containing our animals and birds, which was towing astern, with our crippled negro from Gurupá steering, broke adrift, and I had the utmost difficulty in getting her again; indeed we took in so much water in our efforts to reach her that I thought for a moment that I should have to make sail again, and abandon the menagerie. The canoe, however, would probably not have perished. She was so light that she took in little water, and would have drifted with the ebb-tide to some point of safety.

We had a quick run to an island near the middle of the bay, and about five miles from the shore that we sailed from. The bay on this side of the island has several sand-flats that are barely covered at low water. They seem entirely detached from the land and have deep water close around them.

Our pilot must have steered by instinct, or the direction of the wind; for most of the time he could see no land, so thick and heavy was the rain. He grinned with delight when we ran under the lee of the island, and I nodded my head approvingly to him, and said, "*bem feito piloto*" (well done, pilot).

We breakfasted on the island, and ran with the flood-tide to its southern extremity; where, turning to the north, we had the flood against us, and were compelled to stop.

We crossed the other arm of the bay (about five miles wide) with the ebb-tide, and anchored at the mouth of a small river called Anapui, which empties into the bay near its opening into the main river of Pará.

There are large mud flats near the mouth of this river, which are enclosed with small stakes driven in the mud close together, for the purpose of taking fish when the tide is out. A great many small fish—about the size of a herring—called *mopará,* are taken and salted for the food of the slaves and *tapuios.* The fishermen, in ludicrously small canoes, gathered around us, admiring our birds and asking many strange questions.

This river is about 250 yards wide, and has a general depth of thirty-six feet. Its banks are lined with plantations of cane, sugar-mills, and potteries. Nearly all the rum and the pots for putting up the turtle-oil that are used on the river are made in this district. The owners of these establishments are nearly all away at this time celebrating holy-week in Sta. Ana, or other neighboring villages.

The establishments are left in charge of domestics, and we saw no signs of activity or prosperity among them. Most of them have neat little chapels belonging to them.

The river Sta. Ana empties into the Anapui. We anchored at its mouth to await for the flood-tide. Our pilot, who always sleeps on the arched covering over the stern of the boat, rolled overboard in the night. The tide was fortunately nearly done, and the old man swam well, or he would have been lost.

The village of Sta. Ana is eight miles from the mouth of the river, and 250 miles below Breves. It is the centre of the rum and molasses trade of the district. It is a small, neat-looking village of about five hundred inhabitants; but the country around is very thickly settled.

The river opposite the town is one hundred yards wide, and has a depth of thirty feet. Just above the village we entered the mouth of a creek called Igarapé Mirim. Six miles of navigation on this creek brought us to a canal which connects the Sta. Ana with the river Mojú. We found the Mojú a fine stream of about four hundred yards in width. The water was brown and clear, and the banks everywhere three or four feet out of the water.

Forty-five miles of descent of the Mojú brought us to the junction of the Acará, which comes in from the southeast. The estuary formed by the junction of the two rivers is about two and a half miles wide, and is called the river Guajará. Five miles of descent of the Guajará brought us to its entrance into the Pará River, five miles above the city, where we arrived at half past nine P.M. on the eleventh of April.

I was so worn out when we arrived that, although I had not heard from home, and knew that there must be letters here for me, I would not take the trouble to go to the consul's house to seek them; but sending Mr. Potter and the Frenchman ashore to their families, I anchored in the stream, and, wrapping myself in my blanket, went sullenly to sleep.

The charm of Mr. Norris's breakfast table next morning, however, with ladies and children seated around it, conversing in English, might have waked the dead. Under the care and kindness of himself and his family, I improved every hour; and was soon in condition to see what was to be seen, and learn what was to be learned, of the city of Pará.

Chapter XVIII

Pará

THE CITY OF SANTA MARIA de Balem do Graõ Pará, founded by Francisco Caldeira do Castello Branco, in the year 1616, is situated on a low elbow of land at the junction of the river Guamá with the river Pará, and at a distance of about eighty miles from the sea.

Pará is not fortified, either by land or water. There is a very small and inefficient fort situated on an island about five miles below the city, but it is only armed with a few ill-conditioned field-pieces, which do not command the channel. There is also a small battery in the city near the point of junction of the two rivers, but there are no guns mounted, and its garrison could be easily driven out by musketry from the towers of the cathedral.

The harbor is a very fine one; it is made by the long island of Onças in front, and at two miles distant, with some smaller ones further down the river. There is an abundance of water, and ships of any size may lie within 150 yards of the shore. There is a good landing-place for boats and lighters at the custom-house wharf, and at half tide at the stone wharf, some five hundred yards above.

The corporation was engaged, during my stay, in building a strong stone sea-wall all along in front of the town. This will make a new wide street on the water-front, and prevent smuggling. Formerly, canoes, at high stages of the river, would land cargoes surreptitiously in the very cellars of the warehouses situated on the river.

The city is divided into the *freguezias,* or parishes, of Sé and Campina. Nine other *freguezias* are included in the *municipio* of the capital, but many of these are leagues distant, and should not geographically be considered as belonging to the city, or their population be numbered in connexion with it. The population of the city proper numbered, in 1848 (the last statistical account I have, and which I think would differ very little from a census taken at this time), 9,284 free persons, and 4,726 slaves.

Pará was a remarkably healthy place, and entirely free from epidemics of any kind, until February 1850, when the yellow fever was taken there by a vessel from Pernambuco. It was originally brought from the coast of Africa to Bahia, and spread thence along the coast. The greatest malignancy of the disease was during the month of April, when it carried off from twenty to twenty-five a day.

About the same time the next year (the fever being much diminished), the small-pox broke out with great violence. About 25 percent of the population died from the two diseases. I imagine that the city will now never be entirely free from either, and the filthy condition in which the low tide leaves the slips, in which lie the small trading craft, must be a fruitful source of malaria, and an ever-exciting cause of epidemic.

The crews of these vessels, with their families, generally live in them. They are consequently crowded, and, when the tide is out, they lie on their sides, imbedded in a mass of refuse animal and vegetable matter, rotting and festering under a burning sun.

Pará, however, is an agreeable place of residence, and has a delightful climate. The sun is hot till about noon, when the sea breeze comes in, bringing clouds with rain, thunder, and lightning, which cool and purify the atmosphere and wash the streets of the city. The afternoon and evening are then delicious. This was invariable during my stay of a month.

The rich vegetable productions of the country enhance much the beauty of the city. In nearly all the gardens grow the beautiful *miriti* palm, the cabbage palm, the cocoa nut, the cinnamon, the bread-fruit tree, and rich green vines of black pepper. The rapidity of vegetable growth here is wonderful. Streets opened six months ago in the suburbs of the city are now filled up with bushes of the *stramonium,* or Jamestown weed of full six feet in height. There are a number of almond trees in various parts of the town, which are very ornamental. These trees throw out horizontal branches, encircling the trunk at intervals of five or six feet, the lowest circle being the largest, so that they resemble in shape a Norfolk pine.

We saw, in a walk in the suburbs of the town, what we thought to be a palm tree growing out of the crotch of a tree of a different species, but, upon examination, it appeared that the tree, out of which the palm seemed growing, was a creeper, which, embracing the palm near the ground, covered its trunk entirely for fifteen or twenty feet, and then threw off large branches on each side. It may seem strange to call that a creeper, which had branches of at least ten inches in diameter, but so it was. It is called in Cuba the *parricide* tree, because it invariably kills the tree that supports it.

The most picturesque object, however, in Pará was the ruins of an old opera house near the palace. The luxuriant vegetation of the country has seized upon it, and it presents pillar, arch, and cornice of the most vivid and beautiful green.

The society of Pará is also agreeable. The men, I am sorry to say, seem to be above work. Most of them are *hidalgos,* or gentlemen; and nearly all are in the employ of the government, with exceedingly small salaries. In the whole city of Pará, I am told, there are not a dozen Brazilians engaged in trade of any kind. The women are simple, frank, and engaging in their manners, and very fond of evening parties and dancing. I attended a ball, which is given monthly by a society of gentlemen, and was much pleased at the good taste exhibited in its management. Full dress was forbidden. No one was permitted to appear in diamonds, and the consequence was that all the pretty girls of the merely respectable classes, as well as of the rich, were gathered together, and I had a merry time of it.

But the principal charm of Pará, as of all other tropical places, is the *dolce far niente.* Men, in these countries, are not ambitious. They are not annoyed, as the more masculine people of colder climates are, to see their neighbors going ahead of them. They are contented to live, and to enjoy, without labor, the fruits which the earth spontaneously offers; and, I imagine, in the majority of cases, if a Brazilian has enough food, of even the commonest quality, to support life, coffee or tea to drink, cigars to smoke, and a hammock to lie in, that he will be perfectly contented.

This, of course, is the effect of climate. There was a time when the Portuguese nation, in maritime and scientific discoveries—in daring explorations—in successful colonization—in arts and arms—was inferior to no other in proportion to its strength; and I have very little doubt but that the bold and ambitious Englishman, the spirited and cosmopolitan Frenchman, and the hardy, persevering, scheming American, who likes little that anyone should go ahead of him, would alike, in the course of time, yield to the relaxing influence of a climate that forbids him to labor, and to the charm of a state of things where life may be supported without the necessity of labor.

To make, then, the rich and varied productions of this country available for commercial purposes, and to satisfy the artificial wants of man, it is necessary that labor should be compulsory. To Brazil and her political economists belongs the task of investigation, and of deciding how, and by what method, this shall be brought about.

The common sentiment of the civilized world is against the renewal of the African slave trade; therefore must Brazil turn elsewhere for the compulsory labor necessary to cultivate her lands. Her Indians will not work. Like the llama of Peru, they will die sooner than do more than is necessary for the support of their being. I am under the impression that, were Brazil to throw off a causeless jealousy, and a puerile fear of our people, and invite settlers to the Valley of the Amazon, there might be found, among our Southern planters, men, who, looking with apprehension (if not for themselves, at least for their children) to the state of affairs as regards slavery at home, would, under sufficient guarantees, remove their slaves to that country, cultivate its lands, draw out its resources, and prodigiously augment the power and wealth of Brazil.

The negro slave seems very happy in Brazil. This is remarked by all foreigners, and many times in Pará was a group of merry, chattering, happy-looking black women, bringing their baskets of washed clothes from the spring, pointed out to me, that I might notice the evils of slavery. The owners of male slaves in Pará generally require from each four or five *testoons* a day (twenty *testoons* make a dollar), and leave him free to get it as he can. The slaves organize themselves into bands or companies, elect their captain, who directs and superintends their work, and contract with a certain number of mercantile houses to do their porterage.

I have frequently seen these gangs of negroes carrying cocoa to the wharf. They were always chattering and singing merrily and would stop every few minutes to execute a kind of dance with the bags on their heads, thus doubling their work. When the load was deposited, the captain, who does no work himself unless his gang is pressed, arrays them in military fashion, and marches them back for another load.

For carrying barrels, or other bulky and heavy articles of merchandise, there are trucks drawn by oxen.

Churches are large and abundant in Pará. The cathedral is one of the finest churches in Brazil. Its personnel, consisting of dignitaries (*dignidades*), canons, chorists, and other *employés,* numbers seventy-four.

A large convent of the Jesuits, near the cathedral, having a very ornate and pretty chapel attached, is now used as a bishop's palace, and a theological seminary. The officers of the seminary are a rector, a vice-rector, and six professors; its students number 115; its rental is about $5,000, of which $1,000 is given from the provincial treasury; and it teaches Latin, the languages, philosophy, theology, history, geography, and vocal and instrumental music.

There are but two convents in Pará—one of the order of St. Anthony, and one of Shod Carmelites.

I attended the celebration of the festival of the Holy Cross, in the chapel of the convent of the Carmelites. There was a very large, well-dressed congregation, and the church was redolent of the fragrance of sweet-scented herbs strewn upon the floor. There were no good pictures in the church, but the candlesticks and other ornaments of the altar were very massive and rich. In the insurrection of the Cabanos the church property was spared, but I am told that, though they have preserved their ornaments, the priests have managed their property injudiciously, and are not now so rich in slaves and real estate as formerly.

I imagine that the priesthood in Brazil, though quite as intelligent and able as their brethren of Peru, have not so great an influence in society here as there. This is seen in an anecdote told me of a rigid Chefe de Policia, who forbid the clergy from burying one of their dignitaries in the body of the church during the prevalence of the yellow fever, but compelled them, much against their will, to deposit the body in the public cemetery, and accompanied the funeral procession on horseback to see that his orders were obeyed. It is also seen in the fact that the provincial assembly holds its sessions in a wing of the Carmelite convent, and that a part of the church of the Merced is turned into a custom-house and a barracks.

There are forty-one public primary schools in the province, educating 1,087 pupils. This gives a proportion of one for every 106 free persons in the province. Each pupil costs the State about seven and a half dollars.

There are two capital institutions of instruction in Pará—one for the education of poor boys as mechanics, who are compelled to pay for their education in labor for the State; and the other for the instruction in the practical business in life of orphan and destitute girls. I think that this education is compulsory, and that the State seizes upon vagabond boys and destitute girls for these institutions.

The province also maintains three young men for the purpose of complete education in some of the colleges of Europe.

There are several hospitals and charitable institutions in the city, among which is a very singular one. This is a place for the reception of foundlings maintained by the city. A cylinder, with a receptacle in it sufficiently large for the reception of a baby, turns upon an axis in a window; anyone may come under cover of night, deposit a child in the cylinder, turn the mouth of the receptacle in, and walk away without being seen. Nurses are provided to take charge of the foundling.

Though I pumped all my acquaintances, I could get no statistics concerning this institution, or whether it was thought to be beneficial or not. I judge, however, that for this country it is. Public opinion here does not condemn, or at least treats very leniently, the sins of fornication and adultery. This institution, therefore, while it would tend to lessen the crime of infanticide, would not encourage the above mentioned sins by concealment; for where there is no shame there is no necessity for concealment. In speaking thus, I do not at all allude to the higher classes of Brazil.

The executive and legislative government of the province is in a president and four vice presidents, appointed by the Crown, and in a legislative assembly. The provincial assembly meets once a year, in the month of May. It is a very inefficient representative system. The people in the districts elect electors, who choose delegates and proxies. Most of these proxies belong to the city; they have little knowledge of the wants, and no sympathy with the feelings, of the people they represent.

Persons complain bitterly of the delay and vexations in the administration of justice. I have heard of cases of criminals confined in jail for years, both in Peru and Brazil, waiting for trial. It is said also, though I know nothing of this, that the judges are very open to bribery. I think, however, that this is likely to be the case from the entire inadequacy of the salaries generally paid by the government.

I believe that the Brazilian code is mild and humane, and I am sure that it is humanely administered. The Brazilians have what I conceive to be a very proper horror of taking life judicially. They do not shrink in battle, and sudden anger and jealousy will readily induce them to kill, but I imagine the instances of capital punishment are very rare in Brazil.

The police of the city is excellent, but, except to take up a drunken foreign sailor occasionally, it has nothing to do. Crime—such as violence, wrong, stealing, drunkenness, &c.—is very rare in Pará. Probably the people are too lazy to be bad.

The province covers an area of about 360,000 square miles, and has a population of 129,828 free persons, with 33,552 slaves.

Much as it needs population, it has suffered, from time to time, considerable drainage. It is calculated that from ten to twelve thousand persons were killed by the insurrection of the Cabanos, in 1835. Since that time ten thousand have been drawn from it as soldiers for the southern wars, and the yellow fever and small-pox, in one year, carried off between four and five thousand more.

The war of the Cabanos was a servile insurrection, instigated and headed by a few turbulent and ambitious men. The ostensible cause was dissatisfaction with the provincial government. The real cause seems to have been hatred of the Portuguese.

Charles Jenks Smith, then consul at Pará, writes to the Hon. John Forsyth, under date of January 20, 1835:

After the happy conclusion of the war on the Acará, this city has remained in a state of perfect tranquility, until the morning of the seventh instant, when a popular revolution broke out among the troops, which has resulted in an entire change of the government of this province.

The President and the General-das-Armas were both assassinated at the palace by the soldiers there stationed, between the hours of four and five A.M. Inglis, Commandant of the Defensora corvette and Captain of the port, was also killed in passing from his dwelling to his ship. The subaltern commissioned officers on duty were shot down by the soldiery, who, placing themselves under the command of a sergeant named Gomez, took possession of all the military posts in the city.

About fifty prisoners were then set at liberty, who, in a body, proceeded to a part of the city called Porto de Sol, and commenced an indiscriminate massacre of all the Portuguese they could find in that neighborhood. In this manner about twenty respectable shop-keepers and others lost their lives.

Guards were stationed along the whole line of the shore, to prevent any person from embarking, and several Portuguese were shot in making the attempt to escape.

A new President and General-das-Armas were proclaimed, but they quarrelled very soon. The President was taken prisoner and murdered by his guards, and Vinagre, the General-das-Armas, took upon himself the government. In the conflicts incident to this change about two hundred persons were killed. The persons and property of all foreigners, except Portuguese, were respected. Many of these were insulted, and some killed.

Vinagre held the city, in spite of several attempts of Brazilian men-of-war to drive him out, until the twenty-first of June, when, upon the arrival of a newly appointed President, he evacuated it. During these attempts the British corvettes *Racehorse* and *Despatch,* a Portuguese corvette, and two French brigs-of-war offered their services for protection to the American consul.

On the fourth of August, Vinagre again broke into the city. The English and Portuguese vessels landed their marines, but, disgusted with the conduct of the President, withdrew them almost immediately. The fire of the *Racehorse,* however, defeated Vinagre's attempt to get hold of the artillery belonging to the city.

On the twenty-third of August, the President abandoned the city to the rebels whose leader exerted himself to save foreign life and property, permitting the foreigners to land from their vessels and take from the custom-house and their own stores the principal part of their effects.

The rebels held the city until the thirteenth of May, 1836, when they were finally driven out by the legal authorities, backed by a large force from Rio Janeiro. They held, however, most of the towns on the river above Pará till late in the year 1837. They did immense mischief, putting many whites to death with unheard-of barbarity and destroying their crops and cattle. The province was thus put back many years. I think that the causes which gave rise to that insurrection still exist, and I believe that a designing and able man could readily induce the *tapuios* to rise upon their *patróns.* The far-seeing and patriotic President Coelho always saw the danger and labored earnestly for the passage of efficient laws for the government of the body of *tapuios* and for the proper organization of the military force of the province. His efforts in the latter case have been successful, and, very lately, a good militia system has been established.

The city of Pará is supplied with its beef from the great island of Marajó, which is situated immediately in the mouth of the Amazon. This island has a superficial extent of about ten thousand square miles, and is a great grazing country. Cattle were first introduced into it from the Cape de Verde Islands, in 1644. They increased with great rapidity, and government soon drew a considerable revenue from its tax on cattle.

Before the year 1824, a good horse might have been bought in Marajó for a dollar, but about that time a great and infectious disease broke out among the horses, and swept away vast numbers, so that Marajó is now dependent upon Ceará and the provinces to the southward for its supply of horses. I heard that the appearance of this disease was caused by the fact that an individual having bought the right from the government to kill ten thousand mares on the island actually killed a great many more; and the carcasses, being left to rot upon the plains, poisoned the grass and bred the pestilence which swept off nearly all.

Other accounts state that the disease came from about Santarem and Lago Grande, where it first attacked the dogs, then the *capiuaras,* or river-hogs, then the alligators, and, finally, the horses. It attacks the back and loins, so that the animal loses the use of its hind-legs. Government sent a young man to France to study farriery, in hopes to arrest the disease, but the measure was productive of no good results. The disease still continues, and, ten years ago, appeared for the first time in the island of Mexiana, not far from Marajó. Within the last year, nearly all the horses on this island have died. I believe it has never attacked the horned cattle.

I saw a number of curious and beautiful animals in Pará. Mr. Norris had some electric eels, and a pair of large and beautiful anacondas. I had never heard a serpent hiss before I heard these, and the sound filled me with disgust and dread. The noise was very like the letting off of steam at a distance. The extreme quickness and violence with which they darted from their coil (lacerating their mouths against the wire-work of the cage) was sufficiently trying to a nervous man, and few could help starting back when it occurred. These animals measured about eighteen feet in length, and the skin, which they shed nearly every month, measured eigh-

teen inches in circumference. They seldom ate; a chicken or a rat
was given to them when it was convenient. They killed their food
by crushing it between their head and a fold of their body and
swallowed it with deliberation. I imagine that they would live
entirely without food for six months.

Many gentlemen had tigers about their establishments. They
were docile and playful in their intercourse with acquaintances,
but they were generally kept chained for fear of injury to strangers. Their play, too, was not very gentle, for their claws could
scarcely touch without leaving a mark.

An American had a pair of black tigers that were the most
beautiful animals I have ever seen. The ground color of the body
was a very dark maroon, but it was so thickly covered with black
spots that, to a casual glance, the animal appeared coal black. The
brilliancy of the color—the savage glare of the eye—the formidable
appearance of their tusks and claws—and their evidently enormous strength—gave them a very imposing appearance. They
were not so large as the Bengal tiger, but much larger than the
common *ounce*. They were bred in Pará from cubs.

Electric eels are found in great numbers in the creeks and
ditches about Pará. The largest I have seen was about four inches
in diameter, and five feet in length. Their shock, to me, was unpleasant, but not painful. Some persons, however, are much more
susceptible than others. Captain Lee, of the *Dolphin,* could not feel
at all the shock of an eel, which affected a lady so strongly as to
cause her to reel and nearly fall. Animals seem more powerfully
affected than men. Mr. Norris told me that he had seen a horse
drinking out of a tub, in which was one of these eels, jerked entirely off his feet.

The shops of Pará are well supplied with English, French, and
American goods. The groceries generally come from Portugal. The

warehouses are piled with heaps of India-rubber, nuts, hides, and baskets of *annatto*. This pigment is made from the seed of a bur, which grows on a bush called *urucu* in Brazil, and *achote* in Peru. In the latter country it grows wild in great abundance; in the former, it is cultivated.

It remains for me but to express my grateful acknowledgments for personal kindness and information afforded by many gentlemen of Pará, particularly by Mr. Norris, the consul, and by Henry Bond Dewey, Esq., now acting consul. These gentlemen were unwearied in their courtesy, and to them I owe the information I am enabled to give concerning the history and present condition of the province and the city.

On May 12, by kind invitation of Captain Lee, I embarked in the United States surveying brig *Dolphin,* having previously shipped my collections on board of Norris's clipper barque the *Peerless*.

Chapter XIX

Resumé

MY REPORT WOULD be incomplete were I to fail to bring to the notice of the department circumstances concerning the free navigation of the river that have occurred since my return from the Valley of the Amazon.

These circumstances are clearly the result of my mission, which appears to have opened the eyes of the nations who dwell upon the banks of the Amazon, and to have stirred into vigorous action interests which have hitherto laid dormant. They have an important and direct bearing upon the question, whether the United States may or may not enter into commercial relations, by the way of the Amazon, with the Spanish American republics, who own the headwaters of that noble stream.

The government of the United States had scarcely begun to entertain the idea of sending a commission to explore the Valley of the Amazon, with a view to ascertain what benefits might accrue to its citizens by the establishment of commercial relations with the people who dwell upon its banks, when the fact became known to Brazil. That government, thus awakened to its own (more apparent, however, than real) interests, immediately cast about for means to secure for itself any advantages that might arise from a monopoly of the trade of the river.

She accordingly despatched to Lima an able envoy with instructions to make a treaty with Peru concerning the navigation of the Amazon; and, this done, to proceed to Bolivia for the same purpose, while the Brazilian Resident Minister in Bolivia was sent to the republics of Ecuador, Venezuela, and New Granada, so as to secure for Brazil the navigation of all the confluents of the Amazon belonging to Spanish South America.

The Brazilian envoy succeeded in making with Peru a treaty highly advantageous to his own government. It is styled "A treaty of fluvial commerce and navigation, and of boundary."

Independently of the action of the Spanish American republics concerning the free navigation of their tributaries of the Amazon, we have a special treaty with Peru, negotiated by J. Randolph Clay, our present minister, in July 1851, which entitles us, under the present circumstances, to the navigation of the Peruvian Amazon. The second article of that treaty declares that "The two high-contracting parties hereby bind and engage themselves not to grant any favor, privilege, or immunity whatever, in matters of commerce and navigation, to other nations, which shall not be also immediately extended to the citizens of the other contracting party, who shall enjoy the same gratuitously, or on giving a compensation as nearly as possible of proportionate value and effect, to be adjusted by mutual agreement, if the concession shall have been conditional."

The concession to Brazil is conditional, but we shall find no difficulty in "giving a compensation as nearly as possible of proportionate value and effect"; that is a matter for Peru to decide, and there is little doubt but that she will consider the presence of our people and our vessels in her country, and upon her streams, as being of proportionate value.

It will be thus seen that our citizens have a legal right, by express grant and decree, to trade upon the interior waters of Peru and Bolivia, and it is presumed that Brazil will not attempt to dispute the now well-settled doctrine that no nation holding the mouth of a river has a right to bar the way to market of a nation holding higher up, or to prevent that nation's trade and intercourse with whom she will, by a great highway common to both.

But Brazil has effectually closed the Amazon by her contract with a private entrepreneur; she gives him the exclusive privilege for thirty years, with a bonus of $80,000 per annum, besides guaranteeing to him the $20,000 of Peru. This of course defies competition, though I very much doubt if the contract will endure; the Brazilians are so little acquainted with river steam navigation that the gentleman will run his boats at great cost; the conditions of the contract are also stringent and oppressive; and under such circumstances, even with the bonus of $100,000, I doubt if the trade of the river for several years to come will support the six steamers that he contracts to keep on the line.

Brazil, too, will soon see that in this matter she is standing in her own light. The efforts of this company, though partly supported by the government, will make little beneficial impression upon so vast a country, in comparison with that which would be made by the active competition of the commercial nations of the world.

Were she to adopt a liberal instead of an exclusive policy, throw open the Amazon to foreign commerce and competition, invite settlement upon its banks, and encourage emigration by liberal grants of lands, and efficient protection to person and property, backed as she is by such natural advantages, imagination could scarcely follow her giant strides towards wealth and greatness.

She, together with five Spanish American republics, owns in the Valley of the Amazon more than two millions of square miles of land, intersected in every direction by many thousand miles of what might be called canal navigation. As a general rule, large ships may sail thousands of miles to the foot of the falls of the gigantic rivers of this country; and in Brazil particularly, a few hundred miles of artificial canal would open to the steamboat, and render available thousands of miles more.

This land is of unrivalled fertility; on account of its geographical situation and topographical and geological formation, it produces nearly everything essential to the comfort and well-being of man. On the top and eastern slope of the Andes lie hid unimaginable quantities of silver, iron, coal, copper, and quicksilver, waiting but the application of sience and the hand of industry for their development. The successful working of the quicksilver mines of Huancavelica would add several millions of silver to the annual product of Cerro Pasco alone. Many of the streams that dash from the summits of the Cordilleras wash gold from the mountain-side, and deposit it in the hollows and gulches as they pass. Barley, *quinua,* and potatoes, best grown in a cold climate, with wheat, rye, maize, clover, and tobacco, products of a temperate region, deck the mountain-side, and beautify the valley; while immense herds of sheep, llamas, alpacas, and *vicuñas* feed upon those elevated plains, and yield wool of the finest and longest staple.

Descending towards the plain, and only for a few miles, the eye of the traveller from the temperate zone is held with wonder and delight by the beautiful and strange productions of the torrid. He sees for the first time the symmetrical coffee-bush, rich with its dark-green leaves, its pure white blossoms, and its gay red fruit. The prolific plantain, with its great waving fan-like leaf, and immense pendant branches of golden-looking fruit, enchains his attention. The sugar-cane waves in rank luxuriance before him, and if he be familiar with Southern plantations, his heart swells with emotion as the gay yellow blossoms and white boll of the cotton sets before his mind's eye the familiar scenes of home.

Fruits, too, of the finest quality and most luscious flavor, grow here; oranges, lemons, bananas, pine-apples, melons, *chirimoyas, granadillas,* and many others, which, unpleasant to the taste at first, become with use exceedingly grateful to the accustomed palate. The Indian gets here his indispensable coca, and the forests at certain seasons are redolent with the perfume of the vanilla.

It is sad to recollect that in this beautiful country (I have before me the valley of the Chanchamayo) men should have offered me title deeds in gratuity to as much of this rich land as I wanted. Many of the inhabitants of Tarma hold grants of land in the Chanchamayo country from the government, but are so distrustful of its ability to protect them in their labors from the encroachments of the savages that they do not cultivate them.

About half a dozen persons only have cleared and are cultivating *haciendas.* One of these, the brave old Catalan Zapatero, was building himself a fire-proof house, mounting swivels at his gate, and swearing in the jargon of his province that, protection or no protection, he would bide the brunt of the savages, and not give up what had cost him so much time and labor without a fight for it. It is a pity that there are not more like him. The Peruvian government, however, should assure the settlers of efficient protection. It should not only keep up the stockade of San Ramon, but should open a road down the valley of the Chanchamayo to some navigable point on that stream, or to the Ucayali itself, establishing other stockades along the route for the protection from the Indians of those whom liberal offers may attract to the settlement and cultivation of that delightful country. I feel confident that she will pierce the continent and open a communication with the Atlantic with more facility and advantage by this route than by any other.

The climate of this country is pleasant and healthy; it is entirely free from the annoyance of sand-flies and *musquitoes,* which infest the lower part of the tributaries, and nearly the whole course of the Amazon. There is too much rain for agreeability from August to March; but nothing could be more pleasant than the weather when I was there in June.

The country everywhere in Peru, at the eastern foot of the Andes, is such as I have described above. Further down we find the soil, the peculiar condition, the productions of a country which is occasionally overflowed, and then subjected, with still occasional showers, to the influence of a tropical sun. From these causes we see a fecundity of soil and a rapidity of vegetation that is marvellous, and to which even Egypt, the ancient granary of Europe, affords no parallel, because, similar in some other respects, this country has the advantage of Egypt in that there is here no drought. Here trees, evidently young, shoot up to such a height that no fowling piece will reach the game seated on their topmost branches, and with such rapidity that the roots have not strength or sufficient hold upon the soil to support their weight, and they are continually falling, borne down by the slightest breeze, or by the mass of parasites and creepers that envelop them from root to top.

This is the country of rice, of sarsaparilla, of India-rubber, balsam *copaiba,* gum copal, animal and vegetable wax, cocoa, Brazilian nutmeg, Tonka beans, ginger, black pepper, arrow-root, tapioca, *annatto,* indigo, sapucaia, and Brazil nuts; dyes of the gayest colors, drugs of rare virtue, variegated cabinet woods of the finest grain, and susceptible of the highest polish. The forests are filled with game, and the rivers stocked with turtle and fish. Here dwell the *anta,* or wild cow, the *peixi-boi,* or fish-ox, the sloth, the anteater, the beautiful black tiger, the mysterious electric eel, the boa constrictor, the anaconda, the deadly coral snake, the voracious alligator, monkeys in endless variety, birds of the most brilliant plumage, and insects of the strangest forms and gayest colors.

The climate of this country is salubrious and the temperature agreeable. The direct rays of the sun are tempered by an almost constant east wind, laden with moisture from the ocean, so that one never suffers either from heat or cold. The man accustomed to this climate is ever unwilling to give it up for a more bracing one, and will generally refuse to exchange the abandon and freedom from restraint that characterises his life there, for the labor and struggle necessary even to maintain existence in a more rigorous climate or barren soil. The active, the industrious, and the enterprising, will be here, as elsewhere, in advance of his fellows; but this is the very paradise of the lazy and the careless. Here, and here only, such an one may maintain life almost without labor.

I met with no epidemics on my route; except at Pará, the country seemed a stranger to yellow fever, small-pox, or cholera. There seemed to be a narrow belt of country on each side of the Amazon where bilious fevers, called *sezoens,* or *maleitas,* were particularly prevalent. These fevers are of malignant type, and often terminate in fatal jaundice. I was told that six or eight days' navigation on each tributary, from the mouth upwards, would bring me to this country, and three or four more would pass me through it; and that I ran little risk of taking the fever if I passed directly through. It appeared, also, to be confined to a particular region of country with regard to longitude. I heard nothing of it on the Huallaga, the Ucayali, or the Tapajos, while it was spoken of with dread on the

Trombetas, the Madeira, the Negro, and the Purus. Filth and carelessness in this climate produce ugly cutaneous affections, with which the Indians are much afflicted, and I heard of cases of elephantiasis and leprosy.

I have been describing the country bordering on the Amazon. Up the tributaries, midway between their mouth and source, on each side are wide savannahs, where feed herds of cattle, furnishing a trade in hides; and at the sources of the southern tributaries are ranges of mountains, which yield immense treasures of diamonds and other precious stones.

It is again (as in the case of the country at the foot of the Andes) sad to think that, excluding the savage tribes, who for any present purposes of good may be ranked with the beasts that perish, this country has not more than one inhabitant for every ten square miles of land; that it is almost a wilderness; that being capable, as it is, of yielding support, comfort, and luxury to many millions of civilized people who have superfluous wants, it should be but the dwelling place of the savage and the wild beast.

Such is the country whose destiny and the development of whose resources is in the hands of Brazil. It seems a pity that she should undertake the work alone; she is not strong enough; she should do what we are not too proud to do, stretch out her hands to the world at large, and say, "Come and help us to subdue the wilderness; here are homes, and broad lands, and protection for all who choose to come." She should break up her steamboat monopoly, and say to the sea-faring and commercial people of the world, "We are not a maritime people; we have no skill or practice in steam navigation; come and do our carrying, while we work the lands; bring your steamers laden with your manufactures, and take from the banks of our rivers the rich productions of our vast regions." With such a policy, and taking means to preserve her nationality, for which she is now abundantly strong, I have no hesitation in saying that I believe in fifty years Rio Janeiro, without losing a tittle of her wealth and greatness, will be but a village to Pará, and Pará will be what New Orleans would long ago have been but for the activity of New York and her own fatal climate, the greatest city of the New World; Santarem will be St. Louis, and Barra, Cincinnati.

The citizens of the United States are, of all foreign people, most interested in the free navigation of the Amazon. We, as in comparison with other foreigners, would reap the lion's share of the advantages to be derived from it. We would fear no competition. Our geographical position, the winds of Heaven, and the currents of the ocean, are our potential auxili.aries. Thanks to Maury's investigations of the winds and currents, we know that a chip flung into the sea at the mouth of the Amazon will float close by Cape Hatteras. We know that ships sailing from the mouth of the Amazon, for whatever port of the world, are forced to our very doors by the southeast and northeast trade winds; that New York is the half way house between Pará and Europe.

We are now Brazil's best customer and most natural ally. The President knows this. At a dinner-party given by him at Barra, his first toast was, "To the nation of America most closely allied with Brazil—the United States." And he frequently expressed to me his strong desire to have a thousand of my active countrymen to help him to subdue the wilderness, and show the natives how to work. I would that all Brazilians were influenced by similar sentiments. Then would the mighty river, now endeared to me by association, no longer roll its sullen waters through miles of unbroken solitude; no longer would the deep forests that line its banks afford but a shelter for the serpent, the tiger, and the Indian; but, furrowed by a thousand keels, and bearing upon its waters the mighty wealth that civilization and science would call from the depths of those dark forests, the Amazon would "rejoice as a strong man to run a race"; and in a few years we might, without great hyperbole, or doing much violence to fancy, apply to this river Byron's beautiful lines:

> *The casteled crag of Drachenfels*
> *Frowns o'er the wide and winding Rhine,*
> *Whose breast of waters broadly swells*
> *Between the banks that bear the vine;*
> *And hills all rich with blossomed trees,*
> *And fields that promise corn and wine,*
> *With scattered cities crowning these,*
> *Whose far white walls along them shine.*

Then might Brazil, pointing to the blossoming wilderness, the well-cultivated farm, the busy city, the glancing steamboat, and listening to the hum of the voices of thousands of active and prosperous men, say, with pride and truth: "This much have we done for the advancement of civilization and the happiness of the human race."